South Africa

The Rise and Fall of Apartheid

Second Edition

Nancy L. Clark and William H. Worger

Longman
is an imprint of

Harlow, England • London • New York • Boston • San Francisco • Toronto • Sydney • Singapore • Hong Kong
Tokyo • Seoul • Taipei • New Delhi • Cape Town • Madrid • Mexico City • Amsterdam • Munich • Paris • Milan

PEARSON EDUCATION LIMITED

Edinburgh Gate
Harlow CM20 2JE
United Kingdom
Tel: +44 (0)1279 623623
Fax: +44 (0)1279 431059
Website: www.pearsoned.co.uk

First edition published in Great Britain in 2004
Second edition published in Great Britain in 2011

© Pearson Education Limited 2004, 2011

The rights of Nancy L. Clark and William H. Worger to be identified as authors of this work
have been asserted by them in accordance with the Copyright, Designs and Patents Act 1988.

Pearson Education is not responsible for the content of third party internet sites.

ISBN: 978-1-4082-4564-4

British Library Cataloguing in Publication Data
A CIP catalogue record for this book can be obtained from the British Library

Library of Congress Cataloging in Publication Data
Clark, Nancy L.
    South Africa : the rise and fall of apartheid / Nancy L. Clark and
William H. Worger. – 2nd ed.
        p. cm.
    Includes bibliographical references and index.
    ISBN 978-1-4082-4564-4 (pbk.)
    1. Apartheid–South Africa–History.   2. South Africa–Politics and
government–1948–1994.   I. Worger, William H.   II. Title.
    DT1757.C52 2011
    968.05
                                         2010050190

10   9   8   7   6   5   4
15   14   13

Set in 10/13.5pt Berkeley by 35
Printed in Malaysia, CTP-KHL

Introduction to the Series

History is narrative constructed by historians from traces left by the past. Historical enquiry is often driven by contemporary issues and, in consequence, historical narratives are constantly reconsidered, reconstructed and reshaped. The fact that different historians have different perspectives on issues means that there is also often controversy and no universally agreed version of past events. *Seminar Studies in History* was designed to bridge the gap between current research and debate, and the broad, popular general surveys that often date rapidly.

The volumes in the series are written by historians who are not only familiar with the latest research and current debates concerning their topic, but who have themselves contributed to our understanding of the subject. The books are intended to provide the reader with a clear introduction to a major topic in history. They provide both a narrative of events and a critical analysis of contemporary interpretations. They include the kinds of tools generally omitted from specialist monographs: a chronology of events, a glossary of terms and brief biographies of 'who's who'. They also include bibliographical essays in order to guide students to the literature on various aspects of the subject. Students and teachers alike will find that the selection of documents will stimulate discussion and offer insight into the raw materials used by historians in their attempt to understand the past.

Clive Emsley and Gordon Martel
Series Editors

Contents

List of maps and figures

Publisher's acknowledgements

We are grateful to the following for permission to reproduce copyright material:

Photographs
Plate 1 courtesy of Bailey's African History Archive (BAHA): Drum Photographer; Plate 2 courtesy of Getty Images; Plates 3, 4 and 5 courtesy of Associated Press; Plates 6, 7 and 8 courtesy of Corbis.

Figures
Figure 3.1 based on building plans supplied by the Port Elizabeth Municipality, *The Atlas of Changing South Africa*, 2nd ed., (Christopher, A.J. 2000), published by Routledge; Figure 3.2 after *Die Argitektuur van Steytlerville met Rigline vir Bewaring en Ontwikkeling*, Port Elizabeth: Institute of South African Architects (Herholdt, A.D. 1986) reprinted by permission of Professor A.D. Herholdt; Figures 5.1 and 5.2 based on information supplied by the South African Institute of Race Relations, *The Atlas of Changing South Africa*, 2nd ed., (Christopher, A.J. 2000), published by Routledge; Figure 6.1 from Epidemiological Fact Sheet on HIV and AIDS: Core data on epidemiology and response, *South Africa*, 2008 Update, p. 4 (UNAIDS/WHO Working Group on Global HIV/AIDS and STI Surveillance 2008).

Maps
Map 1 redrawn from official 1:250,000 topo-cadastral maps, various dates, Pretoria: Government Printer. Reproduced under Government Printer's Copyright Authority No. 11153 dated 01 September 2003; Maps 2 and 3 redrawn from South Africa: Time Running Out: The Report of the Study Commission on US Policy Toward Southern Africa. Copyright (c) 1981 Foreign Policy Study Foundation. Published and reprinted by permission of University of California Press; Map 4 redrawn from map produced for Actis by MAPgrafix. Reprinted by permission of MAPgrafix.

Tables

Table 6.1 from Poverty in South Africa: A profile based on recent household surveys, Stellenbosch Economic Working Papers 04/08 (Armstrong, P., Lekezwa, B. and Siebrits, K. 2008), data sourced from Statistics South Africa (2008a).

In some instances we have been unable to trace the owners of copyright material, and we would appreciate any information that would enable us to do so.

Chronology

1919   Jan Smuts became prime minister. Clements Kadalie established Industrial and Commercial Workers' Union (ICU)

1920   Native Affairs Act created separate 'tribal'-based administrative structures for Africans in Reserves. 20,000 African mineworkers went on strike

1922   Rand Revolt, white workers went on strike in support of workplace segregation

1923   Natives (Urban Areas) Act established segregated living areas in cities. SANNC changed name to African National Congress (ANC)

1924   Hertzog's National Party formed government in alliance with the Labour Party. Hertzog became prime minister (until 1939)

1924   Industrial Conciliation Act excluded Africans from definition of 'employee'

1927   Native Administration Act consolidated all policies dealing with Africans under one government department (Native Affairs, later renamed Bantu Affairs)

1929   Hertzog's National Party won national election. Formation of Federation of Afrikaner Cultural Organizations (FAK)

1934   Hertzog and Smuts allied National and United parties to form 'Fusion' government. D.F. Malan broke away from National Party and established Purified National Party (GNP)

1936   Representation of Natives Act abolished Cape African franchise and limited Africans to voting for white representatives

1936   African land ownership extended in theory to 13 per cent of South Africa

1938   Centenary of Great Trek. Formation of Ossewabrandwag (OB, Ox-wagon sentinel)

1939   Hertzog resigned over South African entry into the Second World War on the side of the British. Jan Smuts became prime minister. Hertzog joined with Malan in Reunited National Party (HNP)

1941   Formation of African Mineworkers' Union

1944   Formation of ANC Youth League

1946   Strike by 100,000 African mineworkers, crushed by police

1948   HNP won election and Malan became prime minister. HNP renamed as National Party (NP)

1949   Prohibition of Mixed Marriages Act. ANC Youth League successfully proposed Programme of Action for ANC

1950   Population Registration Act, Immorality Act, Group Areas Act and Suppression of Communism Act

1951   Separate Representation of Voters Act

1952   Natives (Abolition of Passes and Co-ordination of Documents) Act. ANC launches Defiance Campaign. ANC membership rose from 7,000 to 100,000

1953   Reservation of Separate Amenities Act and Bantu Education Act

1953–61	Mandela banned from speaking in public
1954	Dutch Reformed Church declared that biblical justification exists for apartheid
1954	J.G. Strijdom succeeded Malan as prime minister. Bantu Resettlement Act
1955	Sophiatown removals of Africans to Soweto. Freedom Charter adopted at the Congress of the People
1956	Tomlinson Commission report recommended establishment of Bantustans. Federation of South African Women march on Union building in Pretoria
1957–61	Treason Trial of 156 signatories of Freedom Charter
1958	Hendrik Verwoerd became prime minister
1959	Promotion of Bantu Self-Government Act and Extension of University Education Act. Pan-Africanist Congress (PAC) formed by Robert Sobukwe
1960	21 March, shootings at Sharpeville by police of demonstrators supporting a PAC-organised protest against the pass laws. ANC and PAC banned. Albert Luthuli, president of the ANC, received Nobel Peace Prize
1961	South Africa became a republic and left the Commonwealth. ANC and PAC began armed struggle. Mandela went underground to organise sabotage and resistance
1962	Mandela arrested and sentenced to five years' imprisonment for inciting unrest
1963	Ninety-Day Act (General Laws Amendment Act)
1963–4	Rivonia Trial. Eight ANC leaders, including Mandela, sentenced to life imprisonment for treason
1966	Prime Minister Verwoerd assassinated in parliament. B.J. Vorster became prime minister. Botswana and Lesotho declared independent states by Britain. United Nations deemed apartheid 'a crime against humanity'
1968	Swaziland declared independent by Britain
1969	South African Students' Organization (SASO) founded by Stephen Biko. Establishment of Bureau of State Security (BOSS). Sobukwe released after nine years in prison but prohibited from leaving country and subjected to internal banning
1972	Establishment of State Security Council (SSC)
1972–3	Wave of wildcat strikes by African dock workers in Durban
1973	Afrikaner Weerstandsbeweging (AWB, Afrikaner Resistance Movement) founded by Eugene Terre'Blanche. Biko banned
1974	Military coup overthrew Portuguese dictatorship
1975	Angola and Mozambique declared independent with Marxist governments. South Africa invaded Angola. SASO banned
1976	16 June, schoolchildren in Soweto protested inferior education. Hundreds killed by police. Government declared Transkei the first 'independent' Bantustan, followed by Bophuthatswana in 1977, Venda in 1979, Ciskei in 1981 and KwaNdebele in 1984

1977   Biko killed in police detention. Seventeen anti-apartheid organisations
       banned. United Nations established mandatory international embargo on
       trade in arms to South Africa

1978   Sobukwe died in Kimberley while still under banning order. 'Infogate'
       scandal. Vorster resigned and P.W. Botha became prime minister

1979   Industrial Conciliation Amendment Act. Formation of Koevoet (Crowbar).
       Vlakplaas established

1980   Zimbabwe declared independent

1982   Ruth First assassinated in Mozambique by letter bomb sent by South
       African government agents. Right-wing Conservative Party (CP) formed by
       Andries Treurnicht after his expulsion from the NP

1983   White referendum approved new constitution to include separate
       parliamentary representation for Coloureds and Asians, but to exclude
       Africans. United Democratic Front (UDF) formed as multiracial opposition
       to new constitution

1984   New constitution came into force. International businesses and banks
       began divesting from South Africa. Bishop Desmond Tutu awarded Nobel
       Peace Prize

1985   Congress of South African Trades Unions (COSATU) formed. Government
       Declared State of Emergency in 36 magisterial districts

1986   Mandela met secretly with the minister of justice. Repeal of Pass Laws and
       Prohibition of Mixed Marriages Act. State of Emergency extended to entire
       country. South Africa launched military raids into Botswana, Zambia and
       Zimbabwe. US Congress passed Comprehensive Anti-Apartheid Act
       imposing mandatory sanctions on trade with South Africa. Dutch Reformed
       Church declared apartheid an error

1987   Three-week strike by 250,000 Africans. Government covertly bombed
       headquarters of COSATU. Establishment of Civil Co-operation Bureau
       (CCB)

1988   Government covertly bombed headquarters of South African Council
       of Churches. South Africa withdrew military forces from Angola in
       anticipation of defeat by Cuban troops. COSATU and UDF banned

1989   Botha suffered stroke, later met privately with Mandela. F.W. de Klerk
       succeeded Botha as leader of the NP and later as State President

1990   Namibia declared independent. February ANC, PAC, SACP and 31 other
       anti-apartheid organisations unbanned. Mandela and other political
       prisoners released from jail. NP renounced apartheid. Sebokeng massacre

1990–1 Repeal of Natives' Land Act, Population Registration Act, Separate
       Amenities Act, Group Areas Act

1991   ANC declared end of armed struggle. Beginning of formal negotiations
       through the Convention for a Democratic South Africa (CODESA) to
       establish a multiracial government

1992 National referendum of white voters supported de Klerk's political initiatives. Boipatong massacre. Bisho massacre. Goldstone Commission concluded that the government used covert forces against its enemies. De Klerk and Mandela agreed on 1994 as the date for the first national election

1993 Assassination of Chris Hani, leader of Umkhonto we Sizwe, by a white right-wing politician. Death of Oliver Tambo. Killing of Amy Biehl by black extremists. De Klerk, Mandela and leaders of most other political parties endorsed an interim constitution. De Klerk and Mandela awarded jointly the Nobel Peace Prize

1994 March, failure of AWB invasion of Bophuthatswana. April, ANC won first non-racial election. Mandela sworn in as President and formed Government of National Unity with de Klerk as one of his deputy presidents

1996 First public hearings of Truth and Reconciliation Commission (TRC). National Party withdrew from Government of National Unity. Enactment of new South African Constitution giving equal rights to all people irrespective of race, gender, sexual orientation, etc.

1997 National Party renamed as New National Party

1999 Nelson Mandela retired. Second democratic election is won by the ANC with an increased majority. Thabo Mbeki became president

2003 South Africa had more HIV-positive individuals than any other country in the world

2004 ANC won a two-thirds majority in national election. Mbeki received another term as president of South Africa

2005 New National Party disbanded as result of precipitously declining electoral support

2008 Mbeki lost support of ANC and resigned as president

2009 ANC won national election with just under two-thirds majority of votes. Jacob Zuma became president of South Africa

2010 South Africa hosted soccer World Cup, the first time that the tournament has been held on the African continent. Continued to have more people living with HIV/Aids than any other country in the world

Who's who

Biko, Stephen Bantu (1946–77): African political activist most widely credited as author of Black Consciousness ideology. Co-founded South African Students' Organization (SASO) in 1969, Black People's Convention (BPC) in 1972, and worked full-time for Black Community Programmes (BCP) beginning in 1972. Banned in 1973. Arrested and detained under Terrorism Act repeatedly in 1976 and 1977. Died while in detention on 12 September 1977 as a result of a police beating.

Botha, Pieter Willem (1916–2006): Prime minister (1978–89). As deputy minister of internal affairs in the late 1950s oversaw the removal of blacks from Sophiatown. Introduced new constitution in 1984 and pursued destabilisation of neighbouring countries through 'Total Strategy'. Responsible for the extension of security and military control over the country.

Buthelezi, Mangosuthu Gatsha (1928–): Appointed minister of home affairs by Mandela in 1994. Served as chief minister of KwaZulu (1976–94) but refused to accept independence for the homeland under apartheid. Revived the Zulu National Cultural Liberation Movement as a Zulu political party, the Inkatha Freedom Party (IFP), and opposed the ANC in multiracial elections. Held responsible for IFP violence against ANC supporters before the elections.

Dadoo, Yusuf Mohamed (1909–83): President of the South African Indian Council (SAIC) and co-leader of the Defiance Campaign. Fled South Africa in 1960 and worked outside the country on behalf of the ANC and the SACP.

De Klerk, Frederik Willem (1936–): Prime minister and state president (1989–94). As prime minister, lifted the ban on the ANC and released Mandela from prison. Inaugurated negotiations leading to multiracial elections in 1994 and credited with overturning most apartheid laws.

Hani, Martin Thembisile (Chris) (1942–93): Chief of staff of Umkhonto we Sizwe (1987–92) and general secretary of the South African Communist Party (1991–3). Fled South Africa in 1967 and engaged in military actions against both South Africa and Rhodesia before returning to the country in 1990. Assassinated by white right-wing extremists outside his home in 1993.

Hertzog, James Barry Munnik (1866–1942): Prime minister (1924–39) and founder of the National Party. Afrikaner nationalist who fought for the recognition of the Afrikaans language on an equal basis with English. Also responsible for most segregationist policies such as excluding Africans from skilled jobs and the establishment of a separate administrative system for Africans.

Lembede, Anton Muziwakhe (1914–47): Co-founder and first president of the African National Congress Youth League in 1944 and architect of Africanist ideology that argued for African control over Africa. Often seen as the ideological forerunner of Black Consciousness.

Luthuli, Albert John (1898–1967): President of the ANC and recipient of the Nobel Peace Prize in 1960. Under his leadership, the ANC engaged in more active opposition to the government, including the Defiance Campaign. Banned in 1962 and forbidden to speak in public until his death in 1967.

Malan, Daniel François (1874–1959): Prime minister (1948–54). Elected on a platform of 'apartheid' and responsible for enacting most apartheid legislation.

Mandela, Nelson Rolihlahla (1918–): President of South Africa (1994–9). One of the founding members of the ANC Youth League. Convicted under the Suppression of Communism Act in 1952 and banned from public gatherings thereafter. Continued to work for the ANC secretly, launching the M-plan to build mass membership. Convicted under the Terrorism Act in 1963 and imprisoned until 1990. Led ANC negotiations with the South African government that resulted in the country's first multiracial elections in 1994 when he was elected president.

Mbeki, Thabo Mvuyelwa (1942–): Elected president of South Africa in 1999. Left South Africa in 1962 and worked for the ANC in a variety of capacities, organising resistance to apartheid both inside and outside the country. Hand-picked by Mandela as Executive Deputy Vice President in 1994 and as his successor. Lost support of ANC and resigned as president in 2008.

Ramaphosa, Cyril (1952–): Secretary-general of the ANC (1991–7). Previously general secretary of the powerful National Union of Mineworkers (1982–91). Central figure in negotiations between the ANC and the South African government leading to multiracial elections in 1994. Left political life in 1997 to work for greater African participation in the economy through various investment and development companies.

Sisulu, Walter Max Ulyate (1912–2003): Deputy president of the ANC (1991–4). One of the founding members of the ANC Youth League and jailed with Mandela in 1964. Released from prison in 1989 and helped to negotiate the end of apartheid and arrangements for multiracial elections in 1994.

Slovo, Joe (1926–95): Minister of housing (1994–5), secretary-general of the SACP (1984–91). Joined the SACP in 1942, listed as a communist in 1954 and banned from public gatherings. Went into exile in 1963 and emerged as one of the leaders of Umkhonto we Sizwe. Returned to South Africa in 1990 and participated in talks leading to the 1994 elections.

Smuts, Jan Christian (1870–1950): Prime minister (1919–24, 1939–48). Early career as state attorney for the South African Republic and a general in the South African War. Pursued 'conciliation' policy with British following the war, earning him the lifelong enmity of Afrikaner nationalists. Supported segregationist policies but argued that complete separation under apartheid would be impractical. Voted out of office in 1948.

Sobukwe, Robert Mangaliso (1924–78): First president of the Pan-Africanist Congress (PAC). Began his political career in the ANC Youth League in 1949. Became critical of ANC moderation and advocated African nationalism, founding the PAC in 1959. Organised the anti-pass law campaign that ended in the massacre at Sharpeville in 1960. Convicted of incitement to violence and imprisoned until 1963 when the government passed a law, thereafter known as the Sobukwe clause, allowing the indefinite detention of anyone convicted of incitement. Held in isolated confinement on Robben Island until 1969 and banned to Kimberley until his death in 1978.

Strijdom, Johannes Gerhardus (1893–1958): Prime minister (1954–8). Most notable act as prime minister was to increase the size of the Senate, giving his government a two-thirds majority in order to push through a constitutional amendment to remove propertied Coloureds from the voting rolls in the Cape.

Tambo, Oliver Reginald (1917–93): President of the ANC (1967–91). Tambo led the ANC from outside the country after it was outlawed and worked for nearly 30 years to garner international support for the organisation in its struggle against apartheid. He suffered a stroke in 1989 and returned to South Africa in 1991.

Terre'Blanche, Eugene (1941–2010): Began career in the South African Police. In 1973 founded the Afrikaner Weerstandsbeweging (AWB, Afrikaner Resistance Movement) as a Nazi-inspired militant right-wing movement upholding white supremacy. Sentenced to six years imprisonment in 1997 for attempted murder for having beaten one of his black employees for eating while at work. Murdered by farm employees in 2010 after a dispute about wages due.

Verwoerd, Hendrik Frensch (1901–66): Prime minister (1958–66). Developed concept of 'grand apartheid', under which the African reserves were to be considered separate national homelands. Also pulled South Africa out of the British Commonwealth and successfully called a referendum of white voters in 1960 to establish South Africa as an independent Republic. Two attempts on his life, the second successful.

Vorster, Balthazar Johannes (1915–83): Prime minister (1966–78). Leader of the Ossewabrandwag during the Second World War when he was jailed for sabotage. As minister of justice under Verwoerd, he was responsible for legislation empowering the government to detain suspects indefinitely and for the arrest of ANC leaders, including Nelson Mandela, in 1963. As prime minister, he presided over the elaboration of 'grand apartheid', including the independence of the Transkei. Responsible for the brutal crackdown in the wake of the Soweto uprising in 1976 and for the 'Infogate' scandal which ended his political career in 1978.

Xuma, Alfred Bitini (1893–1962): President of the ANC (1940–9). Worked as president successfully to expand membership and reorganise the nearly defunct ANC. Eventually eclipsed by younger members demanding more effective leadership.

Zuma, Jacob Gedleyihlekisa (1942–): Became a member of the ANC in 1959 and of Umkhonto we Sizwe in 1962. Spent ten years incarcerated on Robben Island, then worked in exile for the ANC during the late 1970s and the 1980s. Returned to South Africa in 1990. Elected president of the ANC in 2007, and president of South Africa in 2009.

Glossary

African Mineworkers' Union (AMWU) Formed in 1941 by migrant mining workers. Grew to membership of 25,000 by 1943, and in 1946 organised strike by 100,000 black mineworkers.

African National Congress (ANC) Formed in 1912 as the South African Native National Congress (renamed the African National Congress in 1923). Established originally to protest against racial discrimination and to appeal for equal treatment before the law. Declared illegal in 1960 under the terms of the Unlawful Organizations Act. Unbanned in 1990. Secured a majority of the votes in the 1994 national election and formed the government with Nelson Mandela as president.

Afrikaner Weerstandsbeweging (AWB) African Resistance Movement established by conservative Afrikaners in 1973 in opposition to what they perceived as government reforms that were undermining Afrikaner culture and political power. Consciously adopted swastika-like emblems on flags and uniforms and attacked both white and black opponents of apartheid.

Apartheid Meaning 'apartness' in Afrikaans. The term adopted by the National Party in its successful 1948 election bid to rule the country. Established as a policy to separate physically all races within South Africa in a hierarchy of power with whites at the top and Africans at the bottom.

Black Consciousness Political philosophy that emerged within the black student community in the late 1960s in response to the implementation of apartheid. Student leader Stephen Biko argued that blacks needed to counteract the psychological impact of apartheid by realising that they were not inferior. Viewed Africans, Indians and Coloureds as all suffering under apartheid and used the term 'black' for all of them.

Broederbond Meaning 'brotherhood'. Exclusively an Afrikaner organisation established in the wake of the First World War to celebrate and protect Afrikaner culture. Within a few years organised as a strictly secret society whose membership and actions were not disclosed to English-speaking whites.

Bureau of State Security (BOSS) Established in 1969 to co-ordinate and complement the security activities of the military and police. It reported to the prime minister, and its activities remained secret.

Coloureds Population group that emerged in the Cape in the seventeenth and eighteenth centuries as a result of contact between Africans, Malaysians and Europeans. Despite partial European heritage, subjected to most apartheid legal restrictions.

Congress of South African Trade Unions (COSATU) Founded in 1985 and a leading force in the final struggle against apartheid.

Convention for a Democratic South Africa (CODESA) Multi-party conference convened in 1991 to determine the process for transformation of South Africa from apartheid to multiracialism. Included representatives from the ANC, the NP, and approximately 20 other political organisations.

Defiance Campaign Organised by ANC and the SAIC in 1952 to demand repeal of apartheid laws. Thousands of people refused to go to work and approximately 8,500 people were arrested. Most leaders of the ANC were banned. Nevertheless, ANC membership jumped from fewer than 7,000 at the beginning of 1952 to more than 100,000 by the end of the year.

Democratic Alliance (DA) Formed in 2000 with the brief alliance of the Democratic Party (DP), successor to the PFP, and the New National Party (NNP), successor to the National Party (NP). Has succeeded in winning the votes of white and coloured voters in the Cape Province.

Inkatha Freedom Party (IFP) Originated as a Zulu cultural organisation and was transformed into a political party under the leadership of Mangosuthu (Gatsha) Buthelezi in the late 1980s. Responsible for brutal attacks, with support from South African police, against ANC supporters in the months before the 1994 election. Garnered 10.5 per cent of the national vote in the election, securing a place in the first multiracial cabinet.

National Party (NP) Formed in 1914 by J.B.M. Hertzog in opposition to the Botha–Smuts South African Party (SAP) and to represent the interests of Afrikaners. Gained control of the government in 1924 in a coalition with the Labour Party and took exclusive control in 1928 until joining in a 'Fusion' government with the SAP in 1934. Eschewed co-operation with other parties during the Second World War and re-emerged in 1948 to take control of parliament and form its own government under D.F. Malan.

Ossewabrandwag (OB) 'Ox-wagon sentinel'. Established in 1938 by Afrikaners participating in the commemoration of the Great Trek. Aimed at inculcating a 'love for fatherland' and at instituting, by armed force if necessary, an Afrikaner-controlled republic in South Africa. During the war, some OB members were arrested for sabotage against the government. By 1949 claimed a membership of 250,000.

Pan-Africanist Congress (PAC) Established in 1959 by Robert Sobukwe who believed the ANC should take more direct action to challenge the government. In March 1960, began a national campaign against the pass laws, leading to the police massacre at Sharpeville. The PAC was outlawed in 1960 and continued to operate both underground and outside the country until 1990 when it became a legal political party inside South Africa.

Progressive Federal Party (PFP) Formed in 1977 to represent the views of English-speaking white voters opposed to apartheid. Succeeded by the Democratic Party (DP) in 1989, which in 2000 became the Democratic Alliance (DA) after joining with the New National Party (NNP).

Rivonia Trial Trial of 17 ANC leaders, including Nelson Mandela and Walter Sisulu, on charges of treason. Eight of them, including Mandela, were sent to prison for life, and most remained incarcerated until the end of the 1980s.

Robben Island Site of the prison where Nelson Mandela and other opponents of apartheid would be incarcerated in the twentieth century. Opposite Cape Town, it was also used by the early Dutch administration in the seventeenth and eighteenth centuries as a prison for exiled political opponents from present-day Indonesia, most of them followers of Islam.

Segregation Racial discrimination as practised in South Africa from 1910 to 1948. It legally separated races to the benefit of those of European descent and to the detriment of those of African descent. Segregation policies affected the rights of Africans to own land, to live or travel where they chose, and to enjoy job security.

Sharpeville African township outside the town of Vereeniging. Site of anti-pass demonstration in March 1960 that ended in violence. Police fired on the demonstrators, killing at least 69 of them and wounding 186.

South African Communist Party (SACP) Established in 1921 as the Communist Party of South Africa. Sought to organise African workers into trade unions and to join with whites in class action against employers. Outlawed under the Suppression of Communism Act (No. 44) of 1950. Worked underground with the ANC and other organisations to end apartheid. Unbanned in 1990.

South African Indian Congress (SAIC) Established in 1924 to seek greater rights for Indians. Worked with the ANC and other groups to oppose apartheid and helped to draft the Freedom Charter.

South African Students' Organization (SASO) Established in 1968 by African university students frustrated with the political position of the multiracial National Union of South African Students (NUSAS). SASO membership was limited to black students (Africans, Coloureds and Indians). Under the leadership of Stephen Biko, SASO organised anti-government strikes and rallies in the early 1970s. Banned in 1975.

Soweto Acronym for South West African Township, located outside Johannesburg. The site of mass protests by students beginning in June 1976 that spread throughout the country and resulted in hundreds of deaths. Protests began in reaction to apartheid educational policies but grew to embrace a wide range of economic and social issues.

State Security Council (SSC) Established in 1972 to advise the prime minister on the security of the country. Operated as a *de facto* war cabinet throughout the 1970s and 1980s, superintending the struggle against the ANC, UDF and other anti-apartheid groups.

Total Strategy Proposed as part of the 1977 Defence budget. Outlined a military strategy to protect the country from perceived external and internal threats and later used as justification for increased control of the government by security and military officers in the SSC.

Treason Trial Trial that lasted from 1957 until 1961, when 156 anti-government activists were tried for treason. All defendants were found not guilty.

Truth and Reconciliation Commission (TRC) Established in 1995 under the Promotion of National Unity and Reconciliation Act. Charged to investigate the sufferings of ordinary people under apartheid and to hear testimony from former agents of the state seeking amnesty for the crimes they had committed. Held hearings for two and a half years and heard testimony of over 29,000 people.

Umkhonto we Sizwe (MK) 'Spear of the Nation'. Militant wing of the ANC established in 1961 after the ANC was outlawed. Conducted sabotage inside the country and provided military training for South African exiles outside the country.

United Democratic Front (UDF) Established in 1983 to oppose the government's proposed constitutional reforms. Served as an umbrella for a multiracial group of organisations including unions, churches and community groups.

United Party (UP) Formal union between the National and South African parties in 1934. Remained under the leadership of Smuts when Hertzog resigned in 1939 and in power until 1948 when it lost the election to the National Party. Dissolved in 1977.

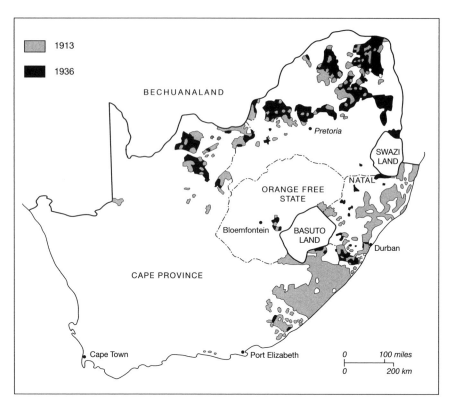

Map 1 Land 'reserved' for Africans, 1913 and 1936

Source: Redrawn from official 1: 250,000 topo-cadastral maps, various dates, Pretoria: Government Printer. Reproduced under Government Printer's Copyright Authority No. 11153, dated 1 September 2003.

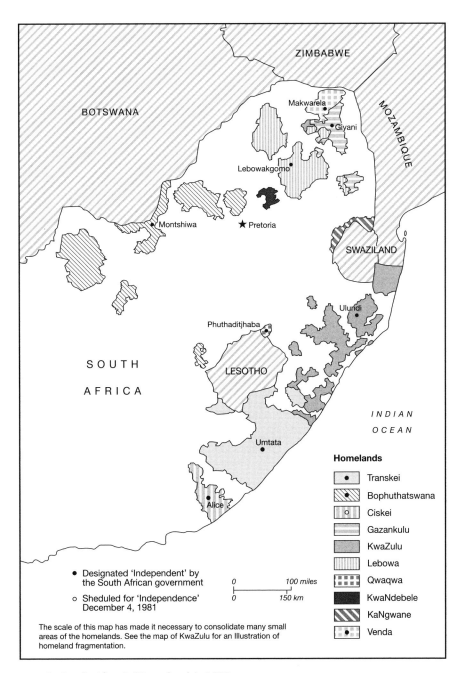

Map 2 South Africa's 'Homelands', 1980

Source: Redrawn from *South Africa: Time Running Out: The Report of the Study Commission on US Policy Toward Southern Africa.* Copyright © 1981 Foreign Policy Study Foundation. Published and reprinted by permission of the University of California Press.

Map 3 KwaZulu, 1980

Source: Redrawn from *South Africa: Time Running Out: The Report of the Study Commission on US Policy Toward Southern Africa.* Copyright © 1981 Foreign Policy Study Foundation. Published and reprinted by permission of the University of California Press.

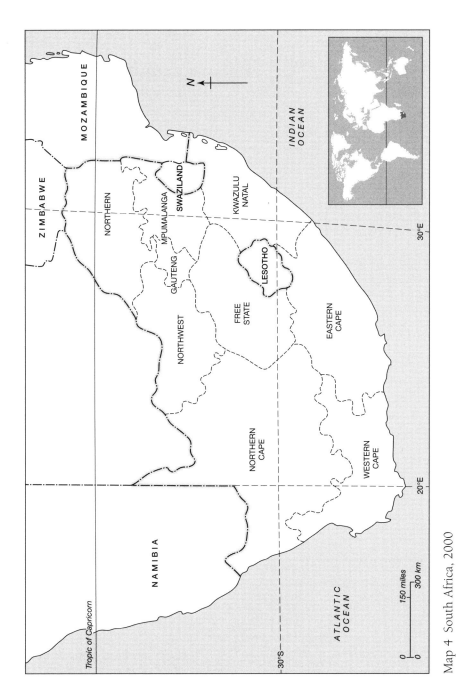

Map 4 South Africa, 2000

Source: Redrawn from a map produced for Actis by MAPgrafix. Reprinted by permission of MAPgrafix.

Part 1

SETTING THE SCENE

1

Introduction

Apartheid, literally 'apartness' or separateness in the Afrikaans and Dutch languages, is the name that was given to a policy of separating people by race, with regard to where they lived, where they went to school, where they worked, and where they died. This policy was introduced in South Africa in 1948 by the National Party government and it remained official practice until the fall from power of that party in 1994.

Racial discrimination did not begin in South Africa in 1948. Indeed, it can be traced back to the beginnings of Dutch colonisation of the Cape of Good Hope in 1652 and the establishment thereafter of an economy based on the use of slaves imported from East Africa and Southeast Asia. Even after the end of slavery in the 1830s, racial discrimination continued in myriad forms as European settlement expanded, the British government conquered African societies, and imperialists and settlers alike spoke of the 'civilising mission' of white rule and favoured, almost without exception, the segregation of black from white.

Neither racial discrimination nor segregationist policies distinguished South Africa from a multitude of other societies, especially those of the colonial world, during the first half of the twentieth century. Before the Second World War no European powers considered that any of their colonies would enjoy full independence in the near future. None allowed colonised people to vote except in the most limited fashion, such as a few representatives to advisory councils. All practised various forms of social and economic discrimination, favouring white settlers and officials in housing and education and jobs at the expense of indigenous peoples. That was colonialism. And people of colour living in the southern United States half a century after the end of the Civil War still experienced many of the same indignities as the colonised peoples of Asia and Africa.

All this changed after the Second World War, with the abrupt ending of colonialism in Asia and Africa during the 1940s and 1950s and the implementation of apartheid in South Africa. The word *apartheid* was coined in the mid-1930s, and was first used as a way of expressing the importance of Afrikaners maintaining a cultural identity separate from that of English-speaking Europeans in South Africa. During the war years, however, the word took on new connotations. Afrikaner politicians, embroiled in a world conflict that they denounced as the product of British imperialism, and appealing for political support to an Afrikaans-speaking, urban, working-class electorate that felt exploited by British capitalists on one side and threatened by cheaper black workers on the other, engaged in a campaign of race-baiting. Although *apartheid* did not appear in a dictionary until 1950, it really entered the public lexicon in 1947 and 1948 as the United and National parties strove against each other for electoral support. As used and developed in the course of election campaigning, apartheid came to stand for support of the physical separation of black and white, this separation to be achieved by legislative policies and state action.

As a proactive and dynamic policy, apartheid marked a real divide from what had gone before, not in general support for the separation of the races, but of the extent of such separation and of the means to be used to attain that separation. Gwendolen Carter, a political scientist who spent a year in South Africa in the early 1950s studying the implementation of apartheid at first hand, remarked that what distinguished the National Party government from its predecessors was the way that it had acted, 'decisively and force-fully', to enact its programmes of racial separation 'through legislation which they have been prepared to put into force in the face of the most bitter criticism . . . from Europeans as well as non-Europeans'. The Nationalists, Carter argued in the first comprehensive study of apartheid, were intent on using legislative action 'to make the African the different kind of person that theory [apartheid] says he is'. She argued that this determination to force theory into reality was based on two fundamental concerns, first 'to try to direct his energies away from his desire for more power and a better return for his labor in the European areas'; second, as a way to deal with the conundrum of 'how to maintain European supremacy in every sphere of life and at the same time advance the industrial revolution in South Africa which helps to make that country independent of outside influences' (Carter, 1958: 15, 411–12).

The implementation of apartheid captured the attention and incurred the wrath of the newly independent states of Asia and Africa. India led the criticism in the late 1940s, objecting especially that the South African government refused to accord to citizens of the 'black' Commonwealth the same rights and privileges given to citizens of the 'white' Commonwealth. Apartheid gained even greater international prominence in 1952 when representatives of 13 Asian and African states (Afghanistan, Burma, Egypt, India, Indonesia, Iran, Iraq, Lebanon, Pakistan, the Philippines, Saudi Arabia, Syria and Yemen) stressed to their fellow members of the United Nations that apartheid was 'creating a dangerous and explosive situation' in South Africa, and that the policy as implemented constituted 'both a threat to international peace and a flagrant violation of the basic principles and fundamental freedoms which are enshrined in the Charter of the United Nations' (United Nations, 1994: 223).

Such international criticism gained wider currency during the 1960s and 1970s as the South African government pursued the implementation of its apartheid policies in brutal fashion, symbolised especially by the police killing in 1960 of 69 Africans demonstrating peacefully at Sharpeville against the country's notorious 'pass' law (see Chapter 3). In December 1966, the United Nations General Assembly condemned 'the policies of apartheid practised by the Government of South Africa as a crime against humanity'. In 1977, after the harsh crushing of the Soweto uprising (see Chapter 4), the UN sought to give teeth to its condemnation by voting unanimously to implement a mandatory embargo on all its member states on the trade in arms to South Africa. The secretary-general at the time, Kurt Waldheim, explained what was an unprecedented action in the following way: 'such a gross violation of human rights and so fraught with danger to international peace that a response commensurate with the gravity of the situation was required' (United Nations, 1994: 50).

But it was during the 1980s that world attention finally focused on apartheid. Whereas in the 1950s and the 1960s the South African government could at least plead for patience from its critics by arguing that it was experimenting with a new policy and needed time to see if apartheid would work in practice, during the late 1970s and the 1980s it had become obvious to most observers that apartheid could never work as espoused by its adherents, and indeed was nothing more than an elaborate yet ultimately flimsy mask attempting to disguise an extraordinarily oppressive system of white rule over blacks. (This view was not news to black South Africans or to many students of the country's history and politics, but it did finally capture world media headlines.) During the 1980s, as South Africa disintegrated into a form of civil war as black opponents of apartheid fought, increasingly successfully, to make apartheid unworkable and South Africa ungovernable, most of the rest of the world joined in the near universal condemnation of the South African government and supported international steps to bring apartheid to an end, especially by enforcing boycotts (economic, political, sporting, and so forth). The high point, symbolically, of this process of a developing international consensus came with the passage in 1986, by a two-thirds vote of the US Congress overriding an attempted veto by President Ronald Reagan (a long-time conservative friend of the South African administration), of the Comprehensive Anti-Apartheid Act. Among other steps, the

Act banned Americans from making new investments in South Africa, from exporting computers (so necessary to the workings of the apartheid police state), from selling oil, and from direct air travel between the United States and South Africa. Within less than five years of the outbreak of civil war and the implementation of international sanctions, the National Party government, to the surprise of all commentators, in 1990 renounced apartheid and stated its acceptance of the principle that all people in South Africa, black as well as white, should participate in the electoral process. Four years later, in 1994, Nelson Mandela, who had spent the years 1963 to 1990 incarcerated as a political prisoner, became the first president of the new South Africa. This book examines the origins of the policy of apartheid, its implementation, its ultimate collapse, and its legacy.

HISTORIOGRAPHY

Writing about South Africa's history and politics has in its authorship and its intellectual and cultural approaches mirrored the divide between black and white that has permeated daily life. The earliest historical writing about South Africa, produced in the latter half of the nineteenth century, reflected the Eurocentric and paternalistic biases of high imperialism. These historians, often civil servants in the colonial administration, wrote of the incursion of Europeans into southern Africa as an essential step in the raising up and improvement of indigenous peoples at a time when popular theories of Social Darwinism remarked on the survival of the fittest within a social order that was assumed to be naturally hierarchical, with Nordic whites at the top and Australian and southern African gatherer-hunter peoples at the bottom. For these writers, the attributes needed by Africans in order to move up the hierarchy, in essence to prove that they were 'civilised', were acceptance of the superiority of European religion – demonstrated by conversion to Christianity – and a willingness to endure the hardships of manual labour, particularly in the diamond and gold mines that were being developed from the 1870s onwards. Refusal to convert or to work (at least on the terms offered by white employers) was deemed a sign of barbarism (Worger, 1999). Much of the content and themes of this nineteenth-century literature continued to dominate the school texts read by elementary and high school pupils, black and white, in South Africa's state education system through to the 1990s (Worger, 1999).

Following this primarily pro-English literature, a distinct settler version emerged in the 1880s and 1890s, and blossomed in the early part of the twentieth century, among the Dutch-speaking settlers who perceived themselves as victims of British imperialism. In their historical works they focused on events such as the Great Trek of the 1830s when Dutch-speaking settlers opposed to British policies favouring the emancipation of slaves had moved beyond British colonial borders into the interior of the subcontinent, on the wars that they had fought with African leaders, whom they depicted without exception as treacherous and unworthy of ruling the lands that the settlers coveted for themselves, and on the wars fought by the British in the late nineteenth century to seize control of the South African gold industry. Alongside the anti-imperial and the anti-black elements, there was a strong radical theme running through the early Afrikaner nationalist literature, linking Afrikaners' struggles for independence as similar to those of the early American colonists, and condemning late nineteenth-century British imperialism as nothing but a mask for the greed of mining capitalism that had left most Afrikaners poor and landless after the South African War of 1899–1902 (Smith, 1988).

Often overlooked in historiographical surveys, a defect of assuming that only academic writing constitutes 'history', have been the considerable contributions of black writers. Literacy became widespread in the second half of the nineteenth century, largely as the result of missionaries who, in carrying the word of God, did so through the technology of the printing press and the founding of newspapers targeted at African audiences. Although missionaries expected their converts to accept and proselytise the word of God and the benefits of European civilisation exactly as taught to them, many of those same converts were struck by the contrast between the theory of what they were taught – that all were equal in the eyes of God – and the discrimination that they suffered in their daily lives. While often praising certain features of European culture – Shakespeare and cricket in particular – these writers also documented the harsh treatment meted out to blacks in the mines and farms of South Africa (Plaatje, 1987 [1916]). Others, especially from the 1920s onwards, took a more radical line, criticising what they perceived as the class basis of imperial rule, and thereby evoking some of the same themes as early Afrikaner writing, albeit from the point of view of a black working class rather than that of a white landless class. For these writers, only class revolution would truly free blacks from their oppressive conditions (Nzula *et al.*, 1979).

The emergence of apartheid as theory and practice in the 1950s and 1960s encouraged the growth of what has sometimes been referred to as the liberal 'school', though few would identify themselves as members, seeing such a label as too much of a straitjacket. In essence, though, the liberals could be seen as those who identified ideas as more important than material conditions in influencing or perhaps determining the way in which people act. Particular lines of interpretation associated with liberal viewpoints are that the racial discrimination so prevalent in apartheid South Africa was a product primarily of Afrikaners as distinct from English-speaking South

Africans, and that these racist attributes of Afrikaners could be traced primarily to experiences that they had undergone in the nineteenth century (frontier wars against Africans and the resulting development of racial antipathies loomed large, as did, in some works, the influence of slavery and slaveholding).

During the 1970s, a time when black workers led strikes and boycotts against their oppressive working conditions, a new line of interpretation emerged and rapidly became dominant. Sometimes styled, not always by the authors themselves, as 'radical' or 'revisionist', this literature, strongly influenced by a reading of Karl Marx, remarked on the benefits of apartheid to business and focused on the historical origins of many of apartheid's most notorious features – racially discriminatory legislation, urban segregation, migrant labour, rural poverty – not in the Afrikaner republics but in the industrial centres of Kimberley (diamonds) and Johannesburg (gold) developed by English capitalists. For the revisionists, racism was not an antiquated feature of the past kept alive by backward-looking Afrikaners, but the very essence of a 'modern' industrial economy that was built, above all, on the exploitation of cheap black labour. The argument ran that South African racism was primarily, though not exclusively, the product of a search by employers for large supplies of state-controlled labour to service colonial industries in which the only cost that was amenable to local control (all machinery had to be imported, and practically all investment capital came from Europe or America) was that of labour. Moreover, the distinctiveness of South Africa lay not in the existence of European (whether English or Afrikaner) racism towards indigenous peoples – because that was a feature of every colonial society – but because South Africa, uniquely among colonial territories, was the only one whose economy was centred on industrialisation and the utilisation of the colonised peoples primarily as an urban working class. Much of this literature followed from, although it was not directly connected with, the earlier black radical tradition of the 1920s and after, and the political views expressed by many leaders of the African National Congress, the Pan-African Congress and the South African Communist Party (Saunders, 1988).

All of this writing was highly political. And in turn the South African government sought to control the ways in which South African politics and history was discussed by banning – that is, making it a criminal offence for people to read and/or possess and/or quote – many works critical of apartheid throughout the 1960s, 1970s and 1980s. The government also sought to muzzle critics with banning orders, home detentions and imprisonment. Likewise, through control of the visa process, the government prevented critics from leaving South Africa, and forbade people deemed 'unfriendly' from entering. The development of separate educational institutions for blacks, many of these being rural universities staffed primarily by Afrikaner academics, further impinged on the ability of those most affected by apartheid to voice their opinions through regular media. As a result, much of the most insightful literature detailing the experiences of ordinary people under apartheid came from black-authored fiction (often banned but sometimes eluding the bureaucratic eye of the censors) and the writings of political exiles (Mphahlele, 1959; Modisane, 1963; Nkosi, 1965; Mokgatle, 1971; Matshoba, 1979; Themba, 1985).

With the formal end of apartheid in 1994, some of the passion and the energy has gone out of the production of scholarship and been transferred into tackling the problems of post-apartheid South Africa. It was practically impossible in 1995 to find anyone who would admit to having been a supporter of apartheid (rather like trying to find a Nazi sympathiser in post-1945 Germany). People had 'moved on': the old supporters and beneficiaries of white supremacy (an overwhelming majority of white voters in the 1980s) to suggest that the past was done and gone and that a needless examination of apartheid-era suffering would only prevent social healing in the new South Africa; the old opponents of apartheid to tackle the immediate problems of urban poverty and black illiteracy and a thousand other pressing concerns. Dwindling funding for state universities left the faculties of the 1970s and 1980s largely intact, primarily white, ageing and with little funding to hire black academics. History is not a growth industry in South Africa. Yet one of the major tasks for a new generation is to take advantage of the fall of white supremacy, of the opening up of records, of the new opportunities for people to express themselves openly as to their thoughts and their experiences, and to document the farthest reaches of apartheid and the struggles of countless people to resist racial oppression.

2

Historical background

The history of modern-day South Africa can be traced back to the settlement of the region by numerous African, European and Asian peoples over the centuries. This region was the site of some of the largest and most complexly organised African kingdoms on the continent. It was also the earliest site of continuous European settlement in sub-Saharan Africa. Slaves were primarily imported into, rather than out of, South Africa, in contrast to the rest of the African continent. And in the nineteenth century, South Africa became the richest region on the continent with the discovery of diamonds and the world's largest known deposit of gold. This combination of factors – diversity, longevity, power and wealth – created the framework for the events that would lead to the introduction of **apartheid** in 1948.

Apartheid: Meaning 'apartness' in Afrikaans. The term adopted by the National Party in its successful 1948 election bid to rule the country. Established as a policy to separate physically all races within South Africa in a hierarchy of power with whites at the top and Africans at the bottom.

THE PEOPLES OF SOUTH AFRICA

Some of the oldest evidence in the world documenting the emergence of humankind has been found in South Africa. Fossils of the earliest hominids (*Australopithecus africanus*) date back at least 3.5 million years, and remains linked to modern *Homo sapiens* date back more than 100,000 years. The oldest evidence of upright posture was discovered on a prehistoric lake shore in South Africa and the entire area is dotted with over 20,000 prehistoric cave paintings indicating early habitation by organised human societies. Humans have existed and interacted in the area since earliest times.

These early groups of people, spread over most of southern Africa, lived by a combination of hunting, gathering and fishing. In the drier interior, most lived in bands of 20–80 related family members. Along parts of the coast, larger concentrations of people gathered and hunted, herded sheep and cattle, and cultivated *dagga* (marijuana, their only crop). They continue to exist into the present, long dispersed to the more arid areas of the north-western Cape, southern Angola and Botswana, and known as Khoikhoi ('men of men') and Nama for those with a mixed economy, San and Tshu-Khwe and other dialectical variations for the hunter-gatherer. All are now viewed by scholars as having a common origin and are referred to as the 'Khoisan' peoples.

Over the past two millennia, additional groups of cultivators speaking Bantu languages began to spread across the south-eastern parts of South Africa from farther north. Archaeological evidence of settled cultivation along the south-eastern coast near the current South Africa/Mozambique border dates from as early as 100 CE, with greater evidence dating from the third century CE for much of current Mpumalanga Province and KwaZulu Natal. By around 1600 these Bantu-speaking peoples occupied practically all of the land that received sufficient rain for cultivation (at least 20 inches a year) or that was watered by springs and rivers. In these areas, comprising most land in the eastern half of present-day South Africa, people lived in extended family communities of fewer than 100 near the coast, and in villages of up to 500 and even 1,000 inhabitants in the interior. They lived in patrilineal communities usually named either after an ancestral figure from whom all were assumed to have descended or else after the name of a ruling family. As they absorbed or expelled most of the hunter-gatherer communities, their languages evolved with the incorporation of many Khoisan words. Trade among all groups was extensive throughout the area, with cultivators and pastoralists developing complementary economies.

Although first Portuguese and then Dutch ships had travelled along the southern African coast from the late 1400s onwards, European settlement in South Africa did not begin until 1652. Well before that date the Portuguese had established ports along the west and east coasts of the rest of the African continent, but they feared the treacherous currents that ran along the southern African coast. The Dutch, however, managed to land at the Cape of Good Hope and established a fort run by the Dutch East India Company. The company was a commercial enterprise with ships travelling between Europe and its trading empire in Asia and the company planned to use the Cape fort as a base to resupply its ships with fresh meat and milk obtained from the Khoi. Initially, the Dutch were not interested in establishing a European settlement at the Cape. However, when the local Khoi objected to the poor terms of trade offered, Company officials embarked on a series of frontier wars with the aim of driving them from their land and replacing them with commercial farms run by European settlers using imported slave labour. From the mid-1650s onwards the Company imported slaves supplied from its vast trading network, including a few from West Africa but most from Mozambique, Madagascar, Malabar, Coromandel, Ceylon and the Malay

Robben Island: Site of the prison where Nelson Mandela and other opponents of apartheid would be incarcerated in the twentieth century. Opposite Cape Town, it was also used by the early Dutch administration in the seventeenth and eighteenth centuries as a prison for exiled political opponents from present-day Indonesia, most of them followers of Islam.

archipelago. The Dutch also used **Robben Island**, the site of the prison where Nelson Mandela and other opponents of apartheid would be incarcerated in the twentieth century, as a site for exiled political opponents from present-day Indonesia, most of them followers of Islam.

During the course of the century and a half that the Dutch East India Company controlled the Cape, new population groups developed as people intermingled in the developing colonial society. In addition to Dutch immigrants employed by the Company, Germans and French Huguenots escaping religious persecution also settled at the Cape. Although the Company did not want to encourage the growth of a permanent settler community, European males denied the company of European women frequently procreated with slave and Khoikhoi women. Some of the offspring were incorporated into the European colonial population without regard to race, although most became part of a rapidly developing 'mixed' community whose members were labelled 'Bastaards' by the Company, and who spoke a new Creole language combining Dutch with elements of Malay and colonial Portuguese, a language that became the basis for Afrikaans. Escaped slaves also intermingled with Africans in the interior, creating a new group of people who called themselves Griqua. The Company tried to control these disparate groups through trade and provided a limited legal framework for settling disputes. In all matters, individual rights were linked to racial designations, however, thus creating a racial hierarchy beginning with Company employees at the top, followed by settlers, the 'mixed' racial groups, and with slaves at the bottom. Despite their limited commercial intentions, the Dutch had precipitated the development of a new, racialised society at the Cape.

British entry into southern Africa in 1795, motivated by their determination to cut Napoleon off from his Dutch overseas empire, did not at first change the population makeup of the south-western Cape. Having taken the Cape in order to keep control of the sea route to Asia, the British, like the Dutch East India Company, did not favour the expansion of European settlement with all its consequent costs and responsibilities. They continued to import slaves and only ceased in 1807 when the British parliament forbade participation in the international trade in slaves, stopping short of outlawing the practice of slavery. They tried to avoid costly frontier wars by ordering Dutch settlers not to expand into the east on to the lands of African farmers. When that failed they tried to create a human physical barrier by importing British settlers to establish small-scale agriculture on the eastern frontier. That too failed when the British settlers found that, because of the environment and the lack of a large local market for their produce, they too needed to engage in large-scale pastoralism to survive. And that meant encroaching on the lands of their African neighbours.

Matters came to a head in the 1830s. Critics of slavery in Britain, the Cape and the Caribbean, denouncing the harsh ways in which slaves were treated, succeeded in having slavery prohibited throughout the British Empire. For the Dutch settlers known as 'Boers' (the Dutch word for farmer), this was a blow. They were frustrated at the refusal of the British to conquer African lands in the east for their use and opposed to the loss of their labour force, and they embarked on what has been called the 'Great Trek', leaving British-held territory for areas where they could still practise slavery and hope to obtain new land. Approximately 20 per cent of the Boer population abandoned the Cape in the 1830s, skirting the greatest concentrations of African settlement as they sought out new lands to farm to the north of the Orange and Vaal rivers and on the eastern coast of Africa. Here they established independent states, Transorangia, Transvaal and the Natalia Republic, all based economically on hunting and pastoralism, and politically on republican ideals (the model was the early American republic) but with a limitation of voting rights to white males only. The British quickly invaded the coastal Boer Natalia Republic in the early 1840s, fearing an antagonistic European population with direct access to the sea, and established their own British colony of Natal. Most Boers fled further inland to their other two republics (later known as the Orange Free State, or just Free State, and the South African Republic) where they remained fairly isolated. As they began to develop their own culture and society separate from their European homelands, the experience of the Great Trek had a huge impact on their historical consciousness. In their retelling of the experience they identified the prime enemies of Boer independence as British imperialism and African treachery: the British by causing them to leave the Cape in the first place, the Africans for resisting Boer encroachment on their lands.

By the middle of the 1860s, alongside the development of a British settler community and South Africa's Boer population, and the large African populations who occupied most of the subcontinent, two other groups had developed relatively distinct identities. In the Cape, emancipated slaves, Khoisan and Griqua continued to mix within a colonial society that distinguished between European civilised and African uncivilised, and sought to find a middle ground by adopting the term '**Coloured**' to refer to themselves. Under apartheid, these people were defined initially as neither white nor 'Native', although within a few years government officials subdivided them into seven supposedly distinct and visibly differentiated groups: Cape Coloured, Cape Malay, Griqua, Indian, Chinese, 'other Asiatic' and 'other Coloured'. The final population group to emerge in colonial southern Africa was composed of Indians, originally brought to Natal to work as indentured servants on sugar plantations, who, despite the preference of their British

Coloureds: Population group that emerged in the Cape in the seventeenth and eighteenth centuries as a result of contact between Africans, Malaysians and Europeans. Despite partial European heritage, subjected to most apartheid legal restrictions.

colonial masters that they return to India once their contracts were completed, in most cases stayed to take advantage of economic opportunities not available in their home communities, becoming shopkeepers and small merchants. Most of these people lived in Natal, although a sizeable community also resided in the Transvaal. The Orange Free State, however, prohibited any Indian from living within its boundaries or even traversing the republic without an official permit. Initially the apartheid proponents envisaged no role for these people in South Africa – they planned to repatriate all of them to India – but by the early 1960s, with the failure of the repatriation schemes, they created a new racial category, 'Asian', to parallel that of Coloureds as somewhere between European and African.

Although all the population groups of apartheid-era South Africa were present in some nascent form by the 1860s, they lived in a variety of political units – two British colonies, two Afrikaner republics and several large African kingdoms. Nor were they economically united. The Boers and the Africans engaged in hunting and pastoralism, often competing for the same resources, and their economies were largely semi-subsistence rather than market-based. The British and Dutch settlers in the Cape exported wine and wool to European markets, and the British settlers in Natal exported sugar. None of these items were in quantities sufficient to produce much wealth in the subcontinent or to attract many new settlers to the area. But that would all change with the discovery of diamonds in late 1860s and gold in 1886.

The discovery of diamonds and gold dramatically altered the economic and political structure of southern Africa. The growing mineral industry created ever-greater divisions between British and Boer, white and black, rich and poor. For the first time, South Africa had an extremely valuable resource that attracted foreign capital and large-scale immigration. Discoveries of gold and diamonds in South Africa exceeded those in any other part of the world, and more foreign capital had been invested in South Africa than in the rest of Africa combined. In the Transvaal, the site of the gold discoveries, the white population expanded eightfold, while hundreds of thousands of Africans sought work each year in the newly developed mines and cities of industrialising areas.

Yet not all shared equally in this new-found wealth. Diamond and, in particular, gold mining industries required vast amounts of inexpensive labour in order to be profitable. To limit the ability of African workers to bargain up their wages, and to ensure that they put up with onerous employment conditions, the British in the 1870s and 1880s conquered the still-independent African states in southern Africa, confiscated the bulk of the land and imposed cash taxation demands. In this way, they ensured that men who had chosen previously to work in the mines on their own terms were now forced to do so on employers' terms. In the new industrial cities, African workers were subjected to a bewildering array of discriminatory laws and practices, all enforced in order to keep workers cheap and pliable. In the much diminished rural areas, the wives and children of these migrant labourers had to survive in large part on the limited remittances sent back by their absent menfolk. In short, many of the discriminatory features so typical of twentieth-century South Africa – pass laws, urban ghettos, impoverished rural homelands, African migrant labour – were first established in the course of South Africa's industrial revolution.

The discovery of minerals also exacerbated tensions between the British and the Boers. Gold had been discovered in the Transvaal, and that was beyond the reach of British rule. Yet the capital invested in the mines, and thus the ownership of the gold industry, was primarily British controlled. Lacking investment capital, the Boers found themselves excluded from ownership and thus from the profits generated in their midst. Indeed, most profits from the mines were reinvested in Europe and the Americas and did not contribute to the growth of additional industries in South Africa. When the Boers sought to gain access to some of this wealth through taxation policies, however, they incurred the wrath of the mine owners, their investors in Europe and, ultimately, the British government itself.

THE CREATION OF SOUTH AFRICA: THE SOUTH AFRICAN WAR AND ITS AFTERMATH

The South African War, fought by the Boers and the British between 1899 and 1902, was primarily a struggle for the control of gold. The British government, exasperated with Boer policies it felt were undermining the profitability of the gold mines, sent troops to southern Africa in October 1899 for the purpose of invading and capturing control of the gold-bearing South African Republic. Less than a week later, Boer militia called 'Commandos' retaliated by invading the British colonies of the Cape and Natal. With Boer forces initially outnumbering the British by almost two to one, the early months of fighting were distinguished by Boer victories and British defeats. But the British were intent on victory and ready to expend as many men and as much money as needed to achieve their goals. Having anticipated in 1899 that they could conquer the South African Republic with an army of 75,000, the British found that they had to mobilise over six times that number (366,000 regular soldiers brought over from Britain, 30,000 men imported from other parts of the Empire, 52,000 troops raised in the Cape and Natal, and 30,000 Africans whom they armed), and spend twenty times the expected invasion cost of £10 million before they were able to achieve victory by May 1902.

The costs of the war in human lives and suffering were enormous, especially because of the readiness of the British military commander, Lord Kitchener, to extend the conflict to civilians. The British lost 22,000 men (two-thirds dying from disease), the Boers 7,000. Losses among non-combatants were far greater, however, due to a British 'scorched earth' policy which devastated the Boer civilian population. In the second year of the war Kitchener ordered the forced removal from their farms of all civilians resident in rural areas of the South African Republic and the Free State, the burning of the homesteads and farm equipment, and the incarceration of all those removed in 'concentration camps', a policy modelled on that adopted by the Spanish in Cuba in 1896–7. The British torched 30,000 farms and placed the Boer men, women and children in their own camps, and set up other camps for African women and children while African men were pressed into service in the British army or in the mines. The conditions of imprisonment were appalling, irrespective of race. Of the 115,000 Africans incarcerated during the war, 10 per cent died. The mortality rate was even greater among the Boer prisoners with 28,000 dying (94 per cent of them women and children) of the 110,000 incarcerated. Back in Britain, opposition politicians shamed the government by calling such measures 'methods of barbarism' rather than honourable warfare.

The Boer leaders remained defiant until they could extract a favourable peace agreement that ensured them a measure of local self-government. Under the terms of the Treaty of Vereeniging, signed in May 1902, the British agreed to compensate Boer farmers for their property losses. The two Boer republics would be incorporated into the British Empire as colonies subject to the authority of King Edward VII, thus losing their independence, but they were promised local self-government, along the lines already enjoyed by the Cape and Natal, as soon as circumstances permitted. These terms were already part of a peace deal the Boers had rejected over a year before. At Vereeniging, however, the British added one crucial change to the terms offered in 1901: 'The question of granting the franchise to natives . . . [would] not be decided until after the introduction of self-government' (Eybers, 1918/1969: 346). Given the commitment by Boer and Briton alike to white supremacy, this was an issue on which they could agree.

Although the British had at times before and during the war referred to Boer mistreatment of Africans as a basis for intervention in the South African Republic, this was more pretext than real concern. African political rights were of little consequence to the British, who assured the Boers at the first peace negotiations in March 1901 that any franchise rights extended to blacks would be granted only on terms that would ensure, in the words of

Alfred Milner, British governor of the newly acquired South African colonies, 'the just predominance of the white race' (Newton and Benians, 1936, vol. 8: 606). Moreover, both Boers and British became increasingly concerned during the war at the extent of black participation in the fighting (even when encouraged by the British), and at Africans' clear expectation that the end of the war would be followed by significant improvements in their economic and political situation. In fact, the Vereeniging negotiations took place in a context of European fears about a 'Native uprising'. Thus, the agreement by Boer and British generals and politicians to sign what was essentially a white man's peace, concluded a war in which southern Africans of every denomination had participated and suffered.

Milner was determined to rebuild the whole of South Africa as a British society. He presided over reconstruction in southern Africa from 1902 until he was recalled to Britain in April 1905. He believed it necessary to have a British majority among white male voters, and that meant encouraging immigration into South Africa. Estimating that English-speakers accounted for 36 per cent of the Transvaal's white population in 1901, he argued that five years of British rule buttressing a much more profitable gold industry would attract so many new immigrants that the British share of the population would increase to 54 per cent by 1906. These immigrants, he believed, would give English-speakers a numerical majority of voters and thereby ensure that local legislatures favoured British interests. At the same time, he embarked on a policy of 'denationalisation' towards Dutch-speakers, forbidding the use of Dutch in public schools and in courts of law, in the hope that they would lose any sense they might have of a distinct identity. Both strategies failed completely, however, as the Dutch became antagonised by his efforts and the British lost interest in the low wages offered by the South African mining industry.

Milner sought to deal with the impact of the labour shortage in the short term by seeking out new supplies of cheap workers. He agreed in 1901 on terms particularly favourable to the Portuguese to renew the so-called 'Modus Vivendi' agreement whereby thousands of Mozambicans (who usually comprised two-thirds of the gold industry's black workforce) annually were forced to migrate to work in the gold mines. Most importantly, he facilitated the importation of 60,000 Chinese indentured labourers in 1904. These men, who accounted for one-third of the mines' workforce, were paid less than African mineworkers and were subjected to much more stringent forms of discipline and control. These measures did indeed alleviate the labour shortage, so that by 1906, when they found that as post-war reconstruction was completed alternative employment opportunities in railway and harbour building were coming to an end, Africans had to seek work in the mines and then at wages lower than had been paid in 1899. Given this result, the mine owners agreed to the eventual repatriation of the Chinese workers.

But the British were concerned to fashion a more lasting solution to the labour problem before leaving South Africa. Godfrey Lagden, Milner's commissioner of native affairs in the Transvaal, argued for the utility of allowing Africans some strictly limited amount of land where their families could live so that they could be treated as temporary migrants in the industrial workplaces, and their wives and children could secure their own living on the rural reserves set aside for African occupation. Or, as Lagden bluntly stated: 'A man cannot go with his wife and children and his goods and chattels on to the labour market. He must have a dumping-ground. Every rabbit must have a warren where he can live and burrow and breed, and every native must have a warren too' (Bundy, 1979: 242).

Lagden was appointed chairman of the South African Native Affairs Commission (SANAC) which framed the key features of a segregationist policy that was to persist throughout most of the century. While the SANAC report laid down general principles rather than specific legislation, these principles formed a foundation of racial discrimination upon which

Segregation: Racial discrimination as practised in South Africa from 1910 to 1948. It legally separated races to the benefit of those of European descent and to the detriment of those of African descent. Segregation policies affected the rights of Africans to own land, to live or travel where they chose, and to enjoy job security.

segregation and later apartheid were built. The gist of the recommendations made by the Commission left Africans, in their own ancestral homelands, without the right to own land, to determine their own government, or even to decide where to live or work. The commissioners recommended that African ownership of land should be limited and that separate 'locations' should be established for Africans. Furthermore, 'no Native shall vote in the election of any member or candidate for whom a European has the right to vote'. Africans should vote for a separate list of candidates 'whose qualification of the member or members to represent the natives should be determined by each Legislature' to represent their concerns (SANAC, 1905: 35–6, 97).

Increasing pressures on Africans to enter the labour market and the acceptance of a segregationist ideology by most white politicians led to growing opposition among blacks. Africans, along with Coloureds and Indians, were dismayed that the British did nothing to eliminate racial discrimination existing throughout the colonies and republics. As a result they began to form new political bodies of their own, ranging from the South African Native Congress, established in 1898 but really expanding after 1902 as it considered how to protect the rights of Africans as British citizens, to the Native Vigilance Association (1901), formed to look after 'the educational and local interest of the Transkeian natives generally', the African Political (later People's) Organization (1902), formed to represent the concerns of Cape Coloureds, the Transvaal Native Vigilance Association (1902), which argued for political and civil rights for all South Africans irrespective of colour, to the Natal Native Congress (1900) and the Natal Indian Congress (founded by Mohandas Gandhi in 1894) which concerned themselves with, respectively, providing a forum for Africans to vent their grievances and defending the voting rights of Indians. Together with these organisations, Africans, Coloureds and Indians developed an expanding and vibrant vernacular and English-language press throughout the country, with only the Orange River Colony lacking a local black-owned newspaper (although a Basutoland newspaper circulated widely in the colony) in the years after the war (Odendaal, 1984).

These groups soon began to flex their muscles. In the Cape Colony Abdullah Abdurahman, a Scottish-trained doctor, became president of the African Political Organization (APO) in 1904 and, through stressing the political discrimination to which Coloureds were subjected, built it into a vital body with 20,000 members by 1910. Mohandas Gandhi began a passive resistance campaign against the pass laws in 1906, leading Indians in Natal and the Transvaal (they were legally prohibited from living in or entering the Orange Free State) in demonstrations and organising stop-work protests that won the support of thousands of people. Opponents of British race policies also began developing links with critics of white supremacy elsewhere, running stories in the African press of the struggles of African Americans to better their conditions, of the need to link up with Africans in other British colonies, and drawing the attention of their readers to the Japanese victory over the Russians in the war of 1905. Most dramatically, in 1906 an armed rebellion led by a Zulu chief, Bambatha, broke out over issues of forced labour, land confiscation and taxation. Although violently repressed (3,000 Zulu were killed for only 30 white casualties, and Bambatha was hunted down, executed, and his corpse mutilated), the uprising increased white fears of future mass rebellion.

At the same time, the basic configuration of white politics also changed substantially. The failure of Milner's post-war immigration schemes meant that Dutch speakers would always constitute a majority of the white voting population. Moreover, steps taken by Dutch speakers to establish their own 'Christian-National' schools, to develop 'Afrikaans' as a language in its own right rather than a linguistically-impoverished dialect of Dutch, and to construct an identity for themselves as a national group – 'Afrikaners' or people of Africa – rather than settlers designated by their occupational status, Boer or farmer, reflected a similar failure for Milner's denationalisation policies. Growing national sentiment, founded especially on bitterness about the South African War, produced two new political parties. In 1905 Louis Botha (with Jan Christian Smuts as his deputy) established a new political party in the Transvaal, Het Volk (The People), while another ex-general, J.B.M. Hertzog, in 1906 formed Orangia Unie in the Orange River Colony. Both parties sought self-government, increased work opportunities for Afrikaners driven from their farms during the war, and the immediate repatriation of the

Chinese (who were viewed as competitors for jobs that poor whites could possibly occupy in the mining industry). In Britain, the general election of 1906 brought the Liberals to power, many of whom had strongly opposed the South African War. Indeed, it was the new prime minister, Henry Campbell Bannerman, who had coined the phrase 'methods of barbarism' to describe British policies during the war. The first policy change of this new imperial administration was to agree to full self-government for the Transvaal and the Orange River Colony by 1907, rather than a process stretched over a much longer period.

But how could the British return the Boers to self-rule without endangering the mining industry and thereby recreating the cycle of events that had led to war in 1899? The solution lay in the realisation by both sides that profits for all could be made at the expense of African workers. As Jan Smuts put it to one of the mine owners, 'their interests [were] in so many ways identical . . . as large property-holders'. At the beginning of 1906 Jan Smuts approached Julius Wernher, the head of the largest mining company, with a proposal that Het Volk would agree to a slow repatriation of the Chinese if the mining companies would agree to employ Afrikaners. These Afrikaners could be employed in place of not the poorly paid Chinese and Africans, but rather the much more highly paid English-speaking workers who occupied, by longstanding industry practice, all the skilled and semi-skilled jobs in mining. At the same time, the ratio between black and white workers would rise, resulting in a substantial overall decrease in the amount the mines spent on wages, white and black. The English-speaking miners went on strike, the mining companies brought in Afrikaner strike-breakers who were protected by British troops, and the strike was broken with many of the English dismissed and Afrikaners employed in their place at lower rates of pay, but still considerably higher than those paid to black workers. As one of the directors of Wernher Beit expressed matters, the world was 'getting topsy-turvy; a Boer government calling out British troops to keep English miners in order while Dutch men are replacing them in the mines. . . . You may rest assured that we are taking every advantage of the strike to reduce working costs as far as possible' (Marks and Trapido, 1979: 73).

A commitment to segregation and to institutionalising white supremacy on a national basis underpinned the establishment on 31 May 1910, of the Union of South Africa. Between October 1908 and May 1909 white representatives from each of the four British colonies in southern Africa met at a national convention to set the terms on which a formal union should be established. Through a process of negotiation and compromise they agreed to form a unitary rather than federal state with a Westminster-style parliament in which a simple majority would give any victorious party power to pass practically any legislation that it wished. The central legislative, administrative and judicial bodies would be shared between the capitals of the Cape (Cape Town), the Transvaal, the pre-war South African Republic (Pretoria), and the Orange River Colony, the pre-war Free State (Bloemfontein), as a means to ensure that all whites felt involved in decision-making in the new state.

While all whites were to be ensured of their participation, they would be the only ones so involved. Despite the protestations of the Natal Native Congress and other bodies that any 'scheme for the Closer Union of the Colonies under the British Crown should include a provision that representation should be accorded fairly to all sections of the community, without distinctions of colour', the members of the convention included in the South Africa Act, 1909, a formal stipulation that all elected representatives in the new parliament be male British subjects 'of European descent' only (Odendaal, 1984: 142). Voting rights in each of the four colonies would remain as they were at the date of the Union's establishment, that is, the franchise would be limited to all white males in the Transvaal and the Orange Free State (as the Orange River Colony was renamed) but not extended to any blacks, by a system of economic qualification in the Cape which included most white men but relatively few Coloureds or Africans (Europeans comprised 85 per cent of the electorate but only 24 per cent of the population in the Cape at the beginning of the twentieth century), and by a mechanism in Natal that included all white males but excluded all Indians and practically all Africans (the latter two groups comprising respectively 0.8 per cent and 0.01 per cent of the eligible voters in 1903). To head this new Union the British governor general, under powers granted him by the South Africa Act, chose Louis Botha as the first prime minister.

UNION AND SEGREGATION

Racial discrimination in South Africa in the years following Union in 1910 and preceding the institution of apartheid in 1948 was enforced through a policy of segregation. Although implemented to varying degrees throughout the new country, the policy of segregation generally separated races to the benefit of those of European descent and to the detriment of those of African descent. Segregation policies affected the rights of Africans to own land, to live or travel where they chose, and to enjoy job security. While segregation was not as sweeping or inclusive as apartheid, neither was it an informal system of discrimination. Segregation policies that increasingly limited African rights were implemented through a series of laws passed during the first half of the twentieth century, and which were often enforced with great brutality. Although sometimes viewed as more benign than apartheid, segregation nevertheless shaped South African society in fundamental ways that still affect the country into the twenty-first century.

Segregation policies attempted to protect white political and economic interests while at the same time drawing Africans increasingly into the country's economy as the chief source of labour. Throughout the twentieth century, whites represented no more than 20 per cent (and closer to 10 per cent at the end of the century) of the South African population, yet they controlled the majority of the country's economic resources. Key to this development was the use of African labour at very low wages and under extremely strict control. One of the first pieces of legislation to emerge from the new South African government that aimed to restrict African employment to menial and unskilled jobs was the 1911 Mines and Works Act. Under this legislation, Africans were excluded from most skilled categories of work in the mines, in effect 'reserving' those jobs for whites. In the same year, the Native's Labour Regulation Act set down the conditions under which Africans would work. They were to be recruited in the rural areas, fingerprinted and issued with a 'pass' allowing them to enter the cities, and if they broke their employment contract or stayed in the urban areas beyond the length of the contract, they were to be arrested and forced to do hard labour for up to two months. As Africans increasingly protested and resisted these oppressive terms of employment through union organisation and industrial strikes, the South African government responded with the Industrial Conciliation Act of 1924, restricting African rights to organise or to negotiate their terms of employment. Under this Act, 'pass-bearing' African males could not be considered under the legal term 'employee', thus excluding them from all rights of labour representation, mediation or organisation. Under segregation, African workers were limited to unskilled jobs, were punished if they quit their jobs, and were robbed of their rights to protest these conditions.

Not surprisingly, Africans tried to avoid such terms of employment and it was necessary for the South African government to take drastic measures to force Africans into the wage workforce. Key to these efforts was the restriction of Africans' ability to earn their own livelihood, as they had before white occupation, on their own farms. Heavy taxes on African farmers had been introduced by the British prior to 1910, including taxes on dogs, on huts and even on heads in an effort to force people into employment in the mines or on white farms. African farmers had responded to these pressures by increasing their agricultural production and successfully participating in the commercial sale of their crops in competition with white farmers. Therefore, in 1913, the South African government passed the Natives' Land Act, restricting African ownership of land to designated areas comprising 7 per cent of the country's total land area. Although the government justified the Act by arguing that these lands approximated African landholdings prior to white occupation, and even increased the percentage share of land to 13 per cent in 1936, most land reserved for Africans was of poor quality and could not meet the needs of the growing African population (Map 1). As the productive capacity of the land waned and taxation proved unrelenting, Africans were increasingly forced into work on white farms, in factories, and in the growing mining industry.

The impact of segregationist policies became most apparent in the cities as white municipalities struggled to deal with the steady influx of Africans seeking work to support their families. While the system of labour contracts and passes encouraged and often forced Africans to return to the rural areas after the completion of their contract, many stayed in the cities rather than return to sure poverty and starvation. In 1923, the government passed the Natives (Urban Areas) Act to establish a uniform policy towards urban Africans. The government had agreed that Africans should remain in the cities only to 'minister to the needs of the white population'. Under this Act, employed Africans were restricted to segregated townships or locations where they could rent accommodation provided by the municipality. Africans coming to town to seek work could stay for only limited periods of time and were returned to the rural areas or imprisoned if they remained without work. The right to live in town was precarious and opportunities for advancement were circumscribed by segregationist limitations on land ownership and business licences.

As segregation became increasingly broad, affecting Africans in the rural areas, urban areas and at the workplace, the government sought to create a more comprehensive system of rule throughout the country. In 1927 the Native Administration Act was passed giving the Department of Native Affairs control over all matters pertaining to Africans. In effect, this Act separated all policies concerning Africans from the rest of the government. Under this Act, the government ruled by decree rather than by law in the African rural areas – deemed the Tribal Reserves – and established separate administrations in the Reserves staffed by bureaucrats and appointed chiefs. As Africans lost the right to reside in the cities and were pushed into the reserves, these policies left most people under despotic rule. In 1936, the few political rights left to Africans under a colour-blind voter franchise in the Cape province were removed under the Representation of Natives Act. Although Africans were allowed to elect a limited number of white representatives, by 1936 they were substantially segregated in the political as well as the economic and social arenas of South African society.

The impact of segregation was devastating for Africans. The rural areas quickly became unable to support the African population and as people sought to work elsewhere they were forced into a system of migrant labour, moving between workplaces where they had no rights, back to rural homes where they could not survive. By the close of the segregation era, African workers and politicians increasingly and aggressively demanded greater rights, staging strikes, protests and boycotts. Laying the foundations for the apartheid era, segregation systematised discrimination and strengthened African resistance – which would both intensify under apartheid.

THE AFRICAN RESPONSE

African National Congress (ANC): Formed in 1912 as the South African Native National Congress (renamed the African National Congress in 1923). Established originally to protest against racial discrimination and to appeal for equal treatment before the law. Declared illegal in 1960 under the terms of the Unlawful Organizations Act. Unbanned in 1990. Secured a majority of the votes in the 1994 national election and formed the government with Nelson Mandela as president.

African opposition to segregation legislation began with the drafting of the Natives' Land Bill in 1911 and led directly to the formation in 1912 of the South African Native National Congress (SANNC, renamed the **African National Congress**, ANC, in 1923). Several hundred members of South Africa's educated African elite met at Bloemfontein on 8 January 1912 and established a national organization to protest against racial discrimination and to appeal for equal treatment before the law. The founding president was John L. Dube, a minister and school teacher who had studied in the United States and who had been strongly influenced by Booker T. Washington. Pixley Ka Isaka Seme, a lawyer with degrees from Columbia University and Oxford University and a prime mover in organising the meeting to establish the Congress, was appointed treasurer. Solomon T. Plaatje, a court translator, author and newspaper editor, who had worked in Kimberley and Johannesburg, became secretary general. The meeting opened and closed with the singing of the hymn 'Nkosi Sikelel'i Afrika' ('God Bless Africa'), which had been composed during the nineteenth century by a Xhosa poet.

The Congress was moderate in composition, tone and practice. Its founders were men who felt that British rule had brought considerable benefits, especially Christianity, education and the rule of law, but who also considered that their careers as teachers, lawyers and court translators were hindered by the racial discrimination so endemic in South Africa. They called not for an end to British rule but for respect for the concept of equality for all, irrespective of colour. Their draft constitution stressed the importance of promoting 'unity and mutual cooperation between the Government and the Abantu Races of South Africa' and 'mutual understanding between the Native chiefs and the encouragement in them and their people of a spirit of loyalty to the British Crown and all lawfully constituted authorities'. In aiming to 'bring about better understanding between the white and black inhabitants of South Africa', the founders of the ANC believed that they could best achieve their aims by dialogue with the British. As John Dube said, the Congress pursued a policy of 'hopeful reliance on the sense of common justice and love of freedom so innate in the British character' (Odendaal, 1984: 273–4). Such reliance, however, proved unfounded. When the Congress sent a deputation to London in 1914 to protest against the Natives' Land Act, the colonial secretary informed them that there was nothing that he could do.

While the petitions and deputations of the SANNC did not persuade white politicians to change their segregationist policies, the increasing movement of Africans into South Africa's towns and cities and into the urban and industrial workforce did pose new challenges for the state. When, for example, the municipal authorities in the Orange Free State capital of Bloemfontein (the population of which had grown tenfold between 1890 and 1904) sought in 1913 to control the movement of African women by requiring them for the first time to carry passes upon their persons, hundreds of these women gathered at police stations, tore up their passes and demanded that they be arrested. At one demonstration held to protest these arrests the leader of the protesters wrapped herself in a Union Jack while those gathered about her defended themselves from the approaching police with rocks, sticks and even their teeth. Because of the determination of their resistance, the municipal authorities backed down and for 40 years African women in South Africa remained free of the requirement that they carry passes.

In the aftermath of the First World War, the retention of wartime controls on wages in a context of rising food and housing prices led to further African challenges to employers and the government. The SANNC petitioned the British king in 1918, stressing the loyalty of Africans to the Empire, noting that during the First World War 17,000 men had fought for the British in East Africa and another 25,000 had laboured on the docks and in the trenches of France, and asking that the king intervene to eliminate 'discrimination on account of colour or creed' in South Africa (http://www.anc.org.za/ancdocs/history/early/petition181216.html). When the British declined to become involved in what they deemed to be the internal affairs of South Africa, the SANNC deputation travelled on to the Versailles peace conference where, though not admitted to the conference, they called for the principles of self-determination to be extended to colonised peoples and not only to Europeans. In 1919 the SANNC, adopting the example of the Bloemfontein women and the non-violent methods used successfully by Gandhi, protested against the pass laws by refusing to carry the documents and courting arrest, although the demonstrations were broken up by police and white vigilantes.

The greatest challenge, however, came from organised black labour. Sanitation workers in Johannesburg and mineworkers on the Rand (short for Witwatersrand, the site of the 1886 gold discoveries) went on strike in 1918. The following year Bloemfontein location workers struck in support of their demand for a minimum daily wage, the SANNC began organising a nationwide campaign against the operation of the pass laws, and in Cape Town an immigrant from Nyasaland (Malawi), Clements Kadalie, began organising

African dockworkers into a new union, the Industrial and Commercial Workers' Union (ICU). The ICU first went on strike in 1919 in support of white railwaymen who had requested assistance in their own dispute over higher wages. The largest African strike came in February 1920 when over 70,000 men in 21 mines walked off the job. Although forced back to work at gunpoint by police and soldiers, and with 11 of their number killed, these strikers caused great concern among employers already concerned at possible 'Bolshevik' influences. The Transvaal Chamber of Mines noted that the work stoppage was 'not, as all previous native troubles have been, a riot; it is a regular strike organised on the European model, obviously by persons who are acquainted with European practices in such matters' (Yudelman, 1983: 150).

Smuts did not hesitate to use force when he thought it necessary to crush resistance to his policies. In May 1921, when 1,000 followers of a religious prophet, Enoch Mgijima, gathered in an area of the eastern Cape marked by a severe shortage of farm labourers and refused to dismantle their settlement, a thousand policemen armed with machine-guns killed 190 men, women and children within the space of ten minutes. When a group of the Nama people in Southwest Africa from 1921–2 protested against land loss, taxes and the forcible deportation of their leader, more than a hundred were killed by a combination of machine-gun fire and aerial bombing.

Black opposition to segregation legislation and policies began to expand throughout the country through various organisations during the 1920s. The ICU under Kadalie's charismatic leadership grew enormously in urban and even more so in rural areas, expanding beyond its origins as a trade union to claim between 150,000 and 200,000 members demanding better wages, the extension of voting rights to all tax-paying Africans, the end of the pass laws, more land and freedom of speech. Members of the South African Communist Party sought to organise African workers into trade unions and to join with whites in class action against employers. These efforts met with considerable success. The Non-European Trade Union Federation formed in 1928 represented more than 12 black unions with a membership exceeding 10,000 and engaged actively in a campaign of strike action in combination with white workers. Even within the African National Congress (as the SANNC had been renamed in 1923), more radical members were moving into leadership positions. Josiah Tshangana (James) Gumede, a founding member of the Natal Native Congress, participant in the SANNC's deputation to the 1918 Versailles peace conference and a supporter of the 1920 African mine-workers' strike, became president of the ANC in 1927 with a call for all critics, whether conservative or radical, of 'the tyranny of European rule' to join together in their efforts. That same year, he attended the first international conference (held in Brussels, Belgium) of the League Against Imperialism, and then travelled to Moscow to join in celebrations of the tenth anniversary of the Russian Revolution. He returned to South Africa in 1928 praising the Soviet Union as a society free of class oppression where racial discrimination was unknown – 'I have seen the new world to come . . . I have been to the new Jerusalem' (Simons and Simons, 1969: 402).

By the mid-1930s, all African organisations were interested in combining their efforts to turn back the determined white tide of segregation. In December 1935, 400 delegates representing practically every African political organisa-tion in South Africa met at Bloemfontein (where the SANNC had been formed in 1912) to establish the All-Africa Convention (AAC). The mem-bers of this new organisation (including leaders of the ANC, Communist Party and the ICU) combined in denunciations of the 'oppressive laws', with expressions of loyalty to South Africa and to the British Crown. They demanded 'full partnership' and citizenship, and rejected political and economic segregation. Yet they were divided as to what measures to take to express their opposition – deputations and petitions of the form favoured by the more conservative leaders of the ANC or mass action in the form of demonstrations and strikes as favoured by the more radical leaders of the Communist Party (CP). Separately, the CP took the lead in organising the establishment of a large number of African trade unions to agitate in the workplace for better conditions of labour and improved wages. The Party encouraged all workers, white, African, Coloured and Indian, to combine together in their struggles against employers, raising considerable concern among members of the government at the growth of 'Bolshevism'. One of the most significant of the unions formed, the **African Mineworkers' Union (AMWU)**, with a leadership comprising both ANC and CP members, grew rapidly from its formation in 1941 to a membership of 25,000 by 1943, raising fears among mining employers of renewed labour struggles on the level of the 1920 African mineworkers' strike. Moreover, the growth on the Rand of autonomous squatter camps, spreading in defiance of the municipal authorities and under the leadership of such men as James Mpanza, one of the delegates to the 1935 meeting that formed the AAC, appeared to threaten white control of the cities.

African Mineworkers' Union (AMWU): Formed in 1941 by migrant mining workers. Grew to member-ship of 25,000 by 1943, and in 1946 organised strike by 100,000 black mineworkers.

THE RISE OF AFRIKANERDOM

While determined African actions continued to stymie the full success of segregation legislation, Afrikaners had started to reclaim their political iden-tity, shattered by the South African War, and to fashion a South African nationalism that was radically exclusionist. Disgruntled with Smuts' support for the mining industry, Afrikaner voters began to turn to J.B.M. Hertzog and

National Party (NP):
Formed in 1914 by J.B.M.
Hertzog in opposition to
the Botha–Smuts South
African Party (SAP) and to
represent the interests of
Afrikaners. Gained con-
trol of the government in
1924 in a coalition with
the Labour Party and
took exclusive control in
1928 until joining in a
'Fusion'   government
with the SAP in 1934.
Eschewed co-operation
with other parties during
the Second World War
and re-emerged in 1948
to take control of par-
liament and form its
own government under
D.F. Malan.

his **National Party (NP)**. Hertzog had formed the NP at the beginning of
1914 to represent the interests of Afrikaners like himself: generally from the
poorer areas of the country (such as the Free State), usually small farmers,
members of the urban working class or professionals such as teachers and
lawyers who felt themselves discriminated against by the English-only policies of the government and who were still embittered by the experiences of
the Afrikaner people during the South African War. The nascent party grew
considerably after August 1914 when Botha and Smuts took South Africa
into the First World War on the side of the British against Germany. For
many Afrikaners, the memory of British brutality and German sympathy
during the South African War made such a move repugnant. When Afrikaner
opponents of South Africa's entry into the world war organised armed upris-
ings, government forces crushed them, killing several men who had been
generals on the Boer side in the 1899–1902 war and thereby providing
martyrs for the new political party. Support for the party grew enormously,
with NP candidates winning the majority of Afrikaner votes from 1915
onwards and gaining control of parliament in 1924 in a coalition, or 'Pact'
government, with the Labour Party.

Hertzog and his supporters attempted to create a broad base of Afrikaner
identity and political mobilisation. They stressed the richness and importance of the Afrikaans language and supported the publication of books and
magazines in Afrikaans. They argued that the Botha–Smuts administration
favoured mining capital and British interests at the expense of all white South
Africans and sent representatives to the Versailles peace talks to press for
international recognition of the right of self-determination for the citizens of
the Transvaal and the Free State. By pooling their limited funds, Afrikaners
created their own financial institutions – the South African National
Trust Company (SANTAM) and the South African National Life Assurance
Company (SANLAM), both established in 1918 – to counter the impact of
the refusal of English-owned banks to loan money to Afrikaners. Young
professionals – teachers, clerks and ministers in the Dutch Reformed
Church – created in 1918 another exclusively Afrikaner organisation, the

Broederbond: Meaning
'brotherhood'. Exclusively
an Afrikaner organisation
established in the wake
of the First World War to
celebrate and protect
Afrikaner culture. Within
a few years organised as
a strictly secret society
whose   membership
and actions were not
disclosed to English-
speaking whites.

Broederbond, or Brotherhood, to bring people together to celebrate and
protect Afrikaner culture. Within a few years they had organised it as a
strictly secret society whose membership and actions were not disclosed to
English-speaking whites.

Hertzog's administration significantly shaped segregationist policies
during the 1920s and 1930s through two initiatives: the introduction of
the 'civilised labour' policy and the passage of the 'Native Bills'. The 'civilised
labour' policy was based on the concept that white workers deserved a
wage that could support a 'civilised', that is, not African, standard of living
(Yudelman, 1983: 225). Employers were encouraged to hire whites with the

promise of protective tariffs from the government in return. Hertzog's 'Native Bills', which were finally passed in the late 1930s, stripped Africans in the Cape of their right to vote, under the same qualifications, as Europeans and established separate government administration for Africans.

Nevertheless, segregationist legislation had not benefited all whites equally. The rural Afrikaner population, beset by landlessness and poverty, had fallen by almost two-fifths between 1921 and the end of the 1930s as poor whites moved into cities seeking jobs in an environment in which English speakers almost without exception owned mining, banking and commerce, and Africans competed with Afrikaners for unskilled jobs. In this context, the leaders of the Broederbond, most of them teachers, lawyers and other professionals, who felt their careers held down by the pro-English sentiments of private business and state bureaucracy alike, sought to mobilise Afrikaners socially, economically and politically. In 1929 the Broederbond had formed the Federasie van Afrikaner Kultuurorganisasies (Federation of Afrikaner Cultural Organisations, FAK) to develop a sense of pride and accomplishment in Afrikaner culture, following the example provided by the Christian National Schools established immediately after the South African War. The FAK organised Afrikaans music examinations, collected folksongs, set up Afrikaner art exhibitions, and called on people to remember their past – one marked by suffering at the hands of British imperialists. Language – Afrikaans – stood at the centre of this emphasis on ethnicity, distinguishing Afrikaners from other whites, especially English speakers. As one Broederbond leader expressed matters:

> Our call to maintain and assert our language is not born out of racial hatred [towards the British] . . . we are here concerned with our highest and holiest ethnic concerns, for defence of language means in the nature of the case defence of the People, because it means the cultivation and confirmation of national consciousness, national pride, national calling, and national destiny.
>
> (Moodie, 1975: 109)

With language as the unifying base, the Broederbond encouraged Afrikaans speakers to invest in the organisations – SANLAM and SANTAM – formed after the First World War to encourage Afrikaner business, and focused on gaining political power to achieve their social and economic goals. At the annual congress of the Broederbond in 1932, the leader of the organisation expressed quite explicitly his ethnic agenda:

> After the cultural and economic needs, the Broederbond will have to dedicate its attention to the political needs of our People. And this aim

must include a completely independent, truly Afrikaans government for South Africa – a government which by its embodiment of our own personal head of state, bone of our bone, flesh of our flesh, will inspire us and bind us together to irresistible unity and power.

(Moodie, 1975: 112)

Afrikaner ethnic organisation expanded aggressively during the 1930s. It was encouraged particularly by Hertzog's negotiation of a political alliance with Smuts in 1933 and the creation of a formal union between the National and South African parties in 1934, with the new **United Party (UP)** government headed by Hertzog with Smuts as his deputy. Many Afrikaners, especially the founders of the Broederbond, opposed this move by Hertzog as, in their eyes, a sell-out to the forces of capitalism and imperialism as represented by English-speaking mine owners and the overly pro-British Smuts. They wanted guarantees that South Africa could remain neutral rather than always having to go to war on the side of Britain, and they wanted a republic. The same year as the Hertzog–Smuts agreement (1933), Hitler came to power in Germany and his movement and theories had considerable influence in South Africa, particularly on the members of the Gesuiverde Nasionale Party (Purified National Party), formed in 1934 by Daniel Malan with the support of the Broederbond. Malan and his allies were strong supporters of capitalism, but not capitalism as they perceived it operating in South Africa, dominated by the British and by Jews. They were also critical of the influence of communist organisers among black and white trade unionists. Alongside the Purified National Party and the Broederbond, admirers of Hitler established Grey Shirt and Black Shirt organisations to combat communism. The Broederbond organised a 'voortrekker' movement for Afrikaner youth as a separate version of the Boy Scouts movement of English speakers. They also assisted in the establishment of trade unions for Afrikaans speakers only, separate from those of other whites and free of socialist influences. Moving on a broad front of ethnic mobilisation, the Purified Nationalists and the Broederbond pressed Afrikaners to engage in 'volkskapitalisme' (people's capitalism) by, for example, paying small monthly subscriptions for a Christian-National 'reddingsdaad' (salvation-deed) – later a formal organisation, the Reddingsdaadbond – that would in turn invest the money in Afrikaner businesses.

Ethnic mobilisation really took off in 1938 when the FAK organised a centenary celebration of the Great Trek and the voortrekkers' defeat of the Zulu king, Dingane, at the Battle of Blood River in December 1838. Stressing the heroic struggles of the voortrekkers fleeing British oppression and facing African treachery, the celebration was not historically accurate (in recreating the trek, the organisers had the wagon trains leave Cape Town whereas in

United Party (UP): Formal union between the National and South African parties in 1934. Remained under the leadership of Smuts when Hertzog resigned in 1939 and in power until 1948 when it lost the election to the National Party. Dissolved in 1977.

the mid-1830s the voortrekkers had left from the eastern Cape) but did have an enormous emotional impact. Wagon parties travelled through every part of South Africa, visiting each town and making collections for the Reddingsdaadbond. Dunbar Moodie, a sociologist who interviewed people in the 1970s for a book on Afrikaner nationalism, records that:

> Every Afrikaner that I interviewed, of whatever political persuasion, recalled the events and activities of the 1938 centenary with deeply personal intensity. The sacred history was constituted and actualized as a general context of meaning for all Afrikanerdom in spontaneous liturgical re-enactments during the 1938 celebrations.
>
> (Moodie, 1975: 180)

The wagon parties converged at two points. First at Blood River in Natal, site of the defeat of the Zulu supposedly because of the intervention of God on the side of the Afrikaners. Second, on a hill outside Pretoria where a foundation stone was laid for a monument that would record and celebrate in stone friezes the ability of the voortrekkers to escape British oppression and defeat African chicanery and to memorialise their *volkseenheid* (people's unity). On the night before the foundation stone was to be laid, torch bearers from all parts of South Africa met at the monument site and, passing before a huge fire, threw their torches into the conflagration. Elsa Joubert, a 16-year-old in 1938 who witnessed the event, recalled vividly the scene 30 years later:

> The hearts of the three thousand Voortrekkers, each of whom in his own town had formed a link in the chain of the Torch Marathon, beat faster when they saw the light of the torch coming towards them over the hills in the dusk. . . .
>
> The hill is on fire; on fire with Afrikaner fire; on fire with the enthusiasm of Young South Africa! You are nothing – your People is all. One light in the dusk is puny and small. But three thousand flames. Three thousand! And more! There's hope for your future, South Africa!
>
> (Moodie, 1975: 183–4)

The future envisaged by those gathered at Pretoria in 1938 was of a white republic ruled by Afrikaners and neutral in any conflict between Britain and Germany. The major organisational development after the voortrekker centenary was the formation of the **Ossewabrandwag (Ox-wagon sentinel, OB)**. Established on the model of Hitler's national socialist movement, the members of the OB (300,000 by the end of 1939) swore loyalty to the *volk* (people) and to the *volksleier* (people's leader). Support for the organisation

Ossewabrandwag (OB): 'Ox-wagon sentinel'. Established in 1938 by Afrikaners participating in the commemoration of the Great Trek. Aimed at inculcating a 'love for fatherland' and at instituting, by armed force if necessary, an Afrikaner-controlled republic in South Africa. During the war, some OB members were arrested for sabotage against the government. By 1949 claimed a membership of 250,000.

among many Afrikaners grew at the end of 1939 when Jan Smuts led a parliamentary coup against Hertzog – who opposed South Africa's entry into the world war that began in September of that year, lost the premiership, and later joined with Malan – and brought South Africa into the war on the side of Britain. The students at the Afrikaans-language university of Potchefstroom expressed the views of many Afrikaners when they stated in their newspaper that:

> Parliament [had] made an unjust decision . . . it was decided that South Africa must wage war against a People which is fighting for its life. . . . For no nation other than England has ever threatened our existence. . . . We as students are therefore decided to shed no drop of blood in the interest of the British empire.
>
> (Moodie, 1975: 192–3)

During the war, although Afrikaners remained divided about the issue of participation – many fought against the Axis powers, while others engaged in a sabotage campaign against the war effort in South Africa – leaders of the Broederbond continued to articulate a political vision of the future that stressed the special role of Afrikaners. Moreover, they underpinned their claims to a special role with references to divine support, as in this 1944 speech by the chairman of the Broederbond:

> In every People in the world is embodied a Divine Idea and the task of each People is to build upon that Idea and to perfect it. So God created the Afrikaner People with a unique language, a unique philosophy of life, and their own history and tradition in order that they might fulfill a particular calling and destiny here in the southern corner of Africa. . . . We must believe that God has called us to be servants of his righteousness in this place.
>
> (Moodie, 1975: 110–11)

While Afrikaner ethnicity was mobilised primarily against the dominance of English speakers in South African business and politics, Afrikaners and English alike were practically unanimous in support of segregation as the policy of choice regarding Africans. Such unanimity reflected the basic fact that white privilege rested on black labour in every part of the country. And while there might be differences in the ways in which such support could be expressed, its practical impact was much the same for Africans. They were denied voting and property rights in practically all of South Africa, especially the cities deemed by Afrikaners and English alike as the preserve of whites even as Africans toiled in the mines and factories, and cleaned the houses of their white *baas's* (bosses). Ralph Bunche, an African-American scholar who travelled through South Africa in 1937–8 on a comparative study of the interaction between western and non-western societies, was struck by the difference from his experiences in the United States. Writing in his journal on 9 December 1938, Bunche noted that 'South Africa is an entire country ridden by race prejudice – unlike [the] U.S. in that there is absolutely no escape at all for these black and colored people' (Bunche, 1992: 249).

After nearly 300 years of white settlement, South Africa was divided on nearly every conceivable level. The numerous racial and ethnic groups, from the descendants of the original Khoi to the latest Indian immigrants, were separated by race, language, wealth, politics, residence, jobs, and on and on in practically every aspect of daily life. Under such a system, few could reap the rich benefits of life in South Africa. The differences between the advantaged and disadvantaged created an unstable situation which would continue to worry the country's white rulers. The answer would be to entrench the existing divisions under an ironclad system of racial separation that would be known as apartheid.

Part 2

ANALYSIS

3

The basis of apartheid

In 1948, white South African voters elected a government dedicated to the ideology of apartheid or, in Afrikaans, 'apartness' or 'apart-hood'. Not content with separation under segregation, the new government would fashion a system that precluded Africans from all rights normally associated with those of citizens. By the 1980s, many Africans in South Africa would no longer legally be considered citizens of that country but would be categorised as foreigners. At the same time, former colonial subjects in Africa and Asia were being given their independence, the civil rights movement was making gains in the US and elsewhere, and it appeared that the world was moving towards greater human rights for all. In comparison, South Africa appeared to be moving backwards at an alarming rate.

WHY APARTHEID?

The reasons for this dramatically regressive turn of events have been hotly debated by scholars, politicians and concerned people everywhere. For some, apartheid was the logical extension of South Africa's own history, a continuation of an intensified form of segregation. Indeed, apartheid rested on a long legacy of racial discrimination. Many apartheid laws merely elaborated on previous colonial policies and segregation legislation. Most South Africans, however, would argue that apartheid made a fundamental and qualitative difference in their lives. The sheer brutality of its implementation and its ultimately overarching impact on the country signalled a dramatic shift. Politicians in opposition to apartheid blamed this shift in race relations on the new Afrikaner Nationalist Party government that came to power in 1948. Opposition politicians, who were primarily English-speaking, accused the Nationalist Party of a regressive 'frontier mentality' derived from years of brutal discrimination towards Africans and economic deprivation experienced by the Afrikaners since the nineteenth century. In other words, they argued that apartheid was a sort of ethnic throwback to the Great Trek, associated exclusively with Afrikaans society and culture. Many scholars in the 1970s and 1980s argued that economic concerns, not history or culture, laid the basis for apartheid. In particular, they asserted that this extreme form of racial discrimination was motivated by white business owners who believed a massive, low-paid African workforce would allow them to make unprecedented profits. Other scholars have argued that white workers and farmers also benefited economically from racially discriminatory laws that protected them from competition with African workers and producers. Historical, cultural and economic forces all undoubtedly played a part in leading South Africa into apartheid.

The immediate causes of the turn to apartheid can be traced to the events of the Second World War. Between 1940 and 1946 South Africa underwent a huge economic and social transformation as the result of the country's participation in the Second World War. Factories expanded to fill the wartime need for many goods, including military supplies, drawing workers into the cities from all over the country. As Africans and whites alike were employed in the new factories, the racial lines between workers became a source of great contention and South Africa experienced serious labour strikes and industrial action. By the end of the war, manufacturing had become the country's most productive economic sector. Nearly half of the population was living in the cities, and competition for jobs between African and white workers worried the white electorate. While the war spurred tremendous economic growth, it also challenged the country's strict segregationist policies in the workplace and in the expanding cities.

Changes in the South African economy began to affect the face of South Africa's cities as increasing numbers of rural dwellers were drawn into the urban areas seeking work. A combination of opportunity in the cities with the expanding numbers of jobs in the war factories and devastation in the countryside as South Africa experienced one of the worst droughts in its history, succeeded in driving nearly a million more South Africans into the cities during the war. Both Africans and whites moved to the urban centres and, for the first time, Africans began to outnumber whites there. The massive influx of Africans created serious problems because of the myriad legal restrictions limiting African entry and residence in the cities. Africans were legally prohibited from entering cities without proper documentation and could live only in specially designated townships, or locations, controlled by the local municipality. Since the strict enforcement of these laws during the war would have overwhelmed the police and seriously impeded the war effort, the government relaxed most restrictions for the duration of the war. The result was the growth of the urban African population under trying conditions, with little accommodation or services provided. Africans were forced to find shelter anywhere and 'squatter' camps – a collection of impromptu shacks without proper sanitation or running water – emerged around the major industrial centres. One of the largest, near Johannesburg in Orlando with more than 20,000 residents, eventually became the basis for the township of **Soweto**. While the government and the local authorities were unwilling to recognise that African workers were becoming part of the permanent urban population, Africans themselves took matters into their own hands and created their own urban communities.

Africans entered the workplace as well as the cities. During the war, the factory workforce grew by 50 per cent, mostly as a result of the expanded recruitment of African workers. Prior to the war, Africans had been prohibited from skilled and even semi-skilled jobs, relegated to menial work and legally categorised as temporary workers. The growth of factory production, however, required workers who were trained to use complicated machinery for the mass production of goods. With more than 200,000 white males serving in the military, employers sought out women war workers to fill some skilled jobs but also increasingly relied on Africans without always paying them at the higher skilled rates. During the war years, from 1939 to 1945, the number of African males working in industry grew by nearly 70 per cent, while the number of women – white and Coloured – grew by 50 per cent. By comparison, white male employment in industry grew by only 30 per cent as many men joined the military. By the end of the war, Africans constituted over 50 per cent of the industrial workforce outside the mining industry for the first time in the country's history.

Changes in African attitudes to politics were best articulated by the African National Congress, the organisation that would finally bring majority rule to the country nearly 50 years later. At the beginning of the war, the nearly moribund ANC was reorganised under the leadership of a new president, Alfred Xuma (1893–1962), a medical doctor with degrees from universities in the United States, Scotland and England. Xuma believed that the ANC should change its tactics in several ways. He encouraged the ANC to work together with other like-minded organisations, such as the Indian National Congress, that also called for universal political rights. He also believed that the ANC should move away from its limited support for constitutional changes to a policy of non-cooperation with the government. Stung by decades of indifference from white politicians, including the wartime prime minister Jan Smuts, Xuma saw no reason to expect action from polite requests. Furthermore, he believed that Africans should link their struggle for greater rights to that of oppressed peoples elsewhere in the world. In 1943 the ANC presented Smuts with a document, 'Africans' Claims in South Africa', which explicitly placed African demands within the principles laid

Soweto: Acronym for South West African Township, located outside Johannesburg. The site of mass protests by students beginning in June 1976 that spread throughout the country and resulted in hundreds of deaths. Protests began in reaction to apartheid educational policies but grew to embrace a wide range of economic and social issues.

down by the Allies (including South Africa) in the Atlantic Charter. Referring to the Charter's affirmation of 'the right of all peoples to choose the form of government under which they live', the ANC stressed that 'the demands of the Africans [throughout Africa] for full citizenship rights and direct participation in all the councils of the state should be recognised. This is most urgent in the Union of South Africa.' In addition to political rights, the ANC called for a 'fair distribution of the land', 'equal pay for equal work', and

> the abolition of all enactments which discriminate against the African on grounds of race and colour. We condemn and reject the policy of segregation in all aspects of our national life in as much as this policy is designed to keep the African in a state of perpetual tutelage and militates against his normal development.
>
> (http://www.anc.org.za/ancdocs/history/claims.html#CHARTER)

In the same year, 1943, young members of the African National Congress, led by Nelson Mandela and Walter Sisulu, among others, proposed establishing a youth group with the aim of invigorating the national organisation and developing forceful popular protests against government segregation and discrimination. In 1944 they formed the ANC Youth League (see the League's manifesto [**Doc. 1, pp. 134–6**]).

While ANC demands met with government silence, other popular organisations took still more direct action. Africans forced to live in makeshift 'shacks' on the outskirts of Johannesburg withstood government attempts to force them out under segregation laws. The 'squatters' set up their own system of local government and taxation, under the leadership of James Mpanza, the self-proclaimed king of the Orlando encampment and leader of the Sofasonke ('We shall all die together') Party. Urban black workers, demanding higher wages and better working conditions, also formed their own trade unions and engaged in a rash of strikes throughout the early 1940s. By 1946 the Council of Non-European Trade Unions (CNETU), formed in 1941, claimed 158,000 members organised in 119 unions. The most important of these new trade unions was the African Mineworkers' Union (AMWU), formed in 1941 by migrant workers (notoriously difficult to organise), which by 1943 claimed a membership of 25,000. In 1946 the AMWU struck for higher wages in the gold mines and succeeded in getting 100,000 men to stop work. Despite the fact that work stoppages were outlawed during the war, there were over 300 strikes by Africans between 1939 and 1945.

Police took direct action to suppress all strikes with great brutality. The mineworkers' strike was crushed by police actions that left 12 dead. Likewise with other strikes, as described by one participant of a 1942 strike by Pretoria City Council municipal workers:

[The Army] put down the demonstration, which they did with brute force. They opened fire on the demonstrators and many African workers lost their lives. The workers had lost their lives, Jan Christian Smuts was the ruler of South Africa, the Second World War was raging, the children of those who lost their lives became orphans with no support.

(Mokgatle, 1971: 236)

These actions demonstrated the potential strength of organised black workers in challenging the cheap labour system and served to throw fear into white employers, workers and politicians alike.

Despite the change in tactics, Africans continued to meet with white intransigence. As Naboth Mokgatle wrote in his moving autobiography, *The Autobiography of an Unknown South African*, Africans were bitterly disappointed during the Second World War. Prisoners of war captured in Europe and held in South Africa were treated better than Africans:

As prisoners of war they entered hotels, restaurants, cafés, cinemas, and enjoyed outdoor life in the parks, all denied to us. Africans who served them were ordered to call them 'master'. Because of Smuts' doctrine of white superiority, the master-race concept, they lived in South Africa far better than we did. . . . South Africa was a paradise for them.

(Mokgatle, 1971)

Indeed, Mokgatle remembered 'the way Smuts used to break our hearts during the Second World War': he had helped to write the Charter of the United Nations after the war, inserting the words that 'the Peoples of the World' deserved equal human rights and liberty. Yet, when asked by Nationalist politician D.F. Malan, 'Do you include them [non-white races] in those words?' Smuts replied, 'You know well . . . that I did not include them in those words. They are not our equal and they will never be our equal' (Mokgatle, 1971: 262–3).

But within the context of white South African politics, Smuts was far more liberal than most of his fellow politicians. The outbreak of war had revealed a radical proto-fascist ideological strain within the white political community. Smuts, then deputy prime minister, favoured entry into the war on the side of the British, J.B.M. Hertzog, the prime minister, supported neutrality, while many of the supporters of D.F. Malan, the leader of the parliamentary opposition, wanted to enter the war on Germany's side. Smuts prevailed, winning the support of a majority of the cabinet and becoming prime minister, while Hertzog resigned and joined with Malan in forming the Herenigde (Reunited) National Party (HNP). South Africa sent troops to fight on the British side in North Africa and in Europe. Nevertheless, German National

Socialism, with its emphasis on the racial superiority of Germanic peoples, its anti-Semitism and its use of state socialism to benefit the 'master race', had garnered many Afrikaner admirers in the 1930s. Oswald Pirow, Hertzog's minister of defence until the end of 1939, formed a movement within the National Party called the New Order, a fascist programme for remaking South African society along Nazi lines. A neo-Nazi Grey-shirt organisation had been formed in 1933 that drew increasing support, especially among rural Afrikaners, in the late 1930s. In 1938 Afrikaners participating in the commemoration of the Great Trek had established the Ossewabrandwag (OB) as a paramilitary organisation aimed at inculcating a 'love for fatherland' and at instituting, by armed force if necessary, an Afrikaner-controlled republic in South Africa. During the war, some OB members were arrested for sabotage against the government, including the future prime minister, John Vorster. By the end of the decade, the Ossewabrandwag claimed a membership of 250,000 out of a total Afrikaner population of a little more than one million. Fears of growing African demands and the government's perceived inability to quell African resistance would only add strength to these radical racist sentiments.

Increasing African dissent and protest – from African unions, African political parties or African squatters – led to demands from white voters for stronger laws and tougher action. As soon as the war ended, the two major political parties representing white voters each began to address what whites viewed as a growing crisis. The United Party (UP), in power throughout the war years and including English- and Afrikaans-speaking whites, issued the Fagan Report in 1948, outlining its proposals for dealing with African urbanisation, while the opposition HNP issued the Sauer Report. Both parties acknowledged that African labour was necessary for economic growth and that African migration to the cities had become a serious issue. They parted company on the implications of this trend and possible solutions. The UP essentially advocated the continuation of business as usual. Its Fagan Report concluded that Africans were in the cities to stay and that complete segregation was 'totally impracticable', but the United Party dismissed any notion of giving Africans political rights. In effect, the Fagan Report was a defence of UP policies throughout the war that offered no remedies for containing African unrest and opposition.

The HNP, on the other hand, blamed African unrest on the effects of urbanisation and argued that Africans should remain in the countryside, later to be called their 'homelands', where they would continue to live in traditional 'tribal' societies. One wing of the HNP, including teachers, lawyers and workers' organisations, favoured total segregation to protect white voters from being 'swamped' by Africans. This group argued that 'total segregation' of the races was politically justified and morally defensible. Total segregation would include the removal of all Africans from the economy in order to protect the jobs, wages and 'dignity' of white labour. Under this scheme, only African male 'migrant' workers would be allowed into the cities, to work in the most menial jobs, and all African women and children would be barred from the cities. This was a radical proposal, conjuring up the threat of huge labour shortages throughout industry despite assurances that white immigration and greater mechanisation of production would meet the need.

More commercially minded HNP members presented an alternative 'practical' apartheid proposal which prevailed. Rather than bar African workers from all jobs in 'white' areas, the commercial wing of the party proposed that Africans could enter the cities only under direct government supervision. The Sauer Report recommended that the government establish special agencies to direct African workers to employment in specific white businesses and thereby regulate the movement of Africans into and out from the cities, a policy and practice that would come to be known as 'influx control'. Not surprisingly, this HNP coalition of Afrikaner farmers and incipient businessmen had been suffering from severe labour shortages during the war and after and hoped that while apartheid would separate the races and keep Africans under strict control, it would also direct African workers their way. The last thing they wanted to see was the disappearance of African workers. As stated in the Afrikaner industrialists' newsletter, the *Volkshandel*, in June 1948:

> It must be acknowledged that the non-white worker already constitutes an integral part of our economic structure, that he is now so enmeshed in the spheres of our economic life that, for the first fifty to one hundred years (if not longer), total segregation is pure wishful thinking. Any government which disregards this irrefutable fact will soon discover that it is no longer in a position to govern.
>
> (Posel, 1991: 54–5)

Practical apartheid not only accepted the presence of African workers in white areas, as did the UP, but went further in advocating direct government intervention in the labour market to ensure the equitable distribution of workers to needy employers (Afrikaners) rather than solely to urban industrialists (the English-speaking mine owners).

The HNP's Sauer Report reflected an idealised vision of white rule that attempted to eliminate African resistance by moving Africans out of the picture altogether. The report advocated total segregation as the 'eventual ideal and goal' while acknowledging that the gradual extraction of Africans from industries in white areas would take many years. The report foresaw a South African future in which Africans would be treated as visitors (*besoeker*) in the cities, that they would be forced periodically to return to the country-side to meet the labour needs of farmers (primarily Afrikaners), and that they could develop political bodies in 'their true fatherland', the African reserves, rather than having any parliamentary representation in South Africa itself. African labour would be controlled through the use of government-run labour bureaux that would move Africans from their rural reserves on to farms or into the cities on a temporary basis only. In this way, the labour needs of Afrikaner farmers and businessmen could be met while retaining the *de jure* denial of African rights in white areas. Africans could move about the country only with the consent of the government and would never con-stitute a permanent, or in any way enfranchised, population in the cities. Contact between blacks and whites would always be mediated through the government, via statute and state enforcement that would protect whites from the threat of African resistance or violence.

The HNP lost no time in promoting this plan to the white voting public. In 1948, renamed the National Party (NP), it began touting its proposals in comparison with the UP, which it misleadingly accused of promoting integration. The NP portrayed itself as offering the only safe solution for white voters, the only party that could prevent integration.

> The choice between us is one of two divergent courses: either that of integration, which would in the long run amount to national suicide on the part of the Whites; or that of apartheid, which professes to preserve the identity and safeguard the future of every race, with complete scope for everyone to develop within its own sphere while maintaining its distinctive national character, in such a way that there will be no encroachment on the rights of others, and without a sense of being frustrated by the existence and development of others. . . . It is the primary task and calling of the State to seek the welfare of South Africa, and to promote the happiness and well-being of its citizens, non-White as well as White . . . such a task can best be accomplished by preserving and safeguarding the White race.
>
> (Krüger, 1960: 402)

How was this to be accomplished? It would require a complete separation of races, and therefore intermarriage between races would be prohibited, including any between Africans, Coloureds and Asians. Furthermore, the NP viewed 'the Indians as a foreign element which cannot be assimilated in the South African set-up. . . . We accordingly have in mind the repatriation of as many Indians as possible.' The 'national home' of Africans would be in the reserves (those marginal areas left in African hands after conquest), Africans in urban areas would be:

regarded as migratory citizens not entitled to political or social rights
equal to those of Whites. . . . The entire migration of Bantu into and
from the cities should be controlled by the State which will enlist the
cooperation of municipal bodies. Redundant Bantu in the urban areas
should be returned to their original habitat in the country areas or the
reserves.

(Krüger, 1960: 405)

Above all, the NP committed itself to protect the 'interests and employment
prospects of White workers in White areas' (Krüger, 1960: 407). In short, the
NP put forward an extremely repressive but clear alternative to the UP's
equivocal proposal to try to regulate 'inevitable' integration in South Africa.

The apartheid alternative won the day with a minority of the votes
cast but winning a majority of the seats contested. In the midst of an economic upswing, but with Afrikaner farmers nevertheless experiencing labour
shortages and African urban protests mounting, the NP took control of the
government. Although the UP won a significant majority of the popular
vote (624,500 to 443,719), the NP won a majority of the seats in parliament
(79 to 71) because of a constitutional provision that provided greater representation in rural than in urban areas. The NP formed a new government
with D.F. Malan as prime minister. He immediately promised to protect 'the
white character of our cities and to provide a forceful and effective way for
the safety of individuals and property and the peaceful life of the inhabitants'.
Africans for their part would be allowed to 'develop along their own lines in
their true fatherland, the Reserves'. Malan also called for the prohibition of
mixed marriages, for the complete banning of black trade unions (they had
had no legal recognition but were not illegal), and for stricter enforcement of
job reservation for whites. Apartheid had been endorsed by a minority of
white voters (a tiny minority of the total population) but would nevertheless
shape the next 40 years of South Africa's history as whites tried in vain to
stifle African voices.

THE IMPLEMENTATION OF APARTHEID

How exactly apartheid would be instituted was not entirely clear in 1948 and
would in fact evolve over the next four decades as successive NP governments attempted to find the means to concurrently ensure economic growth,
the maintenance of white privilege, and a reduction in African protest. In
1948, however, as soon as the NP took control of the government, party
leaders were forced to consider exactly what was meant by 'apartheid', with

its contradictory and radical implications. Taking power with a minority of white voters supporting their policies, they feared they might lose the next election and began to move very quickly to give apartheid a legislative reality that could not easily be overturned should they be removed from office.

The opposition, stunned by defeat, rushed to proclaim the impracticality and lack of realism in apartheid proposals. Speaking in parliament immediately after his election as leader of the opposition rather than as prime minister, Smuts called into question the possibility of ever realising complete segregation. He referred to evidence in his party's Fagan Report that the Native Reserves, envisioned in the rival NP's Sauer Report as the permanent home for Africans, could only accommodate 40 per cent of the African population, thereby raising serious questions concerning their viability as the proper home for all Africans. 'If that is the apartheid which is contemplated then I have no difficulty at all in saying that it is an impossible policy' (Krüger, 1960: 412). He questioned the desirability of such a scenario in any case. If apartheid did work, and all industries were based on cheap black labour, then 'what is going to happen to White South Africa, to White industrial South Africa?' White workers would be out of the picture. And industries would be faced with what Smuts viewed as an inferior workforce:

> The Native has been integrated into our industrial system and into our economic system. He is our worker; he works on a lower level. He is not a competitor in that sense of the White man, but he is part and parcel of the whole which constitutes South African economic society. . . . He has to become more efficient, he cannot remain simply a barbarian, working on the lowest level. He must be shaped into an economic instrument; he must be made economically and industrially efficient.
>
> (Krüger, 1960: 413)

Not only was such a development possibly undesirable from the viewpoint of the white worker, but Smuts argued that it was completely impossible under apartheid. Certainly no provisions would be made for the training and education of African workers under apartheid, leaving South Africa with a cheap but inferior workforce, few jobs for whites, and overcrowded living conditions for Africans. Smuts and his UP were fairly certain that apartheid would face utter failure (Krüger, 1960: 410–14).

The Nationalists themselves were still wrestling with the meaning of apartheid. H.F. Verwoerd, soon to be minister of native affairs in the new Nationalist government and a future prime minister and architect of apartheid ideology, rose in parliament to explain: 'Nobody has ever contended that the policy of apartheid should be identified with "total segregation". . . .

The apartheid policy has been described as what one can do in the direction of what you regard as ideal' (Krüger, 1960: 2–17). Along the same lines, W.M.M. Eiselen, a professor of social anthropology at Pretoria University, chair of the Native Education Commission, formerly chief inspector of schools for native education in the Transvaal and soon to be secretary of native affairs wrote in 1948 of 'The Meaning of Apartheid':

> Separation is a distant goal and can only be achieved by careful long-range planning, and its gradual realisation need not bring about economic dislocation . . . [it] is generally accepted that the whole South African economy depends on a permanent supply of Native labour.
>
> (Eiselen, 1948: 79)

Even by 1950, Prime Minister Malan was still trying to explain the meaning of apartheid:

> Total segregation is not the policy of our party and it is nowhere to be found in our official declarations of policy . . . total territorial segregation was impracticable under present circumstances in South Africa, where our whole economic structure is to a large extent based on native labour. It is not practicable and it does not pay any party to endeavour to achieve the impossible.
>
> (Posel, 1991: 62)

For another view of apartheid see the explanation given in 1950 by the minister of native affairs, Hendrik Verwoerd, to a group of African leaders [**Doc. 2, pp. 136–41**].

If Nationalist politicians could not state clearly what they meant by apartheid, its critics had a ready answer: white supremacy. Writing in 1948 following the election, Naboth Mokgatle sent out a letter to members of the Native Representative Council. 'Apartheid means total segregation of the African people and all non-Europeans in the country, permanent denial of human rights, permanent *baasskaap*, master race, and inferiority for anything non-white. That . . . is the meaning of Apartheid' (Mokgatle, 1971: 271). This became increasingly clear to white voters as well. Trevor Huddleston, an Anglican minister and early critic, wrote in 1955:

> It is not *apartheid* which has provided the Nationalist government with its immense and growing dominance over all the European groups and parties in this country. It is not the thirst for such a negative state of affairs as 'separation' *in itself* that has so stirred enthusiasm and multiplied votes.

It is something much deeper and much more appealing. In a word, it is *'white supremacy, now and always'*. . . . It is not white self-preservation that is considered a sufficient motive force today; it is white *supremacy*, that and nothing less.

(Huddleston, 1956: 252–3)

In the years that followed the NP's initial victory, the UP never seriously challenged the concept of white supremacy and continued to lose votes to a growing Nationalist majority. Rather than question the ethical legitimacy of apartheid, the UP criticised its practicality. Party documents stated that the UP's policies were based on 'recognition of the factual position', meaning that there were, and should be, differences between the positions of whites and Africans but that Africans had a place in white society. Nevertheless, the party opposed any 'equality or assimilation' between the races and supported 'social and residential separation and the avoidance of race intermixture'. The development of 'Native' peoples in their own and the country's interests should take place 'under European guidance' in the Native Reserves and in the European areas. The government should eliminate African slums and shanty towns in the cities and replace them with 'separate Native townships for permanent residence'. While the UP differed from the Nationalists in supporting separate political representation for Africans, it also advocated the same type of labour registration and regulation advocated by the Nationalists (Krüger, 1960: 408–9). Neither Smuts nor his party made a compelling case against the apartheid structure that was being rapidly constructed.

EARLY APARTHEID LEGISLATION

Despite NP ambiguity in defining apartheid, the legislative programme advanced from 1948 through to the 1980s was breathtaking. Every aspect of South African life was determined under law by race. From the most basic rights of citizenship to the most personal choices of association, life in South Africa was dictated by race laws. These laws not only aimed at separating whites and blacks, they also instituted the legal principles that whites should be treated more favourably than blacks, that separate facilities need not be equal, and that the state should exercise the power deemed necessary to deal with any opposition. Not only were blacks and whites punished for transgressing racial laws, they were also prevented from exercising free speech in opposition to these laws, and they were harassed, persecuted and incarcerated under increasingly repressive and arbitrary powers of the police and the state. In retrospect, the maze of laws appear to fit together as a 'grand plan' to systematically separate races and rob all but whites of most rights and opportunities. In fact, apartheid laws emerged over the course of four decades in response to the increasing contradictions inherent in the system and the intensification of opposition from Africans, Coloureds and Indians. By the end of the apartheid era, the South African legal system vested so many powers of surveillance and enforcement in the police – as opposed to the courts – that the country operated for most of its inhabitants as a police state.

In the first few years of Nationalist rule, the party moved quickly to legislate a separation of the races that would make concrete the vague apartheid ideals set forth by the party. Key to all legislation was the fact that people resident within South Africa would enjoy different rights and privileges based on their race. Accordingly, one of the first pieces of legislation passed by the new Nationalist government was the Population Registration Act (No. 30) of 1950 which established mechanisms for determining and registering the race of all South Africans. (On this and all legislation, see Horrell, 1978.) This Act provided the basis for most subsequent apartheid legislation. Under the terms of this Act, all residents of South Africa were to be classified as 'White', 'Coloured' or 'Native' (later called 'Bantu') people. Indians, whom the NP in 1948 had refused to recognise as permanent inhabitants of South Africa, were later included under the category 'Asian' in 1959. The Population Registration Act required that people be classified primarily on the basis of their 'community acceptability'; later amendments (1962, 1964) placed greater stress on 'appearance' in order to deal with the practice of light-coloured blacks 'passing' as whites, and also added descent (1967), again to prevent assimilation. The Population Registration Act also provided for the compilation of a population register for the whole country and for the issuing of identity cards listing the assigned race of the individual. This Act established a rigid system of racial classification and identification which determined any individual's access to legal rights in South Africa.

In order to put this system of classification into practice, the government needed to institute an easy method of identifying South Africans by race at any time and in any place: hence the creation of passes. Passes, or legal documents required of Africans to enter and remain in some 'white' areas, had been in existence in South Africa since the beginning of the nineteenth century. The use of pass laws had varied throughout the provinces and it was not until 1952, with the Native Laws Amendment Act (No. 54) and the ironically named Abolition of Passes and Co-ordination of Documents Act (No. 67), that the use of passes was regularised throughout the country. Under the terms of the Native Laws Amendment Act, African women as well as men were for the first time made subject to influx control and the pass laws and, under Section 10 of the Act, neither African men nor women could remain in an urban area for longer than 72 hours without a special permit stating that they were legally employed. The Act stated that no African, male or female, who had not been born in an urban area could live there unless s/he had lived there continuously for 15 years or worked for the same employer for 10 years. Regional pass documents were abolished and replaced with a document known as a 'reference book', which included an individual's photograph, address, marital status, employment record, list of taxes paid, influx control endorsements, and rural district where officially resident. Not having the reference book on one's person was a criminal offence punishable by a prison sentence. In 1970, similar documents were issued to Whites, Coloureds and Asians under the Population Registration Amendment Act.

The pass system became emblematic of the degree of control the government intended to exert over the African population and was a daily reminder for Africans of the often petty but also determined repression under which they lived. For urban Africans, born and living most of their lives in areas increasingly deemed 'white', obtaining a pass to remain in their homes was a humiliating and embittering experience. Ezekiel Mphahlele, a university-educated school teacher born in Pretoria, poignantly described the experience suffered by millions of Africans after 1952:

> I first had my photograph taken at the Pass Office after being regimented by a man with a very red face with lines round the neck like a rhino's. It cut inside me like a razor-blade to be regimented in this way, and I felt as if there were a liberal leak in a bag of gall somewhere deep inside my stomach. I used to believe that if I had so much sympathy for the utterly illiterate thousands who moved from one job to another to the tune of rubber-stamps and paper-thumbing, I wouldn't feel the humiliation overmuch when I should queue for a pass. I realised I had cheated myself.
>
> The next thing was to present a slip of paper at the first official's desk in a long line. The paper came from the Orlando superintendent, certifying that I was a registered tenant of his location. The clerk then gave me a reference book – the pass – and stuck one photograph to a page. He insisted on having a Sotho first name from me to enter into the book. I told him I was never called by a Sotho name. He looked angry and disgruntled at once.
>
> I moved on to the next clerk. He produced two cards, filled in the information about me and duplicated it. Another photograph of me was stuck on to one card and filed. Then to the next one. The big man in the influx control machinery, armed with a large rubber-stamp that could send a man packing in twenty-four hours to quit the city. He it was who

was supposed to reduce the number of what they called 'redundant natives' in his municipality; to issue a heavily prescribed permit to look for work; to register every employer and his worker or workers so as to control the Black man's movements everywhere and at all times. A rubber-stamp came down on one of the pages of my book, giving me permission to look for work in Johannesburg. When I found employment, my boss would have to sign his name in the book every month and write 'discharged' if and when he should kick me out or I should decide to leave. But this would only be after another rubber-stamp had come down to give me permission to stay in Johannesburg as long as I worked there. If I later failed to get 'suitable' employment and the big man got tired of renewing my permit to look for work, down would come his stamp sending me to Pretoria, my place of birth, there to go through the same process.

(Mphahlele, 1959: 170–1)

With a basic system of identification and control in place, the Nationalist government could then determine where and how Africans would live, what rights they could enjoy and those they could not, whom they could marry, and so forth. The Prohibition of Mixed Marriages Act (No. 55) of 1949 made marriages between whites and members of other racial groups illegal. The Immorality Act (No. 21) of 1950 extended an earlier ban on sexual relations between whites and Africans (the Immorality Act (No. 51) of 1927) to a ban on sexual relations between whites and any non-whites. Moving from the most personal aspects to the most public, in 1950 the government divided the entire country into geographical areas based on race, the Group Areas Act (No. 41). Under this Act, the government could impose control throughout the country over property rights requiring permits, based on race, for ownership and occupation. African land ownership was already limited to approximately 13 per cent of the country's total territory under the Natives' Land Act of 1913 and its 1936 amendments. The Group Areas Act took this separation several steps further by including all racial groups and giving the government the power to 'proclaim' an area as fit for occupation by one group and forcibly removing existing occupants from any other groups. In practice, the Group Areas Act finished the work of earlier legislation (Natives' Land Act, Urban Areas Act) by defining the racial occupation of every inch of South Africa.

With the mechanisms for racial classification and physical separation in place, the government went on to define the political rights enjoyed by each separate group. Most Africans had been denied voting rights since Union in 1910, and the remaining propertied Africans had been taken off the voting rolls in 1936. In 1951, the government, by establishing separate embryonic governments for Africans in the rural areas under the Bantu Authorities Act (No. 68), bolstered the fictive claim that the true home areas of Africans were in their 'tribal reserves'. At the same time, it abolished the Natives Representative Council that had operated in the urban areas as the only avenue of African political expression. The Bantu authorities were to be dominated by chiefs and headmen appointed by the government. The government also sought in 1951 to remove Coloured voters in the Cape from the common roll on to a separate roll and to require that they elect white representatives only (Separate Representation of Voters Act (No. 46) of 1951). The Supreme Court immediately declared the Act invalid on constitutional grounds, but after a long struggle it was successfully re-enacted (the Separate Representation of Voters Amendment Act (No. 30) of 1956). Under apartheid, only whites would enjoy political rights within South Africa.

Not only would life be separate under apartheid, it would also be unequal. The concept of unequal allocation of resources was built into legislation on general facilities, education and jobs. The Reservation of Separate Amenities Act (No. 49) of 1953 stated that all races should have separate amenities – such as toilets, parks and beaches – and that these need not be of an equivalent quality. Under the provisions of this Act, apartheid signs were erected throughout South Africa. And under the Native Labour Act (No. 48) of 1953, all Africans were precluded from legal union representation and from staging any strikes. Africans could not sit on the same seats or even organise themselves in the same manner as whites (Figures 3.1 and 3.2).

But most damaging in the long term was the legislated inequality of education under apartheid. The Bantu Education Act (No. 47) of 1953 was 'by far the most important [legislation] and by far the most deadly in its effect' (Huddleston, 1956: 158). This legislation was the product of a commission on native education appointed in 1949 under the chairmanship of Dr W.M.M. Eiselen. The final commission report decreed that blacks should be provided with separate educational facilities under the control of the Ministry of Native Affairs, rather than the Ministry of Education. Previously the bulk of schooling for Africans had been provided by mission schools which received state subsidies, amounting to 16 times as much for each European child as for each African, for teacher salaries and supplies. In 1945 there were 4,360 mission schools which trained approximately 90 per cent of all African pupils as compared with 230 government schools. The Bantu Education Act removed state subsidies from denominational schools, with the result that most of the mission-run African institutions (with the exception of some schools run by the Roman Catholic Church and the Seventh Day Adventists) were sold to the government or closed. At the university level, the Extension of University Education Act (No. 45) of 1959 prohibited blacks from attending white institutions of higher education,

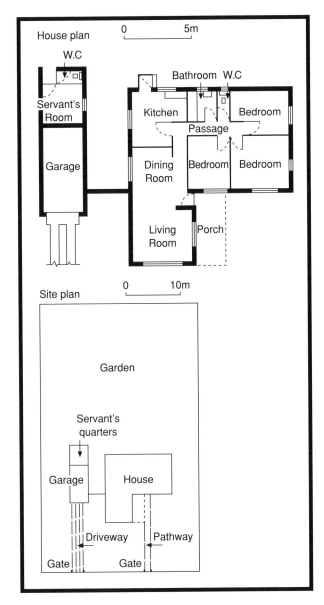

Figure 3.1 House with servant's quarters

Source: Based on building plans supplied by the Port Elizabeth Municipality, from Christopher, A.J. (2000) *The Atlas of Changing South Africa*, 2nd Edition, published by Routledge, Figure 5.1.

with few exceptions, and established separate universities and colleges for Africans, Coloureds and Indians. African students would be isolated from their white counterparts and placed entirely under the control of the government.

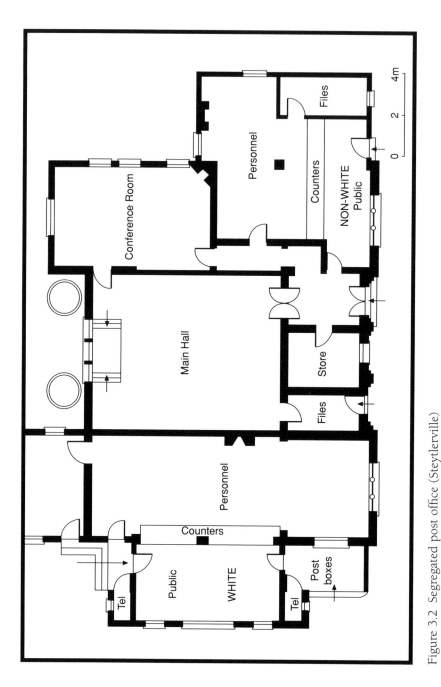

Figure 3.2 Segregated post office (Steytlerville)

Source: Modified after A.D. Herholdt (1986) *Die Argitektuur van Steytlerville met Rigline vir Bewaring en Ontwikkeling*, published by Institute of South African Architects, Port Elizabeth. Reprinted by permission of Professor A.D. Herholdt.

Indeed, the politicians who framed the Bantu Education Act saw it as the keystone that would ensure a smooth transition from the tumultuous years of African unrest during the Second World War to the idealised apartheid future. Under government control, Africans would be taught their cultural heritage and, in the words of Hendrik F. Verwoerd, minister of native affairs, would be trained 'in accordance with their opportunities in life'. For Verwoerd and his fellow Nationalists, Bantu education would mould Africans into compliant citizens and productive workers:

> By blindly producing pupils trained on a European model, the vain hope was created among Natives that they could occupy posts within the European community despite the country's policy of 'apartheid'. This is what is meant by the creation of unhealthy 'White collar ideals' and the causation of widespread frustration among the so-called educated Natives. . . . The school must equip him [the Bantu pupil] to meet the demands which the economic life of South Africa will impose upon him. . . . The Bantu teacher must be integrated as an active agent in the process of the development of the Bantu community. He must learn not to feel above his community, with a consequent desire to become integrated into the life of the European community. He becomes frustrated and rebellious when this does not take place, and he tries to make his community dissatisfied because of such misdirected ambitions which are alien to his people. . . . My department's policy is that education should stand with both feet in the reserves and have its roots in the spirit and being of Bantu society. . . . The Bantu must be guided to serve his own community in all respects. There is no place for him in the European community above the level of certain forms of labour. Within his own community, however, all doors are open. For that reason it is of no avail for him to receive a training which has as its aim absorption in the European community, where he cannot be absorbed.
>
> (Verwoerd, 1954)

But Africans had a very different view of their education. In a statement before the Eiselen Commission, school teacher Ezekiel Mphahlele voiced the existing frustrations of African teachers and students:

> I condemned the textbooks ordered by the Education Department for use in African schools: a history book with several distortions meant to glorify white colonization, frontier wars, the defeat of African tribes, and white rule; Afrikaans grammar books which abound with examples like: *the Kaffir has stolen a knife; that is a lazy Kaffir* . . . and a literature that teems with non-white characters who are savages or blundering idiots to

be despised and laughed at; characters who are inevitably frustrated creatures of city life and decide to return 'home' – to the Reserves.

(Mphahlele, 1959: 166)

The NP's legislative programme nevertheless received increasing support from the white electorate. Such support, while based on a range of socio-economic concerns, also rested on biblical justification when the Dutch Reformed Church gave its imprimatur to apartheid. In a formal pronouncement in 1954 the Church stated that:

God divided humanity into races, languages and nations. Differences are not only willed by God but are perpetuated by Him. Equality between natives, coloureds and Europeans includes a misappreciation of the fact that God, in His Providence, made people into different races and nations. . . . Far from the word of God encouraging equality, it is an established scriptural principle that in every community ordination there is a fixed relationship between authorities. . . . Those who are culturally and spiritually advanced have a mission to leadership and protection of the less advanced. . . . The natives must be led and formed towards independence so that eventually they will be equal to the Europeans, but each on their own territory and each serving God and their own fatherland.

(Huddleston, 1956: 57–8)

The NP won re-election in 1953 and in 1958, each time with increased majorities. Malan retired in 1954 and was replaced as prime minister by J.G. Strijdom, leader of the Transvaal branch of the party. After Strijdom's death in 1958, Hendrik F. Verwoerd, the Dutch-born minister of native affairs as well as a former professor of applied psychology and the pre-eminent ideologue of apartheid, became prime minister. The UP competed aggressively for white votes by adopting a pro-white platform, stressing that all in South Africa should share but that whites were still the bearers of civilisation for Africans, by rejecting government expenditures on acquiring more land for African reserves, and by supporting the removal of Coloured voters from the common roll. In 1959, 11 of the more liberal members of the UP broke away to form the Progressive Party, but with little impact. Practically all Afrikaners and increasing numbers of English-speaking whites voted for the NP. In 1960 a majority of white voters, irritated by growing world condemnation of apartheid, especially by the newly independent Asian and African members of the British Commonwealth of Nations, supported Verwoerd's proposal to make South Africa a republic, whereupon it left the Commonwealth. In the 1961 general election, the NP won 105 seats, the UP 45 and the new liberal Progressive Federal Party (PFP) only one.

CHALLENGE AND REPRESSION

Africans, Coloureds and Indians were all as adamantly opposed to apartheid as they had been to segregation. As these groups watched their lives circumscribed in countless ways under the rash of apartheid legislation enacted between 1950 and 1953, they organised to resist, protest and finally attempt to overthrow the apartheid regime. Each action taken by anti-apartheid forces was brutally suppressed and answered with increasingly repressive legislation. The government outlawed all forms of dissent, to no avail, finally empowering police to detain anyone without charging them with a crime. The complete separation envisioned in apartheid theories would require the transformation of the government into a police state.

The architects of apartheid feared the growing determination and acuity of Africans who had challenged white rule throughout the 1940s. During the Second World War young members of the ANC, critical of what they considered the organisation's passivity, had formed their own organisation, the Congress Youth League (CYL). Anton Lembede, president of the CYL from 1944 until his death in 1947, stressed that South Africa was 'a black man's country', in which the concerns of Africans should take precedence. He argued that African society was inherently socialistic but, because he considered the conflict in South Africa to be primarily a racial rather than a class struggle, he repudiated any alliance with the Communist Party in bringing about 'national liberation'. After the war and Lembede's death, and faced with the ongoing debate among white politicians over how to control Africans, the CYL's leaders, Peter Mda, Jordan Ngubane, Nelson Mandela, Oliver Tambo and Walter Sisulu, strove to take charge of the ANC. In the late 1940s, they called on the organisation to adopt the use of strikes, boycotts, stay-at-homes, and various forms of civil disobedience and non-cooperation to force change in post-war South Africa. It was in the face of such developments within the African community that Malan and the NP came to power with an apartheid solution.

Only one year after the Nationalist victory, Africans began to organise massive protests against the new government. Overcoming the opposition of ANC president Alfred Xuma to such strategies, the CYL succeeded in 1949 in electing James Moroka to the presidency of the ANC and in seating three CYL members (Sisulu, Tambo and Mandela) on the party's national executive body. The ANC adopted a 'Programme of Action' in 1949 to challenge the Nationalists' plans for apartheid. As Nelson Mandela remembered, 'We explained that we thought the time had come for mass action along the lines of Gandhi's non-violent protests in India and the 1946 passive resistance campaign, asserting that the ANC had become too docile in the face of oppression' (Mandela, 1994: 113–14). The ANC annual conference ratified

South African Communist Party (SACP): Established in 1921 as the Communist Party of South Africa. Sought to organise African workers into trade unions and to join with whites in class action against employers. Outlawed under the Suppression of Communism Act (No. 44) of 1950. Worked underground with the ANC and other organisations to end apartheid. Unbanned in 1990.

South African Indian Congress (SAIC): Established in 1924 to seek greater rights for Indians. Worked with the ANC and other groups to oppose apartheid and helped to draft the Freedom Charter.

programmes of boycotts, strikes, civil disobedience and non-cooperation, and a national day of work stoppage. The **South African Communist Party (SACP)**, a multiracial party, also called for greater action, staging a national strike on May Day 1950. The government's promise to separate all races in South Africa – the apartheid vision – would not in itself persuade Africans to relent or frighten them from voicing opposition.

The government reaction was swift and violent, presaging the characteristically brutal nature of the apartheid years. The evening before the ANC strike, police and troops escorted Africans to their places of work to sleep there and also on the day of the strike marched them from their homes to bus stations to make sure that they went to work. As Naboth Mokgatle recalled, the 'police state came out into the open. In Pretoria we were lucky there was no loss of life. In Johannesburg, at locations like Alexandra, police opened fire on the people and there was loss of human life' (Mokgatle, 1971: 285). Indeed, 18 people were killed in Johannesburg after 2,000 police had been called out to prevent the strike. Following this action, Mandela and the ANC leadership called for a National Day of Protest on 26 June 1950 in cooperation with political organisations representing the Coloured (African People's Organisation – APO) and Indian (**South African Indian Congress – SAIC**) communities. In cities most black businesses closed and a majority of workers stayed home.

In what would become a familiar pattern, government repression was followed by new legal restrictions. The government enacted the Suppression of Communism Act (No. 44) of 1950. The Act not only outlawed the Communist Party, which had not to that time posed a significant threat to the government, but defined communism as any scheme that aimed 'at bringing about any political, industrial, social or economic change within the Union by the promotion of disturbance or disorder' or that encouraged 'feelings of hostility between the European and the non-European races of the Union the consequences of which are calculated to further' disorder. The Act empowered the minister of justice to 'list' members of such organisations and to 'ban' them, usually for five-year periods, from public office, from attending public meetings or from being in any specified area of South Africa. The minister of justice could investigate any organisation, declare it illegal, liquidate its assets, and he could ban any gatherings he deemed likely to 'further the aims of communism'.

The Suppression of Communism Act for many years was used to silence any government critics without regard to communist ideology, sentiment or connection. As Naboth Mokgatle discovered, any criticism of the government qualified as 'communism':

On the sixteenth of February, nineteen-fifty-one . . . we began to speak at Pretoria Market. We opened meetings by first singing a song to attract people, and after five minutes we started speaking, one in English and interpreting what was said into Sesotho. . . . We did not mince words in our speeches in denouncing Dr Malan as a fascist, his ministers as a group of fascists – racists who had no legal right to govern the country because they were elected by the minority, for the minority. We stressed strongly that they were an illegal government.

(Mokgatle, 1971: 289)

After a few months, Mokgatle was visited by the police who, under the Act, could question anyone suspected of trying to further 'communism'. At the end of 1951 he was arrested: 'As far as I know we were the first in the country to be arrested under that vicious Act' (Mokgatle, 1971: 299). Although no specific charges of illegal activity were ever brought and his trial was dismissed, Mokgatle was soon served with 'banning' orders, under the terms of which

we were forbidden to attend public gatherings other than social and religious gatherings throughout the country for two years. Further, we were ordered to resign from the African General Workers' Union and the Pretoria Non-European Distributive Workers' Union and never to take part in their activities. We were further ordered to resign from the African National Congress and never to take part in its activities. That was how Malan, fearing the truth we were delivering at the Pretoria market meetings, muzzled us for two full years.

(Mokgatle, 1971: 312)

He left South Africa after the police threatened him with a lifelong ban. As the aeroplane took off, he thought 'Am I really above South Africa? Am I really leaving torture and the pass laws which have been part of my life for the past forty-three years?' (Mokgatle, 1971: 330). The brutal suppression of all dissent was underway.

But government repression could not stop opposition to apartheid. The ANC's new leaders formed a joint Planning Council with leaders of the SAIC and in February 1952 called on the government to repeal all unjust laws or face a '**Defiance Campaign**' starting on 6 April, the tercentenary of Jan van Riebeeck's arrival at the Cape. Malan rejected the ultimatum. The ANC and the SAIC, led by Yusuf Dadoo, then organised mass rallies and stay-at-homes for 6 April and 26 June. These actions drew the support of thousands of men and women. The government reacted by banning leaders and newspapers under the Suppression of Communism Act and by arresting participants in the demonstrations. By December 1952, approximately 8,500 people had been arrested, most of them in the Cape, and the Defiance Campaign had

Defiance Campaign: Organised by ANC and the SAIC in 1952 to demand repeal of apartheid laws. Thousands of people refused to go to work and approximately 8,500 people were arrested. Most leaders of the ANC were banned. Nevertheless, ANC membership jumped from fewer than 7,000 at the beginning of 1952 to more than 100,000 by the end of the year.

largely come to an end without bringing about any change in the laws. The ANC had grown enormously, however. Its paid membership had increased from fewer than 7,000 at the beginning of 1952 to more than 100,000 by the end of the year. Its leadership had also changed. James Moroka had been dismissed in disgrace for having pleaded guilty to charges placed under the Suppression of Communism Act, and Albert Luthuli had been made president.

In response to the Defiance Campaign, the government appropriated the right to suspend all laws and shifted the burden of proof to the accused. The Public Safety Act (No. 3) of 1953 allowed the government to declare a state of emergency and suspend all laws if it believed that any action or threatened action might endanger public safety or the maintenance of public order. Such a state of emergency could stay in effect for 12 months, and could be renewed at that time. The Criminal Law Amendment Act (No. 8) of 1953 stated that anyone accompanying a person found guilty of offences committed while 'protest[ing], or in support of any campaign for the repeal or modification of any law' would also be presumed guilty and would have the burden of proving his or her innocence. Thus any protests, or threatened protests against the government, could prompt a suspension of all laws and the incarceration of anyone suspected of opposing the government.

Nevertheless, government opponents such as Nelson Mandela had determined that violence, imprisonment and worse would not deter them from fighting against the government. By 1953, he believed that 'violence was the only weapon that would destroy apartheid and we must be prepared in the near future to use that weapon'. Although he had earlier advocated nonviolence, 'For me, nonviolence was not a moral principle but a strategy; there is no moral goodness in using an ineffective weapon' (Mandela, 1994: 115, 157). In the wake of the Defiance Campaign, Mandela was banned in 1953 and these orders, which kept him from participating in public meetings, were extended until 1961 [**Doc. 3, pp. 141–8**].

House arrests, bannings and other forms of government restriction limited the ability of ANC and SAIC leaders to organise publicly in 1953 and 1954, but in 1955 approximately 3,000 delegates met on 25 and 26 June near Soweto in a Congress of the People. They represented African (the ANC), white (the Congress of Democrats), Indian (the SAIC) and Coloured (the Coloured People's Congress) political organisations and the multiracial South African Congress of Trade Unions (SACTU). The congress was held to develop a new vision for a future South Africa, one that reached beyond protest politics. The prime document discussed was the Freedom Charter, which had been drafted several weeks before the congress met. The charter emphasised that South Africa should be a non-racial society with no particular group assumed to have special rights or privileges. The charter stated that all people should be treated equally before the law, that land should be 'shared among those who work it', and that the people should 'share in the country's wealth', a statement that has sometimes been interpreted to mean a call for the nationalisation of all economic assets [**Doc. 4, pp. 148–52**]. The congress delegates had ratified almost all the sections of the charter when the police surrounded the meeting, announced that they suspected treason was being committed, and recorded the names and addresses of all those in attendance. The following year, using the information gathered at the meeting, the police arrested 156 leaders, including Luthuli, Mandela, Tambo, Sisulu and others, and put them on trial for treason in a court case that dragged on for five years. The government also responded to the publication of the Freedom Charter by passing two censorship Acts, the Customs and Excise Act of 1955 and the Official Secrets Act (No. 16) of 1956, establishing a Board of Censors to censor books, films and other materials imported into or produced in South Africa.

Although the infamous **Treason Trial** kept most leaders of organised opposition groups restricted for years, mass resistance continued in a variety of forms. The government had amended the Riotous Assemblies Act (No. 17) in 1956 to outlaw any public gatherings which might cause 'feelings of hostility between Whites and Blacks' and to prohibit any 'banned' persons from attending or addressing public meetings. Nevertheless, Africans continued to organise strikes and boycotts. Thousands of people participated in bus boycotts on the Rand, preferring to walk to work rather than to pay high fares to travel on substandard vehicles. Thousands of African women, organised by the newly formed Federation of South African Women (FSAW), protested against the extension of the pass laws. In 1956, 20,000 of them marched on the parliament buildings in Pretoria and presented a petition with the signatures of tens of thousands of people opposed to the pass laws [**Doc. 5, pp. 152–4**]. In response, the government again enacted repressive legislation, the Native Administration Act (No. 42) of 1956, which permitted the government to 'banish' Africans, essentially exiling them to remote rural areas far from their homes.

Despite all these efforts, the failure of the ANC to achieve any practical success in its campaigns against apartheid caused a major split in black resistance groups by 1959. With most leaders still involved in the Treason Trial or otherwise banned, critics within the ANC argued that its alliance with other political groups, particularly the white Congress of Democrats, had caused their organisation to make too many compromises and to fail to represent African interests. Influenced by the writings of Lembede, the Africanists, now led by Robert Sobukwe, called on the ANC to look to African interests first and to take more action to challenge the government. They were, however, forced out of the ANC, and they formed their own

Treason Trial: Trial that lasted from 1957 until 1961, when 156 anti-government activists were tried for treason. All defendants were found not guilty.

Pan-Africanist Congress (PAC): Established in 1959 by Robert Sobukwe who believed the ANC should take more direct action to challenge the government. In March 1960, began a national campaign against the pass laws, leading to the police massacre at Sharpeville. The PAC was outlawed in 1960 and continued to operate both underground and outside the country until 1990 when it became a legal political party inside South Africa.

Sharpeville: African township outside the town of Vereeniging. Site of anti-pass demonstration in March 1960 that ended in violence. Police fired on the demonstrators, killing at least 69 of them and wounding 186.

Umkhonto we Sizwe (MK): 'Spear of the Nation'. Militant wing of the ANC established in 1961 after the ANC was outlawed. Conducted sabotage inside the country and provided military training for South African exiles outside the country.

Rivonia Trial: Trial of 17 ANC leaders, including Nelson Mandela and Walter Sisulu, on charges of treason. Eight of them, including Mandela, were sent to prison for life, and most remained incarcerated until the end of the 1980s.

organisation, the **Pan-Africanist Congress (PAC)**. In March 1960, the PAC began a national campaign against the pass laws and called on Africans to assemble outside police stations without their passes and to challenge the police to arrest them. One such demonstration outside the police station at **Sharpeville**, a 'native' township in the industrial area of Vereeniging to the south of Johannesburg, ended in violence on 21 March when the police fired on the demonstrators, killing at least 69 of them and wounding 186. According to information released years later, most of the dead and wounded had been shot in the back. Protest continued, however, with work stoppages and demonstrations taking place throughout 1960 and culminating in a peaceful march of 30,000 Africans on the Houses of Parliament in Cape Town. Verwoerd's government reacted by declaring a state of emergency, by arresting approximately 18,000 demonstrators, including the leaders of the ANC and the PAC, and by outlawing both organisations.

Prohibited from operating peacefully or even having a legal existence in South Africa, both the ANC and the PAC established underground organisations in 1961 to carry out their struggle against the government. The militant wing of the ANC, **Umkhonto we Sizwe** (Spear of the Nation), targeted strategic places such as police stations and power plants but carefully avoided taking any human lives. Poqo (Pure), the militant wing of the PAC, engaged in a campaign of terror, targeting in particular African chiefs and headmen believed to be collaborators with the government and killing them. Nelson Mandela explained the ANC's adoption of a policy of violent resistance in the following words:

> Firstly, we believed that as a result of Government policy, violence by the African people had become inevitable, and that unless responsible leadership was given to canalize and control the feelings of our people, there would be outbreaks of terrorism which would produce an intensity of bitterness and hostility between the various races of this country which is not produced even by war. Secondly, we felt that without violence there would be no way open to the African people to succeed in their struggle against the principle of white supremacy. All lawful modes of expressing opposition to this principle had been closed by legislation, and we were placed in a position in which we had either to accept a permanent state of inferiority, or to defy the Government.
>
> (Mandela, 1994: 164)

By 1964 the police had succeeded in crushing most resistance. Seventeen Umkhonto leaders, including Walter Sisulu, had been arrested at a farmhouse at **Rivonia** near Johannesburg in July 1963 and, along with Nelson Mandela, who had already been imprisoned on other charges, were tried for treason. Eight of them, including Mandela, were sent to prison for life, and most remained incarcerated until the end of the 1980s. The ANC president Albert Luthuli had been awarded the Nobel Peace Prize in 1960, but the government confined him to his rural home in Zululand until his death in 1967. Tambo escaped from South Africa and became president of the ANC in exile. Robert Sobukwe was jailed on Robben Island until 1969 and then placed under a banning order and house arrest in Kimberley until his death in 1978.

The government campaign to crush internal resistance was orchestrated by John Vorster, then minister of justice, and by General Hendrik J. van den Bergh, of the security branch of the police (and later head of the aptly named **Bureau of State Security – BOSS**). Both were former members of the Ossewabrandwag who had been interned for pro-Nazi activities during the Second World War. Vorster and van den Bergh used a plethora of security legislation to put down the resistance. The most extreme of the new laws enacted was the General Laws Amendment Act of 1963. This legislation empowered the police to detain people for 90 days without charging them and without allowing them access to a lawyer. At the end of that period, the police could re-arrest and re-detain them for a further 90 days, and continue doing so for an indefinite number of times. During the period of detention, no court could order a person's release; only the minister of justice had that authority. Because of his success in defeating (at least temporarily) the ANC and the PAC, John Vorster became prime minister of South Africa in 1966 when Verwoerd was assassinated by a Coloured parliamentary messenger.

During the 1950s, enforcement of these various laws resulted in approximately 500,000 pass-law arrests annually, in the listing of more than 600 people as communists, in the banning of nearly 350 people, and in the banishment of more than 150 individuals.

Bureau of State Security (BOSS): Established in 1969 to co-ordinate and complement the security activities of the military and police. It reported to the prime minister, and its activities remained secret.

THE 'GRAND APARTHEID' SOLUTION

By the end of the 1950s, after a decade in power, the Nationalists faced serious unrest and opposition that could not forever be kept in check by countless security measures. Although African, Indian and Coloured leaders had been imprisoned, the vast majority of the South African public was clearly opposed to apartheid and willing to act to protest against its imposition. The Nationalists began to look for new ways to defuse and undermine resistance in addition to outright repression. Separating the races was not enough to ensure peace. The opposition would have to be marginalised and fractured in a significant manner in order to secure the peace. By the end of the 1950s, the government began to move quickly to implement what would be called 'grand apartheid'.

The grand apartheid project was a massive effort of social engineering that even the government feared was impossible. Verwoerd argued to his white peers in parliament that the government's first priority was the preservation of white autonomy. 'How can we prevent the swamping of the White community taking place in all spheres of life – politically, socially, and economically . . . [only by making sure] that this increased Bantu population is not accommodated in the White urban areas.' Africans, he argued, could be kept out of white cities and still benefit from economic growth if industries were established on the rural borders of the homelands. He staunchly supported the massive social engineering that the state would need to undertake in order to accomplish the removal of Africans from white areas:

> Can this standpoint be justified morally? My reply is 'yes', because every nation has the right to self-protection and self-preservation, and if it exercises that right in such a way that it uplifts the other people and protects them from disorderliness and disease and destruction, and it educates and takes care of them, then it need not do it in a way as to constitute a threat to its own survival.
>
> (Hansard, 1956: cols 5296, 5312)

Nevertheless, even the government-appointed Tomlinson Commission had concluded in 1956 that the areas set aside for Africans would never, even under the best of conditions, be able to support more than two-thirds of the African population. Moreover, without further land purchase the reserves could not even support the 50 per cent of the African population then resident in them. Ignoring the Commission's findings and recommendations, the government refused to allocate more land to Africans and expanded its policy of removing blacks from areas officially designated for whites. Still, Verwoerd estimated that by the year 2000 there would be 6 million Africans resident in South Africa's cities, albeit all of them migrant workers without permanent rights of residence. An additional 4 million Africans would be resident on white farms but those were, he argued, places 'where the problem of apartheid presents no difficulty to us and where apartheid is maintained locally', that is, by the autocratic power of white farmers supported by the police. While not accomplishing complete separation, this version of apartheid would result in a huge rearrangement of the population of South Africa and its regional disbursement.

With African audiences, Verwoerd adopted a more paternalistic tone. At the 1957 opening of the Transkeian Territorial Authority, in a building now occupied by the Nelson Mandela Museum, he used metaphor and simple language to try to secure support for apartheid:

> When one thinks big, one can do great things. The big idea I want to talk about is that of separate development. These are words of great hope for the Bantu. Every man wants to have something which is his own – something which is separately his. He likes to be with other people but he also wants to be separated from them at times. 'Separateness' means: Something for oneself. The other word refers to what is bigger still, viz., 'development', which means growth. . . . Separate development means the growth of something for oneself and one's nation, due to one's own endeavours. . . . Separate development is a tree, a fruit tree which this Government gave the Bantu of South Africa. It planted the tree, but that tree must be tended in order to grow. . . . Let it grow slowly. Do not be impatient. Let the branches become strong so that they can bear many fruits . . . do not look at the more developed tree of the white man with jealous eyes because then you will neglect your own small tree which will one day also be big. . . . When I went to Europe there was always a desire in my heart to return to my own country and my own coast. I could not become a Frenchman, or Italian or anything else because I am an Afrikaner. . . . Should it not be the same with the Bantu? Should his children there in Cape Town, Port Elizabeth and East London not always hanker after their Chiefs, Authorities, and own people here? . . . Every child who is lost there [the urban areas] is like a branch broken from a tree. If it is a fruit-bearing bough, everything on it is lost.
>
> (Verwoerd, 1958)

Within six years of this speech, Verwoerd's government in 1963 proclaimed the Transkei a 'self-governing' territory, beginning the process of cutting the area and its inhabitants off from white South Africa. In 1976 the Transkei was declared 'independent', although it relied entirely on the South African government for its budget and the training of its police force, and no country except South Africa recognised the new state. Other homelands were prepared for 'independence', although they were even less economically viable than the Transkei. Bophuthatswana consisted of 19 separate pieces of land spread hundreds of kilometres apart, and KwaZulu (formed out of Zululand and other parts of Natal) was divided into at least 11 fragments interspersed with white farms. All the coastal areas were also allocated to whites. Despite the lack of economic viability for such 'states', the South African government moved ahead with preparing them for independence and thereby ensuring that no African would be a citizen of South Africa (Maps 2 and 3).

By the end of apartheid's first decade, its intent and form had become clear: racial separation under white supremacy. And in the short term it was proving extremely profitable for the white economy even if, in the long term, it seemed a fantastic feat to accomplish. Despite protests and dislocation, South Africa entered an economic boom in the 1960s. Foreign investors had withdrawn their funds and white immigration had come to a halt in the immediate aftermath of Sharpeville, but Vorster's harsh measures rebuilt confidence in the security of investments and the stability of the state, and money and people returned. Foreign investment in South Africa, attracted by rates of return on capital often running as high as 15 to 20 per cent, more than doubled between 1963 and 1972, while high immigration levels boosted the white population during the same period. Investment and immigration fuelled an impressive economic boom, with the country's annual economic growth averaging 6 per cent for the decade. Smuts' earlier dismissal of apartheid as impractical and impossible in the 1940s rang hollow by the end of the 1960s.

4

Growing contradictions

Apartheid had been implemented inside South Africa through an intricate series of laws and regulations carefully constructed to separate the races into a hierarchy of power with all groups subservient to white rule. Throughout the 1950s, the South African government had enacted legislation that controlled every aspect of its citizens' lives based on race. Members of each racial group were classified, told where to live, what schools to attend, whom they could marry, and how much money they could earn at work. Despite its all-encompassing reach, however, the apartheid structure had been designed on an ad hoc basis in response to ongoing challenges from the African population. In this manner, apartheid also created some glaring contradictions and unintended results that threatened to destabilise the entire structure. By the 1960s, these contradictions began to emerge.

Many apartheid laws produced results that were counterproductive to the intentions of Nationalist politicians. African students, who were educated to believe that they deserved no more than a subservient position in South Africa, instead came to understand that apartheid left them nothing to lose in opposing the government by violent means. Employers found that there was no practical way to settle disputes with workers who were legally denied union representation or visible leadership. Africans who found themselves 'citizens' of their 'homelands' were too poor to buy the myriad products being produced at great rates of profit in South Africa's expanding industries. And all credible African leaders capable of exerting real leadership and control in the African community were in jail or dead. Rather than creating the well-ordered world of white supremacy foretold by apartheid's architects, South Africa's new legislation was creating a chaotic wreck of human waste.

The South African government turned increasingly to brute force and, in a desperately hypocritical move, even staged a mock 'reform' to blunt opposition. Throughout the 1960s and 1970s, the government imprisoned all of the country's most experienced African leaders, outlawed their organisations and prohibited all forms of protest against government policies. Public speeches, newspapers, songs and even T-shirts critical of the government or in any way supportive of racial integration were illegal inside South Africa. The government tried to force an acceptance of apartheid. Nevertheless, the show of force only served to radicalise further opposition when Africans came to understand that there was no hope for them under apartheid. When the government offered a farcical constitutional 'reform' in 1983, African frustrations boiled over and signalled the beginning of unrelenting opposition that spelled the final downfall of apartheid.

THE IMPACT OF APARTHEID

While the government increasingly repressed the majority of its citizens, South Africa nevertheless saw a steady growth in its economy as foreign investors returned to the country, eager for the astounding profits that repression earned. Relying on extremely low wages, firms operating in South Africa earned profits averaging annually nearly 25 per cent by the early 1980s, as compared with rates of 6.5 per cent in Britain and 4.1 per cent in Germany. There were approximately 2,000–2,500 foreign businesses operating in South Africa by that time – including 1,200 British, 350 German and 340 American firms – investing about $30 billion by the early 1980s and accounting for approximately 20 per cent of all industry in the country. The overall value of companies operating inside South Africa increased by an astounding 400 per cent in the 1970s. For the first time, Afrikaners began to partake of this wealth at something near the level of the English-speaking South African community, with an annual per capita income of over 70 per cent that of the English, rising from less than 50 per cent in the pre-war decades. The white community enjoyed a standard of living higher than that in most western industrialised countries.

But all of this wealth came at the expense of South Africans who were not part of the white community. Despite the overall increase in the economy, African wages did not rise. The real value of African mine wages was less in 1971 than it had been in 1911. And the African factory workers who were making South Africa's manufacturing sector its most productive earned only 18 per cent of the wages of their white co-workers. Overall, white per capita income was ten times that of Africans. By the early 1980s, South Africa ranked as the country with the most inequitable distribution of income in the world, with the bottom 40 per cent of the population earning only 6 per cent of national income. This gap between whites and other communities did not simply result in lowered standards of living, but also threatened lives. The mortality rate for African and Coloured infants was 13 times higher than for whites. As many as 25 per cent of African and Coloured children died before their first birthday.

THE FAILURE OF GRAND APARTHEID

The centrepiece of apartheid strategy was the belief that the complete separation of all races and ethnic groups would ensure stability and control. Nationalist politicians believed that Africans, Indians and Coloureds would come to accept conditions in their communities if their contact with white South Africa was limited. In Verwoerd's words, the African should not 'desire to become integrated into the life of the European community', but should understand that 'within his own community, all doors are open' (Huddleston, 1956: 159). To that end, all races should live in their own geographically defined areas, with whites holding most rural and urban space, Indians and Coloureds relegated to their own townships in urban areas, and Africans increasingly removed from urban townships and moved into ethnically defined 'homelands' in the rural areas. In this manner, contact between the races would be limited and groups would remain racially and ethnically defined and fragmented, discouraging multiracial organisation or resistance.

Under the provisions of the Group Areas Act, urban and rural areas in South Africa were divided into zones, in which members of only one racial group could live. All others had to move. In practice, however, it was blacks who had to move, often under the threat or use of force. With the enactment of the Bantu Resettlement Act (No. 19) of 1954, the government began to remove Africans from the western Johannesburg suburbs of Sophiatown, Newclare and Martindale. The residents had been in the area since the beginning of the century and had acquired freehold rights from the original developer (who had hoped to sell to whites but the presence of a nearby sewage treatment plant had put them off). The government used the excuse that the process of removal was really only 'slum clearance' for the 'benefit' of the 'natives'. The government began to 'remove' residents physically, beginning on 10 February 1955, when 60,000 people were moved by army trucks and armed police from Sophiatown to an area set aside for Africans. One white observer described the manner in which Africans were moved:

> It was a fantastic sight. In the yard [opposite the local bus station] military
> lorries were drawn up. Already they were piled high with the pathetic
> possessions which had come from the row of rooms in the background.

> A rusty kitchen stove; a few blackened pots and pans; a wicker chair;
> mattresses belching out their coir stuffing; bundles of heaven-knows-what;
> and people, soaked, all soaked to the skin by the drenching rain.
>
> (Huddleston, 1956: 179–80)

The Africans were moved out and replaced with white Afrikaners who renamed the suburb, Triomf, or 'triumph'. Sophiatown to Triomf was the first of the removals but the process was played out again and again throughout South Africa – the removal of Coloureds from District Six in Cape Town is probably the best known – as the government sought to give physical effect to its policy of separation, and whites seized the property of their black former neighbours. The means remained much the same: forced ejection of people who protested against their removal, and the demolition and destruction of what little property they possessed. Twenty-five years after Sophiatown, here is how Africans whose families had lived in a rural area of northern Natal since 1885 described the implementation of apartheid:

> On the 19th August 1980 we saw the Municipality and the Drakensberg
> Administration Board as well as police, all armed with guns, and a
> bulldozer. They started to break down houses. Most of the owners of these
> houses were not at home but at work or fetching wood. When they came
> home from work they found their houses broken down.
>
> (Platzky and Walker, 1985: 269)

During the three decades that the South African government pursued this policy, from the mid-1950s to the mid-1980s, approximately 3.5 million Africans were removed from 'white' areas in a process the government came to refer to as 'erasing black spots'. In addition to the physical removal of entire communities, the very rigid application of pass laws doubled the number of Africans ejected from the cities between 1962 and 1967.

Where were Africans to go? To their 'homelands', areas originally defined by the colonial British government as African land and established as 'reserves' under the Natives' Land Act of 1913. Comprising 7 per cent of South Africa's land area in 1913, they were theoretically expanded to be equivalent to approximately 13.5 per cent in 1936, though the process of government purchase of the additional land was slow and incomplete. In the 1950s the government asserted that these lands corresponded with traditional African kingdoms and landholdings, although in most cases they were the areas left in African possession after conquest in the 1870s and 1880s and comprised mostly land deemed uneconomic for white habitation and cultivation. Of the ten homelands, only one (Qwaqwa) had contiguous borders while the rest consisted of scattered bits of unwanted territory (KwaZulu was made up of approximately 70 segments). The government established ten homelands, also referred to as Bantustans, based on ethnicity: Transkei, Ciskei (both Xhosa), Bophuthatswana (Tswana), Venda (Venda), Gazankulu (Tsonga), Lebowa (North Sotho), Qwaqwa (South Sotho), KwaZulu (Zulu), KaNgwane (Swazi) and KwaNdebele (Ndebele) (Map 2).

In 1959, Prime Minister Hendrik Verwoerd announced government plans to grant them all 'independence' under the Bantu Self-Government Act and to relinquish responsibility for these territories and their inhabitants. To that end, the South African government had to assemble 'national' political institutions in each homeland. Following more than a century of conquest and white rule in most parts of South Africa, resurrecting chiefdoms seen as legitimate in African eyes in these areas was by all accounts suspect. Nevertheless, these representatives were then given powers of limited self-government in territorial legislatures. Finally, they were granted full 'independence' for their own affairs by the South African government. In 1976 the government proclaimed the Transkei an independent nation-state and followed this move by granting independence to Bophuthatswana in 1977, Venda in 1979, and Ciskei in 1981. Citizens of these states, including the half who lived outside their borders, were then deemed aliens in South Africa. Another six ethnically based homelands were granted limited self-government in the 1980s in preparation for eventual independence: they were KwaZulu, Lebowa, Gazankulu, Qwaqwa, KaNgwane and KwaNdebele. None of these states received international recognition.

In this way, the government not only tried to dispel the appearance of political repression of its own citizens, but also cut financial costs associated with what it considered an 'unproductive' segment of the population. Fewer hospitals, schools, electricity lines, water supplies and so forth were needed inside 'white' South Africa. Africans were to live in their 'homelands', therefore it was unnecessary to provide them with amenities in the 'white' areas. Consequently, the government stopped building houses for Africans in urban areas (where they were not allowed to own property and were forced to live in townships designated under the Group Areas Act). In South Africa's capital, Pretoria, not a single house for an African family was constructed between 1967 and 1976. By the late 1970s there was, according to a government study, a housing backlog of 141,000 units (almost one-third of existing urban housing for Africans) and a shortage of 126,000 beds in workers' hostels (equal to 40 per cent of existing hostel accommodation). The average number of residents in a typical four-room home in Soweto at that time was 14. While apartheid success depended on African labour, government leaders still viewed Africans as visitors in South Africa who should be treated as transitory and disposable and afforded no rights or services in 'white' South Africa.

Since neither the proffered incentive of political participation in the homelands, the enforced disincentive of limited housing in the 'white' areas, nor even physical 'removal' seemed to be successful in keeping Africans out of the cities, the government simply decreed that they were no longer citizens of South Africa. Joseph Lelyveld, the *New York Times* correspondent in South Africa in the late 1970s, travelled throughout the country and described the process in action. 'Apartheid double bookkeeping, subtracting blacks every time there was an independence ceremony in a homeland, made this miracle possible. Who could have imagined that?' (Lelyveld, 1985: 122). The 'subtracted' citizens of South Africa showed up, either physically or statistically, in the apartheid homelands. Despite a high birthrate, the official number of blacks registered in the South African census regularly showed a decline throughout the 1970s and 1980s. In 1976 there were 18.5 million Africans; by 1977, the official estimates claimed, there were only 15.7 million. Between 1973 and 1982 there had been virtually no rise at all. In contrast, in 1970 the homeland of KwaNdebele had a population of 32,000; by 1980 it had, according to official statistics, 465,000 'citizens'. This scenario was repeated throughout the country with the establishment of each homeland. In 1960, 39.8 per cent of the total black population was in homelands; by 1980 resettlement led to 53.1 per cent in homelands. In absolute terms, the population in the homelands increased from 4.4 million to 11 million.

Although many Africans successfully evaded the move to the homelands, population densities in these outposts still rose to unacceptable limits. Whereas the 'white' areas in the Cape hosted a population of 2 per square kilometre, and in the Transvaal 11 per square kilometre, the corresponding figures for the homelands in 1980 were Bophuthatswana: 29, Lebowa: 65, KwaNdebele: 193, Transkei: 55, Ciskei: 82, and Qwaqwa: 298. Agricultural cultivation became impossible under such crowded conditions with defor-estation and soil erosion quickly marking the landscapes of these semi-fertile areas. The results were disastrous. Even by South African government esti-mates, 80 per cent of the population in the homelands was living in poverty by 1983.

One of the most shocking examples of the crowded conditions obtaining in the homelands was in Qwaqwa, an intended national state that consisted of a quarter of a million people crushed into an area of only 25 square miles. When Joseph Lelyveld visited Qwaqwa in 1983 he tried to find a way to capture the experience:

> For an hour or so, I experimented with taking pictures of these hillside settlements, hoping to get an image that conveyed the hive-like density of the place, but gave up in frustration. One picture of mud houses squeezed together in a barren landscape looked more or less like another. It wasn't

the houses themselves that accounted for the overwhelming sense of abandonment and claustrophobia that you might expect to find in a refugee camp; it was the accumulation, the totality of them, with little in the way of a visible, supporting economy. It required a panoramic shot with a precise depth-of-field calculation, which was beyond my competence. And it required the immediate contrast of white South Africa, in all its plenitude and spaciousness, next door. How else could you make an image of exclusion?

(Lelyveld, 1985: 138)

Although the homelands were economic disasters, what of their so-called political 'independence'? Situated within the borders of South Africa, they could either harbour Pretoria's enemies or remain under firm South African control. The South African government took few chances, installing leaders who would cooperate with Pretoria and provide no challenge to white rule in South Africa. Their national budgets relied heavily on assistance from Pretoria, and most security legislation (Internal Security Act, detentions, bannings, etc.) continued to operate until formal independence was granted. Some homeland leaders voiced opposition to the South African government but with little effect. Mangosuthu (Gatsha) Buthelezi, the government-appointed head of the KwaZulu homeland, successfully opposed accepting independence but at the same time he encouraged Zulu nationalism, building up an ethnically oriented power base with his **Inkatha Freedom Party (IFP)**.

In the Transkei and the Ciskei, familial dictatorships – the Matanzima brothers in the former, the Sebes in the latter – provided 'indigenous' leadership for regimes in which state power was exercised without even a veneer of respect for the rule of law. Lelyveld captured best the appearance of Lieutenant General Xhanti Charles Sebe, director of state security for the Ciskei:

a flamboyant black cop who sometimes wore a black Stetson with his smoked glasses and Christian Dior suits . . . [who had] a helicopter and a couple of planes at his disposal and also a fat-cat BMW sedan with frosted glass so that the assassins who were presumed to be lurking in wait for him could never know whether he was inside or where he was sitting.

(Lelyveld, 1985: 158)

Before becoming a general in the homeland security force, Sebe had been a sergeant in the South African police in which one of his last jobs had been to spy on Stephen Biko, founder of the **Black Consciousness Movement**, and his supporters. For Sebe the real enemy was communism and it took many forms:

Inkatha Freedom Party (IFP): Originated as a Zulu cultural organisation and was transformed into a political party under the leadership of Mangosuthu (Gatsha) Buthelezi in the late 1980s. Responsible for brutal attacks, with support from South African police, against ANC supporters in the months before the 1994 election. Garnered 10.5 per cent of the national vote in the election, securing a place in the first multiracial cabinet.

Black Consciousness: Political philosophy that emerged within the black student community in the late 1960s in response to the implementation of apartheid. Student leader Stephen Biko argued that blacks needed to counteract the psychological impact of apartheid by realising that they were not inferior. Viewed Africans, Indians and Coloureds as all suffering under apartheid and used the term 'black' for all of them.

in my context a liberal is a Communist. . . . The struggle in South Africa is not between a black struggle and a white. It is a communistic oriented ideology professed by the African National Congress for the Communists to take over in South Africa as it is stated in their blueprint. . . .

You [speaking to a group of Afrikaner students] all heard about Mandela. . . . You all heard about Moses Kotane, Alfred Nzo, Oliver Tambo, but because of *commu-u-nism*, where are they now with their brains, with their academic backgrounds?

(Lelyveld, 1985: 158, 172–3, original emphasis)

But grinding poverty and political repression had enormous costs and not just for the victims of apartheid. By the end of the 1970s, the government began to acknowledge that the homelands were a failure. In 1979 the Commission of Inquiry into Legislation Affecting the Utilisation of Manpower (Riekert Commission) determined that poverty in the homelands was so crushing that tens of thousands of Africans were faced with no choice but to enter the cities, risking arrest and imprisonment, in order to survive. The government also admitted that 'grand apartheid' had equally grand costs. Moving Africans from their separate living areas, sometimes more than a hundred miles, to their urban workplaces on a daily basis required an enormous transportation network, primarily buses in which people were crushed for hours a day. With African wages kept low to benefit industry, the real cost of the transportation could not be charged completely against the commuters, with the result that the state by the late 1970s was subsidising African bus passengers at the rate of $1,000 per commuter per year. Lelyveld reported that the 'KwaNdebele bus subsidy . . . was higher than the KwaNdebele gross domestic product. This is basic apartheid economics' (Lelyveld, 1985: 122). While the government did not want to spend the money to build schools, hospitals or housing for urban Africans, it was also reluctant to continue subsidising a scheme that was not working. But it would be almost another decade before the government would publicly acknowledge this failure by rescinding the pass laws in 1986.

Too poor to sustain the African population and ignominiously discredited as corrupt regimes, the homelands represented the largest and most expensive failure of apartheid policies. Most importantly, they utterly failed to stem the tide of African urbanisation, with the number of Africans in the cities doubling by the 1980s. Through overcrowding and insufficient investment in basic economic infrastructure, the homelands offered Africans no alternative to employment in the white areas of South Africa. Moreover, the illegitimacy of homeland governments and leaders left Africans few alternatives to the political leadership of the ANC, Black Consciousness, and other groups staunchly opposed to any accommodation with apartheid.

ESSENTIAL WORKERS: THE FAILURE OF LABOUR CONTROL

The same Africans who travelled back and forth to the empty independence of the homelands were also the backbone of South Africa's economy and wielded more power at the urban workplace than in their homelands. South Africa's prosperity was inextricably linked with apartheid, a system that produced huge profits through the exploitation of the workers and in turn relied on those profits to implement exploitation, often through the police force. Brutality towards workers was not new in South Africa, and had been a feature of the slave economy at the Cape in the seventeenth century and in the mining economy starting in the nineteenth century. In most cases, employers relied on the fact that workers had little recourse against ill treatment and in any case could easily be replaced if they proved too troublesome. By the middle of the twentieth century, however, the situation began to change. While workers in the mines or on farms might be replaced with little trouble, doing so in South Africa's burgeoning factories would incur considerable expense in retraining Africans and possibly halting production altogether. African workers were indispensable not only in the traditional mining and farming sectors, but also in the most productive sector of the South African economy, manufacturing.

White governments in southern Africa had always viewed Africans as labourers who should be closely controlled, and by 1948 a formidable network of laws governed African workers. They were barred from certain skilled work (Mines and Works Act, 1911) and could be found guilty of a criminal offence if they broke an employment contract (Native Labour Regulation Act, 1911). Africans were not included in the legal definition of 'employee' and therefore could not join legally registered unions. Nor could African unions be officially recognised in labour negotiations (Industrial Conciliation Acts, 1924 and 1937). It was also illegal for African workers to engage in strike activity (War Measure 145, 1942) (Horrell, 1978: 8, 265). If African workers had any grievances, they had no effective or legal means of expressing their concerns.

Under apartheid after 1948, elaborate controls were extended to all African workers to ensure that labour was still provided to white businesses in spite of the strict separation of races. Beginning in 1952 under the Bantu Laws Amendment Act, the government established 'labour bureaux' where unemployed African men between the ages of 16 and 64 were required to register with a local employment officer, much like the US Selective Service system for military registration (Horrell, 1978: 173–4). These bureaux were first established in areas designated under the Group Areas Act for whites, but additional bureaux were established in the African homelands in 1968 under Bantu Labour Regulations. The labour bureaux acted as a sort of clearing house for African labour, with African work-seekers increasingly stuck in the homelands without legal means of entering the cities to find work, and at the mercy of the employment officers. The bureaux notified workers of employment opportunities and required them to sign a legally binding contract to take a job. If an African lost his job, the labour bureau in that locality required him to register for new work and gave him six weeks to find a job. At the end of that time, if still unemployed, he would be bussed out to his 'homeland'. At that point, he was forced to register again with the labour bureau in his homeland and could only re-enter white areas if he was assigned a job through the homeland labour bureau. It was illegal for employers to hire an African who was not registered with a local labour bureau and employers were required to sign an African employee's reference book, commonly known as their 'pass' book, monthly, as proof of their continued employment and therefore their right to stay in a 'white' area. The labour bureaux worked to funnel workers into specific areas and to ensure that no African resided in a white area without serving white economic interests.

African workers were also subject to strict control over what types of job they could take. While earlier legislation, especially the Mines and Works Act, 1911 and the Apprenticeship Act, 1922, excluded Africans from employment in most 'skilled' industrial jobs, apartheid legislation began in 1956 to 'reserve' specific jobs for specific racial groups. By that time, increasing mechanisation in factories had created new semi-skilled jobs into which Africans were being placed at rates of pay that white workers would not accept. The white labour unions argued that these rates of pay were too low to provide for a 'civilised' standard of living. In such a case, the white workers could ask the employer to raise the rates of pay or, if such action failed, the workers could request an investigation by a government-appointed Industrial Tribunal under the provisions of the Industrial Conciliation Act, 1956. The Tribunal could recommend that a 'Job Reservation Determination' be made by the minister of labour, legally reserving stated types of work to a specified racial group. The minister of native affairs could also exercise a type of job reservation by refusing to register labour contracts for specific types of work in specific areas, such as prohibiting Africans from working as managers in stores in white areas (Group Areas Act, 1950 and Bantu Laws Amendment Act, 1970).

All avenues of African representation were effectively closed. The government moved to deny Africans access to any union representation by continuing to exclude them from the legal definition of employee (Native Labour Settlement of Disputes Act, 1955), and by barring any mixed-race unions from being legally registered (Industrial Conciliation Act, 1956). It therefore became impossible for African, Coloured or Indian workers to make any legal representations through many of the white-led unions that had been sympathetic and had tried for years to represent their concerns. Instead, the government established a completely separate process and set of institutions for the resolution of African workers' complaints (Native Labour Settlement of Disputes Act, 1955). At the top of this structure was the government-appointed Bantu Labour Board and Bantu Labour Officers. At the factory level, 'works committees' were established to deal with the conditions of employment in each establishment. Nevertheless, Africans still had no access to industry-wide organisations and the works committees were ineffective and largely non-existent.

By the 1970s, this system began to break down under the pressure of worker discontent. Economic recession in the early part of that decade, followed by inflation and a contraction in the job market, resulted in a dramatic upsurge in labour unrest. With over 165,000 African industrial workers, Durban became the focus of this unrest. In January 1973, a prolonged series of illegal strikes there began at a brickworks employing 2,000. The men went on strike arguing for higher wages, marching down the street chanting 'Man is dead, but his spirit lives'. When the brickworkers won a wage increase, strikes immediately spread throughout Durban to textile factories notorious for low wages and poor conditions, and moved on 'like a wave. As one factory won a wage increase and returned to work, another group of workers would come out on strike' (MacShane *et al.*, 1984: 21). In the first three months of 1973, some 160 strikes involving more than 60,000 industrial workers took place, mostly in Durban but also spreading to the Eastern Cape and the Rand.

In addition to the high level of participation they engendered, the strikes were also significant in bringing about new and more successful organising methods for Africans with no rights of representation and under heavy police surveillance. The workers engaged in sudden 'wildcat' strikes rather than the protracted negotiations used by African workers in the 1940s. In this way, employers and police had little time in which to take preventive and repressive measures. And the workers went a step further by choosing not to form representative bodies or to elect a leadership, learning from previous decades of labour and political protests that police would move quickly to arrest and jail any person who organised a strike. This was especially frustrating for employers who found themselves faced with the prospect of negotiating with '1,500 workers on a football field' rather than with credible leaders presenting workers' demands in order to keep their factories running (MacShane *et al.*, 1984: 51). Once again, apartheid had created its own contradictions by making it impossible to control workers through outright repression.

Under pressure from workers and employers alike, the government began to allow for some legal worker representation. In July 1973, the Bantu

Labour Relations Regulation Amendment Act for the first time granted Africans direct legal rights in wage negotiations. Africans, rather than their white representatives, could represent their own interests at the industrial councils, conciliation and wage boards that determined their conditions of employment. Strikes by African workers were also legalised, and a system for organisation within the factories through elected committees was also created. By 1976, nearly 3,000 such committees had been formed. Although the Act stopped short of allowing for industry-wide African unions, it was an acknowledgement by the government that the economy could not exist without the cooperation of African workers.

Nevertheless, the political and economic situation in South Africa continued to worry employers. The strikes brought working conditions in the factories to the attention of the world since many of the businesses operating in Durban and the Eastern Cape were owned by international firms. Worldwide criticism began to mount through the 1970s and 1980s with successful calls for disinvestment in South Africa. Pressured by investors and worried about the continuing stability of the South African economy, companies began to re-examine their operations in South Africa. Those who stayed were faced with a growing labour shortage in the country's factories. During the 1960s, the number of jobs in manufacturing had grown by nearly 70 per cent as compared with only 10 per cent in mining and negative growth in farming jobs. The very workers who were threatening apartheid's control of the economy were in high demand in the factories. Employers could not afford high turnovers or dissatisfaction within this labour force.

When tensions inside South Africa erupted in student demonstrations in Soweto in 1976 (see below), employers became even more concerned. Most of the student political groups involved in the demonstrations, including Stephen Biko's Black Consciousness Movement, had close ties with workers and the labour union movement. The political groups had worked with the incipient unions throughout the 1970s, helping to organise community self-help efforts. And workers themselves had increasingly argued for the connection between economic and political disadvantage in South Africa. With the outbreak of country-wide community protests in 1976, employers feared the worst in their factories.

In order to forestall the politicisation of the workforce and the union movement, the government appointed in 1977 a Commission of Inquiry into Labour Legislation (known as the Wiehahn Commission). The Commission report was published in 1979 and opened with the admission that

There were simply not enough [white] skilled workers available to fill all the vacancies [in manufacturing] . . . with the result that increasing numbers of unskilled and skilled workers, particularly Blacks, had to be trained and utilised to perform higher-level skilled jobs.

(Price, 1991: 30–1)

Under such circumstances, employers needed legally recognised workers' representatives with whom to bargain, and the Commission recommended that blacks should be allowed to register trade unions and to have them recognised as part of the official conciliation process. The Commission also recommended the elimination of statutory job reservation by race that had restricted Africans from higher paid and more skilled jobs, although it left it up to individual firms as to whether they wanted to practise segregation in the workplace.

Legislation incorporating the recommendations of the Wiehahn Commission was passed in 1979 (Industrial Conciliation Amendment Act, 1979, permitting Africans to form trade unions, Labour Relations Amendment Act, 1981, permitting the formation of trade unions with a mixed membership, that is Africans, Coloureds, Indians and whites could be in the same union) and resulted in a surge of strikes and a huge growth in African trade unionism in the early 1980s. Whereas an annual average of 2,000 African workers had gone on strike in the 1960s and nearly 100,000 in the turbulent conditions of 1973, throughout the early 1980s nearly 90,000 Africans were out on strike each year. By 1984, 550,000 Africans were members of organised trade unions. The impact of union activities was apparent as the earnings of African workers began to increase, with African wages as a percentage of whites' doubling in the manufacturing industries and more than tripling in the mining sector.

In addition to working towards improving life in the factories, the new unions also became increasingly involved in larger community issues. The impact of apartheid on African workers reached far beyond the workplace, and unionists became involved in establishing 'civic' organisations calling for better housing, health care and political rights. These workers would eventually join with an energised student movement to help force political change in the 1980s.

BANTU EDUCATION AND BLACK CONSCIOUSNESS

By the 1970s, Bantu Education had been in operation for nearly 20 years and had produced its first generation of African students. Educated to understand their 'place' within South African society – with no rights, privileges or opportunities – the Bantu Education generation envisioned by Verwoerd should have docilely taken its place as the servant of the whites and never have dreamed of any other life. However, Bantu Education backfired badly with a new generation that saw the naked truth: apartheid held no benefits for them and they were being 'brainwashed' into thinking that they were inferior, lesser human beings. Stephen Biko would articulate the response of this generation with his political philosophy of 'Black Consciousness'.

The frustrations of youths growing up under apartheid were most intensely crystallised in the school systems. Most African students were in the urban areas since the government had decided to expand the number of African schools there, in spite of the homeland scheme, because of the increasing shortage of labour in the cities. Elementary and secondary school black enrolment rose from 1 million in 1955 to 2.5 million in 1969, and the black university population went from 515 in 1961 to 3,000 in 1972. During the same period, the amount of GDP spent on black education steadily declined, resulting in massive overcrowding in the schools. From 1970 to 1975, African high school enrolment grew by 160 per cent. In 1975, half of Soweto's population was under the age of 25, and there were 16,000 families for every high school compared to 1,300 families for every white high school. At Morris Isaacson High in Soweto, there were 70 students in each classroom.

By 1969, African university students were especially frustrated with their deteriorating situation and broke away from the multiracial National Union of South African Students (NUSAS) to form their own group, the **South African Students' Organisation (SASO)**. Objecting to the fact that the avowedly anti-apartheid NUSAS still adhered to apartheid laws in its daily practice (by, for example, requiring that black and white students occupy segregated dormitories at its national convention), the founder of SASO, Stephen Bantu Biko, argued that blacks should take matters into their own hands. First, they needed their own representative organisations: 'Blacks should work themselves into a powerful group so as to go forth and stake their rightful claim in the open society rather than to exercise that power in some obscure part of the Kalahari.' Second, they could not rely on whites, no matter how well meaning, as allies in the struggle against apartheid: 'White liberals vacillate between the two worlds [of black and white] verbalising all the complaints of the blacks beautifully while skilfully extracting what suits them from the exclusive pool of white privileges.' Third, blacks had to remake themselves psychologically:

> as long as blacks are suffering from an inferiority complex – a result of 300 years of deliberate oppression, denigration and derision. . . . What is

South African Students' Organization (SASO): Established in 1968 by African university students frustrated with the political position of the multiracial National Union of South African Students (NUSAS). SASO membership was limited to black students (Africans, Coloureds and Indians). Under the leadership of Stephen Biko, SASO organised anti-government strikes and rallies in the early 1970s. Banned in 1975.

necessary . . . is a very strong grassroots build-up of black consciousness such that blacks can learn to assert themselves and stake their rightful claim.

(Biko, 1986: 15–16, 21)

Stephen Biko, born in 1946, had received his elementary and high school education in missionary-run institutions, and then experienced the full ramifications of 'Bantu Education' when in 1965 he entered the 'Non-European' section of the medical school at the otherwise all-white University of Natal. He was strongly influenced by the writings of earlier ANC activist Anton Lembede and by the Black Power movement in the United States. In developing the major tenets of Black Consciousness he defined 'blacks' as including people from all racial groups denied basic civil rights under apartheid, including Africans, Coloureds and Asians. In bringing about change, he stressed the need for 'blacks' to free themselves first from their psychological chains and then to work together for liberation. He did, however, reject the policies of violence adopted by the ANC and the PAC in the early 1960s and emphasised that only non-violent methods should be used in the struggle against apartheid [**Doc. 6, pp. 154–7**].

Although government officials at first welcomed the development of Black Consciousness because they mistakenly believed that the philosophy complemented the racial separation inherent in apartheid, they quickly learned that Black Consciousness was not meant to restrict Africans to their homelands. In 1972, SASO organised strikes on university campuses, resulting in the arrest of more than 600 students. In 1974, SASO and the Black People's Convention organised rallies to celebrate the overthrow of Portuguese colonialism in Angola and Mozambique. The students made clear the connection that they saw between the end of colonialism in these neighbouring countries and the fight against apartheid, brandishing posters and banners saying:

Frelimo fought and regained our soil, our dignity. It is a story. Change the name and the story applies to you. The dignity of the Black Man has been restored in Mozambique and so shall it be here. Black must rule. We shall drive them to the sea. Long live Azania. Revolution!! [Samora] Machel will help! Away with Vorster Ban! We are for Afro black Power!!! Viva Frelimo. Power!!! We shall overcome.

(Price, 1991: 52)

But the government responded with a predictable combination of repression and intimidation. Biko himself was banned in 1973 after strikes that year, and he was arrested and charged with fomenting terrorism following the pro-Frelimo rallies. By 1975, SASO was banned on all black campuses. The message of Black Consciousness was not silenced, however, as Biko used his trial – as had Nelson Mandela ten years earlier – as a platform to explain his message to South Africa and to the world. Biko's trial dragged on for most of 1975 and 1976 and during his testimony he explained the problems for Africans in South Africa:

> I think the black man is subjected to two forces in this country. He is first of all oppressed by an external world through institutionalised machinery, through laws that restrict him from doing certain things, through heavy work conditions, through poor pay, through very difficult living conditions, through poor education, these are all external to him, and secondly, and this we regard as the most important, the black man in himself has developed a certain state of alienation, he rejects himself, precisely because he attaches the meaning white to all that is good, in other words he associates good and he equates good with white. This arises out of his living and it arises out of his development from childhood.
>
> (Biko, 1986: 100)

The sheer arrogance and brutality of apartheid made clear to all blacks that under this system they had no worth and no hope, and this left them with two choices: submit or rebel.

Apartheid, in the form of Bantu Education, again failed in its primary aim. While the government planned to educate Africans to submission, it instead witnessed the beginning of apartheid's final downfall with student demonstrations in Soweto. The situation in Soweto began in 1974 when the newly appointed minister of Bantu Education, Michael C. Botha, and his deputy, Andries Treurnicht, decided to enforce a previously ignored provision of the Bantu Education Act that required Afrikaans to be used on an equal basis with English as a medium of instruction. A shortage of Afrikaans-speaking teachers and a lack of suitable textbooks had resulted in English and African languages being used as the languages of instruction. Because Afrikaans was identified by Africans, especially by the young and by those sympathetic to Black Consciousness, as the language of the oppressor, opposition to this new policy grew throughout 1975 and into 1976. Some African school boards refused to enforce the policy and saw their members dismissed by the government. Students began to boycott classes. On 16 June 1976, hundreds of high-school students in Soweto, the African township south-west of Johannesburg, marched to Morris Isaacson High School and then towards Orlando Stadium (the main soccer venue) where they planned to protest against having to use Afrikaans.

Plate 1 Nelson Mandela and Ruth First at a Bloemfontein meeting of the African National Congress in December 1951. Mandela was banned in 1952 by the South African government from speaking in public, and imprisoned from 1962 until 1990. Ruth First went into exile in 1964, and was killed in Mozambique in 1982 by a letter bomb mailed by Craig Williamson, a member of the South African police.

© Bailey's African History Archive (BAHA)

Plate 2 H.F. Verwoerd in March 1951, when he was Minister of Native Affairs. Often regarded as the architect of apartheid in practice, Verwoerd served as prime minister of South Africa from 1958 until he was stabbed to death by Dimitri Tsafendas, a parliamentary messenger, on 6 September 1966.

Plate 3 Aftermath of the Sharpeville massacre. Police fired into the backs of hundreds of PAC supporters protesting the pass laws, in Sharpeville township, on 21 March 1960. The bodies of the over 69 killed and those of the wounded were left in the street and photographed the next morning.

© Associated Press

Plate 4 Steve Biko, the African political activist who founded SASO and developed Black
Consciousness ideology in South Africa. He died in police custody on 12 September 1977, after
being severely beaten during interrogation.

Plate 5 Young people in Johannesburg, 18 October 1976, hold up a banner protesting the death in police custody of 16-year-old Dumisani Mbatha, arrested a month earlier for demonstrating in memory of the 16 June 1976 Soweto uprising.
© Associated Press

Plate 6 ANC supporters at a rally on 16 June 1993, held to commemorate the 17th anniversary of the 1976 Soweto uprising, wave a banner threatening the lives of Afrikaners.

Plate 7 Three members of the AWB lying beside their Mercedes Benz after their organisation invaded the Bophuthatswana homeland in March 1994 in an attempt to overturn a coup by ANC-supporting soldiers. Moments after this photo was taken, the Bophuthatswana soldier shot dead the AWB men.
© Corbis

Plate 8 Jacob Zuma, Nelson Mandela and Thabo Mbeki at an ANC party in August 2008 celebrating Mandela's 90th birthday. Mbeki resigned as prime minister a month later after having lost re-election to the presidency of the ANC. Zuma became president of South Africa in April 2009.

© Corbis

As news of the protests spread, police began to converge on Soweto, shooting at school children and throwing tear gas. By 9 a.m. on the morning of 16 June, chaos began to sweep through the township. The first victim was Hector Petersen, a 13-year-old protestor shot by the police, who died on the way to hospital. As different groups of students came together and learned what was happening, they were shocked and then outraged. The police responded with tear gas and then with gunfire that left at least three dead and a dozen injured. The demonstrators, joined by angry crowds of Soweto residents, reacted by attacking and burning down government buildings, including administrative offices and beer halls [**Doc. 7, pp. 157–60**].

The next day, the government closed down the schools and put the South African military on alert. The deputy minister of Bantu affairs, Andries Treurnicht (nicknamed 'Dr No'), announced: 'In the white areas of South Africa [including Soweto], where the government erects the buildings, grants the subsidies and pays the teachers, it is our right to decide on language policy.' The minister of justice, Jimmy Kruger, accused the students of being communists: 'Why do they walk with upraised fists? Surely this is the sign of the Communist Party?' And Prime Minister John Vorster announced: 'The government will not be intimidated. Orders have been given to maintain order at all costs.' Those costs would include the lives of 174 Africans and two whites who were killed that day, as well as hundreds more who would be killed in the following months. News of the shootings swept around the world and the South African economy began to feel the shock with both gold and diamond shares dropping. Nevertheless, the South African government was prepared to deal with protests as it always had, with extreme force and repression.

The radicalisation of African youth evident in the violence that began in Soweto reverberated within the black community. Parents who had seen their children take to the streets, risking and sometimes losing their lives, were stirred to action. Throughout the urban African townships, parents began to organise new political groups for the first time since the Defiance Campaign of the 1950s. Over the next year, the 'Committee of 10', formed in Soweto, worked on a plan to remedy African grievances. In July 1977, the Committee issued a programme for the election of a new community board to have total autonomy in Soweto, including the power to levy taxes and to control education, the police and local elections. The plan was widely supported within the African community, including youth and parents. The minister of justice rejected the programme out of hand, and the government remained committed to controlling all African townships through the Bantu Administration Board. Immediately following the government announcement, unrest in African townships, especially those near Johannesburg and Pretoria, erupted.

THE APARTHEID POLICE STATE

To argue that apartheid failed in many of its primary goals – control over workers, complete separation of races, submission of youth – is not to say that apartheid did not wreak terrible destruction in the African, Coloured and Indian communities. Once the government began to realise that Africans would not automatically follow the dictates of the apartheid legislation of the 1950s, harsher and even more repressive state powers were established to force Africans into acquiescence. If African resistance could not be combated through separation, education or impoverishment, then the government would simply kill or imprison anyone who spoke out.

Throughout the 1960s, the government had steadily increased the police powers of the state in response to African challenges at Sharpeville and from the ANC and its armed wing, Umkhonto we Sizwe. These organisations had all been outlawed under the Unlawful Organizations Act of 1960, and all of their leaders 'banned' under the Suppression of Communism Act. In 1963 the General Laws Amendment Act enabled the government to institute the 90-day, later extended to 180-day, detention of individuals without charge, trial or legal representation. In the same year, the notorious 'Sobukwe Clause' was also inserted in the same Act, allowing the minister of justice to extend detention past the prison term handed down by the courts of anyone convicted under the Suppression of Communism Act (Robert Sobukwe was the only person ever held under this clause). The Terrorism Act of 1967 further expanded upon the types of activity that could be deemed dangerous to public safety, including any action that could encourage resistance to the government, causing a disturbance, furthering any political aim, or causing feelings of hostility between races. Although similar to the Suppression of Communism Act, the Terrorism Act dropped any reference to ideology and allowed for the imposition of the death penalty for those found guilty.

In addition to the increasing web of legal restrictions placed on Africans, the government was also busy constructing an elaborate apparatus of state security organisations to monitor resistance. Beginning in 1963, the government decided to establish a number of bodies – many secret – to coordinate security and intelligence matters. In that year, the State Security Committee was established to consider these issues. In 1969 the government formally established the Bureau for State Security (BOSS) to coordinate and complement the security activities of the Security Branch of the police and the military intelligence division of the Defence Force. It reported to the prime minister and its activities remained secret. In 1972, the **State Security Council (SSC)** was established to advise the prime minister on the formulation of national policy and strategy in relation to the security of the country. Members of the SSC included the prime minister (later the president), the

State Security Council (SSC): Established in 1972 to advise the prime minister on the security of the country. Operated as a *de facto* war cabinet throughout the 1970s and 1980s, superintending the struggle against the ANC, UDF and other anti-apartheid groups.

ministers of defence, justice, police and foreign affairs, as well as intelligence officials. By this time, the state had the intelligence network to uncover resistance and the legal tools to prosecute all who opposed the state.

These weapons would be used with great brutality following the Soweto uprising. Within the year, a total of 21 Africans died while being held in police custody. Many more had been tortured while imprisoned [**Doc. 8, pp. 160–2**]. All public gatherings had been banned throughout the country. By May 1977, the South African Institute of Race Relations reported that 617 Africans had died by violence since June 1976 in the townships. In an effort to appear to be making some moves towards reform, the government announced in August 1977 plans to write a new constitution, including limited representation for Asians and Coloureds, but not for Africans. Violent unrest continued in over 70 African townships throughout the country.

Mounting criticism and pressure on the government came to a head following the death in detention of Stephen Biko in September 1977. He had been held in indefinite detention and died from massive head injuries sustained during police interrogation. His public notoriety raised this incident to a level of national and international interest despite the fact that such deaths were being repeated in many South African jails. An inquest was held into the death and the police supplied the following official explanation:

Maj. Snyman reports that on 7/9/77 at about 07:00 he and [officers] Siebert and Beneke at the security offices in Sanlam offices interrogated Stephen Bantu Biko. The detainee was extremely arrogant, went berserk, took one of the chairs in the office and threw it at Snyman. With his fists he then stormed at the other members and the other members overwhelmed him. After a violent struggle, he fell with his head against the wall and with his body on the floor and in this process he received injuries on the lip and body. Warrant-Officer Beneke received an elbow injury and nonetheless did not go off duty. The district surgeon was informed and visited the detainee.

(Official notation from the police record book)

The officer in charge of Biko's interrogation, Major Harold Snyman, 20 years after the event, told in his testimony to the Truth and Reconciliation Commission (TRC) how the 'official version' of Biko's death was fashioned:

The instruction from Col. Goosen [Snyman's superior] to all the members of the security branch who had been involved with Biko; the Saturday after his death, he called all of these members into his office. . . . During this meeting Col. Goosen explained that the death of Biko was a great embarrassment to the security branch and the South African Government or could be a great embarrassment. It was clear that this event would have a negative impact on the image of South Africa abroad and that perhaps this could lose foreign investments for the country. . . . Col. Goosen explained that it was in the interest of the Government of the day that the matter had to be managed in such a way that the interests of the security branch and the South African Government could be protected. During this meeting there were instructions for everyone involved that the true facts with regard to this incident had to be adapted or simply not mentioned.

(http://www.justice.gov.za/trc/amntrans/pe/snyman.htm)

[**Doc. 9, pp. 162–4**]

The circumstances surrounding the death of Stephen Biko became a flashpoint for continuing resistance as well as increasing international attention to the brutal implementation of control in apartheid South Africa. The United Nations and the US government expressed concern over the circumstances of his death and the US Congress proposed that an international group examine South African laws and practices relating to detention and in particular the death of Stephen Biko. The South African government responded with a massive spate of bannings and detentions. On 19 October 1977, the government declared 18 organisations unlawful, arrested over 70 African leaders (including eight of the Soweto 'Committee of 10'), placed a number of people under banning orders, and closed down newspapers critical of the government. The minister of justice, Jimmy Kruger, who had already gained international notoriety by stating publicly that Biko's death had left him cold, justified these measures by declaring that the organisations and individuals affected were a threat to 'law and order'.

THE TOTAL STRATEGY

However, it was apparent by the end of the 1970s that neither the implementation of apartheid nor police intimidation was successful in halting continuing resistance and unrest within South Africa. The contradictions inherent in a system that depended on the submission of the overwhelming majority of the population had become glaring, with African workers, students and parents ready to risk their lives to challenge the state. Moreover, through widely reported events such as the Soweto uprising, the killing of Biko, and the violence in the townships, the world outside South Africa had become increasingly aware that apartheid was an inhumane system and anomalous in a world in which the last white-ruled colonial regimes of Angola, Mozambique and Southern Rhodesia had all fallen and been replaced by black-majority governments committed to freeing their African compatriots to the south.

Until the 1970s, apartheid was only one variant of continued colonial rule under white settler populations in Africa and elsewhere. By the end of that decade, however, South Africa stood alone and most significantly had no remaining white-ruled neighbours to secure the country's borders. Botswana and Lesotho had achieved independence in 1966, Swaziland in 1968, though they remained surrounded by white-ruled areas and their economies continued to be dependent on that of South Africa. In 1972, Africans in Rhodesia began a full-scale guerrilla war against the renegade white minority Smith regime that was attempting to perpetuate white settler rule. By 1978 the war covered 80 per cent of the Rhodesian countryside and all whites lived in a state of military siege. Although supported covertly by police and soldiers from South Africa, the settlers were forced to the negotiating table and capitulated in 1980, but not without ensuring that the lands confiscated from Africans during conquest in the early part of the century remained in the ownership of white farmers. Things fared worse for white settlers in the Portuguese colonies of Angola and Mozambique when the government of premier Marcello Caetano in Portugal was overthrown in 1974 and the Portuguese military withdrew from all colonies. White settlers fled to South Africa and to Portugal, while both Angola and Mozambique became independent with governments avowedly Marxist and strongly committed to the overthrow of apartheid. Angola granted the South West African People's Organisation, a movement fighting for the independence of South West Africa (under South African control since the First World War but whose 'trusteeship' of the territory, originally accorded by the League of Nations, had been terminated in 1969 by the United Nations), the right to establish military training bases and transit and refugee camps in the central and southern parts of the country. Mozambique entered diplomatic relations with the ANC and permitted Umkhonto we Sizwe (MK) guerrilla fighters to establish transit facilities to Swaziland and South Africa. Feeling threatened, South Africa invaded Angola in August 1975 (with secret encouragement from the United States), but its troops were forced to pull back when Cuban troops arrived. Seeking both to destabilise the Angolan government and to prevent infiltration of guerrilla fighters into Namibia, as South West Africa was known by those opposed to apartheid, South Africa maintained a military force in southern Angola for the next decade although never admitted to this fact publicly until after the fall of apartheid. In testimony to the TRC, the South African Defence Force submitted that invasion and occupation had been necessary in order to counter 'further Soviet-led expansion in the region' (TRC, 1998, vol. 2: 21).

The PAC and the ANC also embarked on new campaigns to bring an end to white rule. Between 1975 and 1977 the PAC initiated plans to infiltrate arms and guerrillas into South Africa, especially from Swaziland where it began military training among post-Soweto refugees from South Africa. However, these plans were brought to a halt in 1977 when the Swaziland government banned the organisation and deported all its members to other southern African countries. The ANC in the late 1970s, influenced in part by the findings of a delegation that had visited Vietnam in 1978 and met with the famous General Giap, who had been responsible for the military strategies of the victorious communist forces there, moved from an emphasis on rural guerrilla warfare to a focus on urban areas and a combination of political and military action. The new strategy aimed at an 'escalation of armed attacks combined with the building of mass organisations' within South Africa and had a goal of creating a general uprising or 'people's war' (TRC, 1998, vol. 2: 27–8).

With hostile neighbours and increasing internal unrest, the South African government in 1977 announced a '**Total Strategy**' to overcome this 'Total Onslaught'. Although the 'Total Strategy' initially referred to military strategy, as outlined in South Africa's defence budget, it soon became apparent that Prime Minister P.W. Botha envisioned a radical restructuring of the South African government. In 1979 Botha, in consultation with the chief of the South African Defence Force, General Magnus Malan, established the National Security Management System (NSMS). This 'system' organised cabinet committees into four – constitutional affairs, economic affairs, social affairs and security – with the last being the most important. As part of the NSMS from 1979 onwards over '500 regional, district and local Joint Management Centres were put into place, theoretically enabling a coordinated security system to reach from the highest level to the smallest locality' (TRC, 1998, vol. 2: 29). The South African Police was given responsibility for counter-insurgency in South Africa and in Swaziland, the South African Defence Force (SADF) for the rest of southern Africa, and an official policy was adopted permitting police and defence force personnel to engage in clandestine operations beyond South Africa's borders.

Between 1979 and 1983 the South African government in the form of the South African Police and SADF was responsible for at least 30–40 assassinations (of which the letter-bomb killing of the prominent anti-apartheid activist Ruth First in Maputo in 1982 was the most publicly notorious), many more failed attempts (including at least three abortive attempts on the Umkhonto we Sizwe leader, Chris Hani), dozens more abductions (many ending in the murder of the victims once in South Africa), and thousands more deaths as a result of raids and other military operations carried out deep into Angola, Lesotho, Mozambique, Zambia and Zimbabwe. Given that no government-

Total Strategy: Proposed as part of the 1977 Defence budget. Outlined a military strategy to protect the country from perceived external and internal threats and later used as justification for increased control of the government by security and military officers in the SSC.

ordered assassinations have been documented for the period 1960–73, and only a few letter-bomb attacks for the years 1974–9, it is evident that there was a huge increase in state-sanctioned violence from 1979 onwards.

At the same time, Botha attempted to neutralise internal opposition to apartheid by offering Africans some limited rights. Immediately following his announcement of the 'Total Strategy' budget in April 1979, the government announced two fundamental shifts in policy towards Africans. African labour unions were to be recognised legally in wage negotiations for the first time, and urban Africans were to be given certain rights, including limited participation in administration boards and expanded opportunities for African entrepreneurship and home-ownership. Both of these moves represented dramatic reversals in longstanding government policies but were greeted with substantial African suspicion. Most African unions initially refused to register with the government for fear of providing officials with information that would lead to arrests and bannings. Also, a large majority of Africans, as well as Coloureds and Asians, steadfastly refused to participate in the urban councils established by the government. The government was attempting to create allies with a vested interest in maintaining the status quo but it was having no success.

Botha went a step further, announcing plans for a much more sweeping re-envisioning of apartheid. In July 1979, he convened a government commission to consider plans to rewrite South Africa's constitution to expand voting rights to the disenfranchised (the Schlebusch Commission). This would eventually lead to a proposal for separate parliaments to represent Coloureds and Asians, but not Africans. At the same time, Botha also vowed to promote South Africa's alliance with a 'constellation of African nations' – in reality the sham homelands, which he tried to present as viable independent African countries. This new vision of apartheid was intended to present an image of rights and freedom for all, within group-identified institutions that in reality had little power and remained firmly under the control of the white South African parliament. Nevertheless, Botha calculated that his proposals would garner enough support to blunt opposition at home and abroad.

For those who refused to accept or support such reforms, the government took increasingly brutal steps to force capitulation. In addition to the secretive activities of police and military units, the government also continued to pursue official and public repression. Against a background of intensified arrests and mysterious deaths in detention, a new Internal Security Act allowed the government to investigate any person or organisation, and the minister of justice gained the power to ban any person without explanation. The SADF was given expanded authority over areas inside South Africa, granting the armed forces the role of policing their own citizens. In addition, the SADF – armed with South African-manufactured weapons in the wake of an international arms embargo against South Africa – invaded the neigh-bouring countries of Zambia, Mozambique, Lesotho and Zimbabwe in raids against suspected ANC camps and offices. To man these efforts, the govern-ment instituted a military call-up of all white males between the ages of 17 and 65 to double the size of the armed forces. Throughout this period, the government maintained a relentless policy of removing Africans from white areas, or 'erasing black spots' from white South Africa, in an attempt to enforce the apartheid fiction.

While intent on punishing dissent, the government nevertheless did not want to advertise its actions. Under successive legislation, the South African press was prohibited from publishing news on a variety of subjects. Information on deaths in detention could not be reported under the Inquest Act, and allegations of brutality and maladministration by the police were outlawed under the Police Act. Under the Protection of Information Act, the press was prohibited from reporting on arrests unless it could be proved that the report would not endanger state security. Television and radio news was controlled by the government and a growing number of newspapers were closed down or silenced through these laws.

Despite these efforts, protest and resistance intensified during this period. In the wake of the Soweto uprising, hundreds of young Africans had slipped across South Africa's northern borders and volunteered to fight as guerrilla soldiers for the ANC and the PAC. In the late 1970s, some of these people began to re-enter South Africa secretly to carry out sabotage attacks on various targets that were seen as symbols of apartheid. Bombs were set off at numerous municipal buildings such as post offices and court houses. Most spectacular were bomb attacks on the government-owned South African Coal, Oil and Gas Corporation (SASOL) plant in 1980, the Koeberg nuclear power station in 1982, and the intelligence headquarters of the South African Air Force in Pretoria in 1983. In 1983 alone, there were a reported 42 ANC attacks on government installations. In addition to these spectacular attacks, African unions mounted increasing numbers of strikes and students shut down most schools throughout the country through boycotts. Once again, repression wreaked incredible damage on the country but did not ensure the peace and security that Botha sought through the Total Strategy.

FROM FAILURE TO REFORM?: THE 1983 CONSTITUTION

The centrepiece of Botha's efforts to convince those inside and outside South Africa that ANC criticisms were unfounded was the creation of a new constitution. Under this, separate parliaments were created for whites, Asians and Coloureds, while Africans were represented by the homeland governments. Botha explained the overarching plan in 1980:

> The basic reasoning could be formulated as a 'confederation' of the RSA with Black States; the recognition of the urban Blacks with a say in such a union of interests in a confederal framework; a joint general citizenship; and the development of the common interests of Coloured, White and Asian in the South African Parliament.
>
> (Price, 1991: 147)

While African interests inside 'white' South Africa were entirely ignored, the constitution also provided little power to Coloureds or Asians. Parliament was divided into three racially determined constituent bodies: the House of Assembly for whites with 178 members, the House of Representatives for Coloureds with 85 members, and the House of Delegates for Asians with 45 members. Each body was limited to issues which dealt with their 'own' racial groups, and laws covering all groups could only be enacted in a joint session of all Houses where whites would have a majority of 178 votes to a combined Coloured/Asian vote of 130. The executive was headed by a state president, who held vast powers. He could dissolve parliament at any time and could rule instead through an executive council. He had the power to appoint and dismiss the country's judges. He was not elected through a popular vote but was chosen by an 88-member electoral college that mirrored the racial ratio between whites, Coloureds and Asians in the parliament (that is, 4:2:1). If Africans had been included, these percentages would have been quite different. Whereas whites had accounted for 21 per cent of South Africa's population in 1936, by 1980 they constituted only 16 per cent. Government projections at the time estimated that by 2010 the white proportion would be less than 10 per cent and falling, while the African population would make up 83 per cent of the total and would be increasing. By excluding Africans, Botha could pretend that whites represented a majority.

Although the constitutional proposal was clearly intended to allow whites to retain overall political control, it still unleashed bitter white opposition by conservatives and reopened old rivalries within the National Party. P.W. Botha had in fact come to power as the result of a bitter internecine fight in the NP between those who favoured a reformist strategy and the hardliners (die-hard proponents of Grand Apartheid) – *verligtes* (enlightened) and *verkramptes* (narrow-minded) in the parlance of the 'reformers'. Botha assumed office when the former prime minister, John Vorster, and a small group of supporters, including the head of BOSS, General H.J. van den Bergh, were caught illegally using government funds to manipulate the news media in

South Africa and to try to purchase newspapers overseas, including the *Washington Star*. Vorster resigned his position as prime minister for the largely ceremonial post of president; his preferred successor, Connie Mulder, was purged from the NP, and Botha, minister of defence since 1966, became prime minister in 1978. When Botha introduced his constitutional pro-posals in 1982, 16 NP members, including Andries Treurnicht, were expelled for refusing to sign a motion of confidence in Botha's leadership. Treurnicht formed the Conservative Party of South Africa in 1982, bringing together old enemies of Botha, such as Connie Mulder, once aspirant heir to Vorster, and supporters of the *verkrampte* faction of the NP. The Conservative Party argued that each racial group should have its own political structure and authority, and viewed the proposed constitution as an imposition of 'non-white' influence over white matters.

Botha proceeded with his plans, calling for a referendum in which only white voters would be asked whether or not they approved of the prime minister's plans for constitutional change. Some liberal opponents of the government, such as Frederik van Zyl Slabbert, leader of the Progressive Federal Party (PFP), and Harry Oppenheimer, head of the Anglo-American Corporation, denounced Botha's plan because it would permanently exclude Africans from having any political role in South Africa. Many other politi-cians and businessmen, English- and Afrikaans-speaking alike, argued that any change in apartheid would be an improvement since the system was proving too costly and unwieldy. Most white voters agreed, and two-thirds of those who participated in the referendum voted 'yes'.

Although the constitutional referendum revealed sharp disagreement among white politicians over the direction of South Africa's future, it also galvanised black opposition in the form of a new and potent organisation, the United Democratic Front (UDF), which was established by a handful of community groups in 1983 as an umbrella for organisations that opposed the constitutional reforms. At the national launch of the organisation in August 1983 at a Coloured township near Cape Town, approximately 1,000 people of all South Africa's 'racial' categories, representing community organisations, unions and sporting groups, gathered to announce their support for a united democratic South Africa, in which all residents would be represented in government, and their opposition to apartheid, especially in the form that it had taken through the imposition of the homelands policy and the Group Areas Act. Although not publicly stating support for the ANC, which would have made those in attendance punishable for committing a criminal act under South African law, the people who established the UDF clearly adhered in everything but word to the basic ideals of the Freedom Charter. Individually, none of the groups was overtly political and thus evaded banning. The UDF relied on leadership from its constituent groups, with no one person or group of persons identified as the 'leader' or 'head' of the organisation. Essentially, it was the political equivalent of the worker groups that had organised successful wildcat strikes on the Durban waterfront in 1973. Without an identifiable leadership cohort, the organisation could not easily be broken by the arrest of that cohort. Although the government arrested nearly 60 UDF activists during its first year of existence, the organisation continued, hydra-like, to grow at an enormous pace, attracting committed supporters – people who were ready to support boycotts, go on strike, engage in various forms of passive resistance – throughout urban and rural areas of South Africa. It formed a potent symbol of continuing peaceful black opposition to the alleged reforms that South Africa's white leaders claimed were ending discrimination and injustice inside the country.

The implementation of the new constitution in 1984 sparked continuing protests and opposition throughout the country. Between January and May of that year, over 14 armed attacks and explosions, mostly organised by the ANC, took place throughout the country. Students boycotted their classes. Police increasingly moved into the African townships, arresting and shooting protesters. When elections for the Indian and Coloured representatives to the new parliament took place, over two-thirds of the eligible voters boycotted them. In September, the government banned all meetings and political discussions inside the country in an attempt to stop the violence. By the beginning of 1985, Botha was so desperate to end the unrest that he offered to release Nelson Mandela from prison if he renounced violence. When Mandela refused the offer, the government was faced with a choice: endure continuing unrest or consider meaningful change.

5

The collapse of apartheid

S tate President P.W. Botha in January 1984 opened the first session of parliament in a triumphal mood. 'In the history of constitutional development', he argued, 1983 would 'go down as a year of great significance for the Republic of South Africa and her peoples'. The South African electorate had, in its November vote for a new constitution, 'demonstrated its preference for consensus politics, acknowledged the need for sound inter-group relations and accepted constitutional renewal as a prerequisite for progress and prosperity'. Still, the government had to be vigilant because 'public statement[s] by terrorist leaders [he was alluding to the ANC] and acts of sabotage provide[d] conclusive proof of the objectives of South Africa's enemies, namely the destruction of order and our democratic way of life'. Moreover, externally the situation was more troubling since there was, Botha argued, 'irrefutable evidence that the Soviet Union is engaged in stockpiling arms in some of our neighbouring countries' (especially Angola) in order to develop 'springboards' into South Africa. Despite these problems, he was especially sanguine about the financial health of the nation. South Africa at the beginning of 1984 had 'no foreign debt problem', it had 'an excellent credit rating', and pursuit of a conservative fiscal policy should allow the country to continue to 'ensure a sound balance of payments and to curb inflation' (Hansard, 1984: cols 4, 6, 8).

REFORM AND REPRESSION

Botha's minister of internal affairs, F.W. de Klerk, spoke on the same occasion about 'the long-term objectives of the Government'. These objectives, he stated, were:

> first . . . to preserve the security, safety and identity of every people and group in South Africa . . . second . . . to create – on the foundation of the

safeguarding of group identity, on the preservation of the right of every group to self-determination, to retain its identity and to cherish what is precious to it – a spirit of co-operation between the various peoples and population groups, because we perceive that there is a multitude of common interests.

The electors he argued, had in their referendum vote,

said that they rejected integration and that they rejected rigid separation as a solution, and that they believed that meaningful co-operation among peoples and groups in this country was possible; but that this should in fact be done with retention of the security and the established rights of every group.

The National Party was not, as the white opposition on the left (the PFP) argued, 'merely engaged in cosmetic changes', nor was it, as the white opposition on the right (the Conservative Party) argued, 'selling out the Whites'. Each 'group' would have its 'own political power base' and through that base be able to pursue 'self-determination' and provide the means by 'which co-operation and joint decision-making on matters of common interest can occur'. Even blacks, he continued, benefited from the changes in place:

We are not merely removing the political shackles, we are giving economic incentives . . . to promote economic decentralisation . . . we have made negotiation available to the Black worker . . . we are encouraging industrialists and employers to train people in the negotiating process.
(Hansard, 1984: cols 47–9, 52, 54)

The mathematics of South Africa's new constitutional dispensation underlay Botha and de Klerk's sense of political supremacy. In the new parliament, the all-white House of Assembly, with 178 members, would always be able to outvote the 85-member House of Representatives (Coloureds only) and the 45-member House of Delegates (Indians only) since the constitution stipulated that parliamentary membership would always have to adhere to a 4:2:1 (white: Coloured: Indian) ratio. The constitution also gave to the state president, Botha, sole authority to determine which issues would be decided by which of the three constituent houses of parliament, and also the power to dissolve parliament.

As chair of the State Security Council (SSC), Botha presided over an enormous and closely integrated security apparatus dedicated to implementing the Total Strategy campaign initiated in the late 1970s. At the national level the ministers of defence, foreign affairs, justice and law and order met regularly with the other members of the SSC, the chiefs of the military and the intelligence services, the commissioner of police, and the chief of the security police, to develop and coordinate policies and strategies to defeat those they deemed South Africa's internal and external enemies. These policies and strategies were in turn implemented by Joint Management Centres (JMC) headed by military or police officers and directing a network of municipal officials, postmasters, fire chiefs and other officials in combating insurgency. With its defence forces 'the most formidable military force in Africa', a police establishment of close to 50,000, a local armaments industry capable of meeting the country's *matériel* needs as well as engaging in a highly profitable international trade, and with the ability to construct nuclear warheads (the South African government constructed six crude atomic bombs during the 1980s), Botha's government felt that it could combat successfully any military challenge.

But just to be sure of the success of his reform programme, Botha's government engaged also in a campaign of covert warfare and assassination. Craig Williamson, a member of the South African Police who infiltrated antiapartheid groups and worked undercover for the security police from 1971 to 1980, testified to the **Truth and Reconciliation Commission (TRC)** that in 1979,

Truth and Reconciliation Commission (TRC): Established in 1995 under the Promotion of National Unity and Reconciliation Act. Charged to investigate the sufferings of ordinary people under apartheid and to hear testimony from former agents of the state seeking amnesty for the crimes they had committed. Held hearings for two and a half years and heard testimony of almost 22,000 people.

> the security forces were told to take the gloves off in the fight against the revolutionary enemy. . . . My security force colleagues and I did not see the liberation movements and their members as fellow citizens in our society. We regarded them as an alien enemy which threatened our society. Our job was to eliminate that threat.
>
> (http://www.doj.gov.za/trc/special/forces/sap.htm)

The first body established in accordance with these strategic aims was Koevoet (Crowbar), founded in 1979 along the lines of the Rhodesian Selous Scouts and RENAMO in Mozambique, to fight against the supporters of the South West African People's Organization (SWAPO), who were trying to win independence for Namibia. The members of Koevoet, a combination of approximately 250 white officers drawn from the South African Police (with previous experience fighting for Ian Smith's regime in Rhodesia) and 750–800 local Owambos, gained a reputation for torture and brutality as teams competed to kill as many suspected guerrillas as possible in exchange for bounty payments. Lance Corporal Sean Callaghan, in requesting amnesty from the TRC, described his daily activities as follows:

> A Koevoet team spent a week in the bush and a week back in camp. . . . There was a scoreboard and a map in the operations room in the Koevoet base and on the weeks that we were not in the bush, we were checking

the scores of the teams that were in the bush. Koevoet was much more effective than SADF units because of its bounty policy. . . . I can remember . . . loading bodies onto and off Casspirs [armoured vehicles]. After a contact bodies were tied onto spare tyres, bumpers, mudguards and were left there until we got back to the base camp, until they could be unloaded. This could be days of driving through thick bush, and the skin could be worn right off the bodies.

(TRC, 1998, vol. 2: 75)

The government also attempted to kill ANC leaders and other anti-apartheid activists living within and outside South Africa. These were, as determined by the investigations of the Truth and Reconciliation Commission, 'targeted' killings, that is 'those which aimed to ensure the victim's "permanent removal from society". . . . The people concerned were frequently high-profile political figures' (TRC, 1998, vol. 2: 222). Between 1980 and 1984 there were at least 12 assassination attempts on people living in Botswana, Lesotho, Swaziland and Zimbabwe, including three (all unsuccessful) on the life of Chris Hani, the head of Umkhonto we Sizwe in southern Africa, as well as a Security Police-organised bombing of the ANC headquarters in London. The most prominent of these assassinations was the killing by letter bomb in 1982 of Ruth First, a long-term critic of apartheid and the wife of Joe Slovo, the head of the South African Communist Party. Although the South African government always denied its involvement in First's death, the long-suspected official linkage was confirmed in 1999 when one of those involved in the assassination, Craig Williamson, applied for amnesty to the TRC. In approving his amnesty application, the TRC summarised the way in which Williamson had acted on orders from his superior officer in the South African Security Police:

he received an official police envelope containing a smaller envelope and with instructions to go to [Brigadier] Goosen [his superior]. On his arrival Goosen asked him [Williamson] whether Raven [Williamson's colleague] could replace the documents of the smaller envelope which was an intercepted letter with an explosive device. . . . After a few days Raven reported back that he had carried out the instruction and on looking in the envelope Williamson asked whether it was in fact a bomb that could kill both of them if it would now explode. Raven confirmed this and he requested him to take the envelope to Brigadier Goosen. . . . He [Williamson] was not surprised by the instruction he received to have a bomb prepared as it formed part of the overall political and military strategy against the ANC at the time.

(http://www.doj.gov.za/trc/decisions/2000/ac20082.htm)

The bomb exploded on 17 August 1982, killing Ruth First at her faculty office at Eduardo Mondlane University, Maputo, Mozambique.

INSURRECTION

Neither constitutional reform nor covert action provided the consensus, progress and prosperity hoped for by Botha. Denounced as divisive and reactionary, the new constitution, critics argued, extended apartheid by further institutionalising the exclusion of the majority black population from political participation and from the ownership of land within South Africa. **The United Democratic Front (UDF)** denounced apartheid and called on Coloureds and Indians to boycott the electoral process; less than one-third of eligible voters cast their ballots. Mass protests began in the African townships of Vereeniging (including Sharpeville) and other parts of the Vaal Triangle in September 1984 – when the minority-elected Coloured and Indian parliamentarians were being sworn into office – against increased rents and electricity charges. These charges were in turn a product of South Africa's declining economic situation as international oil prices rose and gold prices fell. The ANC added its voice to that of the community activists, calling in April 1985 for people to 'Make apartheid unworkable! Make the country ungovernable!'

United Democratic Front (UDF): Established in 1983 to oppose the government's proposed constitutional reforms. Served as an umbrella for a multiracial group of organisations including unions, churches and community groups.

The protestors attacked targets that symbolised Botha's system of black local government. They burnt down police stations and other government buildings (including municipal beer halls), along with the homes of black policemen and town councillors and, on occasion, killed the occupants of these buildings (12 councillors by April 1985). Stay-at-home protests and school boycotts followed as resistance spread throughout the Transvaal and then to the Orange Free State, Natal and the Cape. The protests were remarkable in their extent, far exceeding Soweto and the anti-apartheid campaigns of the 1950s, and in the widespread community involvement of young and old, female and male.

The apartheid system of local and township governance largely collapsed by the middle of 1985 to be replaced by an alternative structure of community-organised bodies such as street committees, residents' associations and people's courts. These community organisations enforced, often through the agency of young people, UDF-supported boycotts and punished those who transgressed. In May 1985, for example, young people monitoring a consumer boycott of beer halls in Port Alfred, forced Ms Nontina Matyumza to eat washing detergent because she had bought beer; she died the following day (TRC, 1998, vol. 2: 381). Young people were also especially prominent in attacks in the homelands on people they identified as government collaborators. This reflected the impact of the migrant labour system with most working-age males and many females absent in the cities and a very high proportion of young people in the homelands. In Lebowa, for example, north of Johannesburg, 72.3 per cent of its population in 1985 was aged 20 or under, living in an area devastated by overpopulation, overstocking and erosion – 'a dust bowl with mountains' – with abysmal conditions in the schools and ruled over by government-appointed chiefs who demanded taxes, tribute and forced labour. The youth responded with witchcraft accusations and attacks on the homes and persons of those they identified as their immediate oppressors (van Kessel, 2000: 87).

Black trade unions, many formed after the Wiehahn Commission, took an increasingly prominent role in economic and political protests in the mid-1980s. These new unions, such as the National Union of Mineworkers (NUM), formed under the leadership of Cyril Ramaphosa, joined together to create larger cooperative bodies, the most important of which was the **Congress of South African Trade Unions (COSATU)**. COSATU represented more than 30 trade unions and 500,000 individual members. Its leadership adhered to the ANC's Freedom Charter and was closely allied with the UDF. The unions organised strikes in East London, on the Rand and elsewhere, protesting against economic conditions, supporting local activists in their struggles and denouncing apartheid. Triple the number of working days were lost in strike action in 1984 as compared with 1983, and there was a doubling again of days lost in 1985.

Congress of South African Trade Unions (COSATU): Founded in 1985 and a leading force in the final struggle against apartheid.

Botha vacillated as the political and economic situation in South Africa unravelled. In January 1985 he rhetorically offered Mandela release from prison so long as the ANC leader 'unconditionally rejected violence as a political instrument'. Determined to 'reaffirm to the world that we were only responding to the violence done to us', Mandela rejected the offer in a written statement that his daughter read out aloud at a UDF rally in Soweto, the first time that his words had been legally heard in South Africa in 25 years:

> What freedom am I being offered while the organisation of the people remains banned? What freedom am I being offered when I may be arrested on a pass offence? . . . What freedom am I being offered when I must ask for permission to live in an urban area? . . . What freedom am I being offered when my very South African citizenship is not respected?
>
> (Mandela, 1994: 521, 523)

In February Botha had the top leadership of the UDF arrested and charged with high treason. In the same month he announced that Africans in the Cape would be able to acquire 99-year leases on their property, not freehold ownership, but seemingly a step in that direction. In March, on the 25th anniversary of the Sharpeville massacre, police fired on a funeral procession in Uitenhage in the Eastern Cape, killing 21 people. Local people, outraged by the shooting, responded with a new form of protest – 'necklacing' – placing tyres around the necks of a town councillor and his three sons and setting them on fire. These deaths were the first of over 60 necklacings that year.

With the country, in the words of the minister of law and order, Adriaan Vlok, 'at the edge of anarchy and bloody revolution', Botha proclaimed a state of emergency on 21 July 1985, the first imposed since Sharpeville 25 years earlier and on the same day that Matthew Goniwe was buried in the Eastern Cape (http://www.justice.gov.za/trc/amntrans/1998/98072031_pre_cosatu1.htm). Goniwe, along with three friends, Sparrow Mkhonto, Fort Calata and Sicelo Mhlawuli, were all activists with the UDF, each of whom had been, on numerous occasions, arrested and tortured by the police. On 27 June the four friends, who became known in the news media as the 'Cradock Four' after the town in which they lived, had been abducted when returning home from a UDF meeting by persons unknown, murdered (Goniwe with 27 stab and bullet wounds), and their bodies mutilated and burned in order to make them appear as though they had been killed by the same people engaging in necklacing. At the time, and for a decade after, the police denied responsibility, as did the South African government. Only in 1998 did the identity of the perpetrators become known when five members of the Port Elizabeth Security Police – a major general, two colonels and two majors – applied for amnesty for their part in the killings.

The abduction and murder of the Cradock Four was part of a vastly expanded campaign by Botha's government to crush popular resistance. At the highest level of government, the State Security Council (SSC), the words recorded in the minutes of council meetings referred to the need to 'eliminate', 'neutralise', 'obliterate', 'track down and destroy', 'remove permanently from society'. Participants in the council meetings, such as the minister of foreign affairs, Pik Botha (no relation to P.W. Botha), claimed in the aftermath of apartheid that the use of these words did not mean that the highest levels of government were authorising the killing of anti-apartheid activists, although he admitted that members of the security forces may well have interpreted such language as an order to murder (http://www.justice.gov.za/trc/special/security/1securit.htm).

Members of the security forces remembered things differently. Eugene de Kock had fought in Rhodesia in the 1970s, been a member of Koevoet (in whose service he claimed over 400 'contacts' or kills), bombed the ANC's London headquarters in 1982, and in July 1985 became commander of a secret police unit based on a farm, Vlakplaas, near Pretoria. Vlakplaas had been established in 1979 as a place where 'askaris' – captured ANC and PAC operatives who had been 'turned' – could be trained to work undercover for the police in counter-insurgency actions. Under de Kock's command, Vlakplaas became the base of an assassination and abduction operation, and his unit worked with other parts of the security forces in covering up official involvement in the killing of opponents of the government such as the Cradock Four. In his autobiography, published in 1998 after he had been convicted of at least six charges of murder (he claimed far more kills) and sentenced to two life terms of imprisonment plus another 212 years, de Kock named the high-ranking officials, police generals and government ministers who had 'assembled us [the members of Vlakplaas and other similar covert units] into the murderous forces that we became, *and which we were intended to be all along*' (de Kock, 1998: 249, original emphasis). Craig Williamson in his TRC testimony emphasised the covert nature and deniability of government actions. 'The eleventh commandment was well known, especially to those in the covert or the special force elements of the security forces, this was *thou shalt not be found out*' (http://www.doj.gov.za/trc/special/forces/sap.htm, original emphasis).

Under the terms of the state of emergency decreed by Botha, the police were given the power to arrest people without warrants and to detain them indefinitely without charging them or even allowing lawyers or next of kin to be notified. It also gave the government even greater authority than it already exercised to censor radio, television and newspaper coverage of the unrest. Police and troops were deployed in African townships throughout South Africa and thousands were detained, including, by the organisation's own estimate, 8,000 leading members of the UDF. Most of those detained (85 per cent according to one study) were tortured, with the most common methods used being beatings, electric shock and strangulation. One victim, Peter Jacobs, a former member of Umkhonto we Sizwe, in 1997 confronted his torturer, Jeffrey Benzien, a former policeman from the Cape, in an especially poignant exchange:

JACOBS: So, you would undress me, tie my blue belt around my feet, throw me on the ground, put the handcuffs with the cloth over my arm to prevent marks. You do that [electric shocks] quite a few times. But at some point, I think it is about the fourth time, when I thought I am dying, you woke me up and you said, 'Peter, I will take you to the verge of death as many times as I want. But you are going to talk and if it means that you will die, that is okay.' Do you remember that?
BENZIEN: I concede I may have said that, Sir.
JACOBS: I want you to tell me, because this is important for me. The truth commission can amnesty, but this is important for me. Did you say that?
BENZIEN: Yes, I did say that.

(Meredith, 1999: 131–2)

Police killings, most of them shootings at protest marches, funerals (at which UDF and ANC symbols were often prominently and defiantly displayed) and 'riots', increased enormously from fewer than 100 in 1984 to more than five times that number in 1985. The increased death rate reflected new directives from the SSC which called for the 'physical gunning-down of leaders in riot situations' and the 'removal of intimidators' (TRC, 1998, vol. 2: 176). The torture of those detained also showed a similar rate of increase during the same period.

The security forces also enlisted large numbers of African men, usually unemployed, illiterate and sometimes with criminal convictions, as special constables, known colloquially as 'kitskonstabels' (instant police), to destroy the new community organisations established by UDF and ANC supporters. These kitskonstabels, along with other state-employed vigilantes such as the 'witdoeke' (white scarves) who terrorised the African squatters in the Cape settlements of Crossroads and Khayelitsha, were ill-trained, loosely super-vised and perpetrators of many crimes, 'including murder, robbery, assault, theft, and rape' (TRC, 1998, vol. 2: 183, 184, 186). The witdoeke killed at least 60 people and destroyed the homes of over 60,000. Government officials denied any association with the vigilante groups, arguing instead that the 'black on black' violence that captured the attention of the local and international media in the mid-to-late 1980s was reflective of the innate inability of Africans to govern themselves. Testimony to the TRC in the late 1990s, however, proved the link between state policy and local terror. As the head of the security police in the Transvaal remembered the situation from his point of view, 'it was war. . . . Full-scale guerrilla tactics were used against the liberation movements. . . . It didn't matter what was done or how we did it, as long as the flood-tide of destabilization, unrest, and violence was stopped' (Meredith, 1999: 119).

State repression, however, led to an international backlash. The pariah status of the country greatly increased, with considerable world attention focused through the news media on images of the police and the military, especially in the townships. The most important impact was on the economy. Foreign bankers and investors, concerned that their investments were at risk, began to pull out of the country. In 1984, 40 US companies pulled out of South Africa; another 50 followed suit in 1985. At the beginning of 1985, Citibank declared that it would make no new loans to the South African government for the foreseeable future. In July 1985, Chase Manhattan Bank caused a major financial crisis in South Africa by refusing to roll over its short-term loans, and its lead was followed by most other international banks. Barclays announced in March 1986 that it would lend no new funds to South Africa until the government could demonstrate its ability to pay its current debts and eliminate apartheid.

In the face of local and international protest and pressure, Botha continued to prevaricate. On the one hand, he continued to claim that he was engaged in a process of reform. In January 1986, he announced in parliament that South Africa had 'outgrown the outdated concept of apartheid', and the following month stated that the pass laws would be repealed and influx control ended. He agreed to the visit to the country of several leading Commonwealth heads of state, the 'Eminent Persons Group', and permitted them to meet with Nelson Mandela in March. Botha hinted to the media in the middle of the year that he would be making a speech at some point with announcements in it equivalent in significance to Julius Caesar's crossing of the Rubicon. And in June he permitted his minister of justice, Kobie Coetsee, to meet Mandela (who had initiated contact with the minister in late 1985). Coetsee asked Mandela:

> under what circumstances would we suspend the armed struggle . . . [and] whether I envisaged any constitutional guarantees for minorities in a new South Africa. . . . I sensed the government was anxious to overcome the impasse in the country, that they were now convinced they had to depart from their old positions. In ghostly outline, I saw the beginnings of a compromise.
>
> (Mandela, 1994: 530–1)

On the other hand, Botha acted in a way befitting his popular nickname, 'die Groot Krokodil' (the great crocodile). In May 1986, soon after the departure of the members of the Eminent Persons Group, he launched commando raids on ANC and PAC bases in Botswana, Zambia and Zimbabwe. In June he extended the earlier regionally-based state of emergency to the entire country and ordered the security forces to step up their crackdown on anti-apartheid activists. His Rubicon speech, when finally given in August, was a resounding let-down, containing no promise to release Mandela (as had been present in the first draft written by Pik Botha) and just a concession that the homeland policy was unworkable (hardly surprising news to anyone by that point).

International pressures intensified, especially for economic sanctions on South Africa. In October 1986, the US Congress, overriding President Reagan's veto, passed legislation implementing mandatory sanctions against South Africa. These sanctions included the banning of all new investments and bank loans, the ending of air links between the United States and South Africa, and the banning of many South African imports. This measure, on top of the earlier actions taken by US banks, led to a 50 per cent fall in American investment in South Africa, from $5 billion in 1984 to $2.78 billion by 1988.

The UDF, the ANC and black trade unions responded to Oliver Tambo's call to 'render the country ungovernable' and, as Mandela has noted, 'the people were obliging' (Mandela, 1994: 529). The unions and the ANC at the beginning of 1986 issued jointly a statement reiterating their commitment to overthrow white supremacy. There was a huge increase in strikes (double the number in 1986 compared with 1985) and an enormous rise in workdays lost (from 680,000 days in 1985 to just over one million in 1986 and to nearly six million days in 1987). In 1988 COSATU, in commemoration of the twelfth anniversary of the Soweto uprising, launched the largest strike in South Africa's history, securing the compliance of 70 per cent of the workers in the manufacturing sector. The ANC embarked on a programme of mass mobilisation and the initiation of a 'people's war'. Armed supporters from bases in southern Africa infiltrated South Africa, engaging in a campaign of bombings, especially of buildings (police stations, bars, restaurants) at which members of the security forces were known to gather. The number of such attacks rose from 45 in 1984, to 137 in 1985, 230 in 1986, 235 in 1987, and peaked at 281 in 1988. The UDF, building on the earlier development of community-based organisations in place of apartheid local authorities, embarked on a programme of 'People's Organs for People's Power', expanding the development of local area committees, people's courts and youth groups (*amabutho*) to regulate communities and organise rent strikes. By 1989, rents had largely ceased to be paid, and the arrears were in excess of half a billion rand. Prohibited at risk of arrest from engaging in any sort of political demonstration, thousands of people turned to funerals as a symbolic occasion at which they could express their unity and their opposition to the government. Tens of thousands of people attended these funerals, prominently displaying ANC and UDF banners, and generally found themselves teargassed and shot at by the police. Cases of necklacing peaked at 306 in 1986 and declined thereafter in response to general condemnation of the practice. The PAC, independently of these other organisations, also embarked on a new programme, through its armed wing, the African People's Liberation Army (APLA, which had replaced Poqo), of attacks on police and civilians. Official statistics tracked the proliferation of 'unrest-related incidents': 14,000 in 1986 (then the introduction of the national state of emergency), 4,000 in 1987, 5,000 in 1988, and 17,000 in 1990. Figures 5.1 and 5.2 illustrate graphically the exponential growth in political violence from 1985 to 1990. The number of people detained for engaging in these unrest-related incidents were, by unofficial estimates, in excess of 30,000 at the beginning of 1987. Those detained, according to emergency regulations, did not have to be charged, nor their detention reported to next of kin, nor legal representation permitted, nor their period of detention limited to any set term.

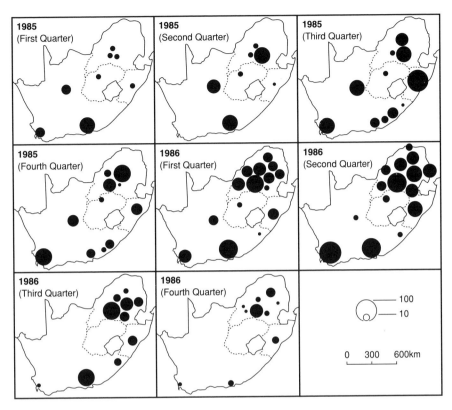

Figure 5.1 Deaths due to political violence, 1985–6

Source: Based on information supplied by the South African Institute of Race Relations, from Christopher, A.J. (2000) *The Atlas of Changing South Africa, 2nd Edition*, published by Routledge, Figure 6.6.

South Africa was embroiled in a civil war and the government continued to target for elimination those it regarded as attempting 'to set the trend for revolution' (http://www.justice.gov.za/trc/amntrans/1998/98072031_pre_cosatu1.htm). In 1987 and 1988 members of the security forces covertly bombed the headquarters of COSATU and the headquarters of the South African Council of Churches (SACC), while publicly the government denied any involvement and blamed the events on internecine warfare within the anti-apartheid movement. In testimony given to the TRC ten years after the events, Adriaan Vlok took responsibility for giving the orders, while testifying that he had acted at the direction of the state president himself. With regard to the COSATU bombing, Vlok stated that he and the national head of the Security Branch of the police believed that members of Umkhonto we Sizwe were based in the headquarters building and that the building's destruction would eliminate it as a base for terrorists. With regard to the bombing of Khotso House, headquarters of the SACC, Vlok detailed the planning of the action – the only testimony given to date directly linking P.W. Botha with the

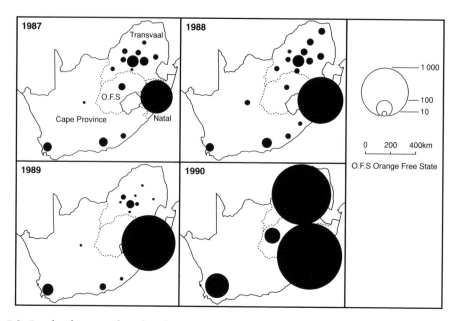

Figure 5.2 Deaths due to political violence, 1987–90

Source: Based on information supplied by the South African Institute of Race Relations, from Christopher, A.J. (2000) *The Atlas of Changing South Africa, 2nd Edition*, published by Routledge, Figure 6.7.

issuance of orders for the security forces to engage in illegal activity. In early August 1988, after a meeting of the State Security Council (SSC), Botha engaged Vlok in a private conversation. The state president told his minister that the SACC had a long history of civil disobedience and something had to be done. A week later, Botha told Vlok that 'you must make that building [Khotso House] unusable', though he also stressed that whatever means chosen should not result in the loss of life. After further discussion between Vlok and the head of the Security Branch, a plan was developed to blow up the building, and on 31 August Khotso House was bombed without loss of life. When Vlok reported the results to Botha at a meeting of the SSC the state president congratulated him on his accomplishment (http://www.justice.gov.za/trc/amntrans/1998/98072031_pre_cosatu1.htm) Publicly, Vlok blamed the bombing on a female ANC supporter and ordered her and her 16-month-old son to be detained.

Despite Vlok's claims that people's lives were never targeted, killings by the security forces increased, not just in public-order policing but also in assassinations. In 1987 yet another covert organisation, the Civilian Co-operation Bureau (CCB) was established (by which agency of the state remains unclear since all records relating to it were later destroyed), and this Orwellian-named body sought to eliminate those identified as enemies of the state. Perhaps the most dramatic such action, although responsibility was not formally attributed to the CCB until the assassin applied for amnesty in 2000, was the killing of David Webster, a university lecturer and critic of the apartheid regime, outside his Johannesburg home in May 1989. The assassin, Ferdinand Barnard, an employee of the CCB, in response to questioning by the TRC, recounted his actions as follows:

> MR BARNARD: Sir, I just killed Dr Webster from a moving vehicle and the same thing can happen to me [he had feared that his employers would turn on him and with good reason; the same year, 1989, South African security police attempted to assassinate in London a former commander of the Vlakplaas unit who was speaking out about that organisation] . . .

> MR BARNARD: . . . the reason why I used it [a shotgun] was because I would be firing at close range and I wanted one shot to go off, not a variety of shots. If it had to take place during the day or something like that, the sound of the single shot would be the same as a car backfiring.
> (http://www.justice.gov.za/trc/amntrans/2000/201002ct.htm)

Despite such actions, the South African government was not able to quell the insurrection. Even the banning of COSATU, AZAPO, the UDF and 14 other anti-apartheid organisations did not prevent strikes, boycotts and continued mass refusal to comply with apartheid regulations and practices. Moreover, at the end of 1987 and the beginning of 1988 two events took place which were ominous for the long-term future of white supremacy. First, on 30 December 1987, Bantu Holomisa, head of the Transkei's armed forces, took control of the 'independent' homeland in a coup. Perceived (rightly) as a supporter of the ANC, Holomisa was viewed thereafter by Botha's government as providing refuge and a base for ANC fighters.

If the Transkei could fall, then so too could the other homelands, all of whose leaders were generally perceived as collaborators with the South African state (the South African government preferred to view them as potential middle-class black allies in the struggle against world communism). Botha attempted in particular to shore up support for Mangosuthu Buthelezi in KwaZulu, the largest homeland. Although Buthelezi in the 1950s had been a supporter of the ANC, he later opposed its plans for destabilisation of the South African economy. Since the late 1970s, he and the ANC's leaders had become bitter enemies, the ANC calling him a sell-out and Buthelezi believing that he was a target for assassination. When the UDF targeted local authorities in the mid-1980s many of these in KwaZulu were staffed by members of Buthelezi's Inkatha organisation. Buthelezi consequently sought a closer association with the South African government, and in the late 1980s Inkatha members, supported by members of the security establishment, such as Eugene de Kock, attacked and killed people they identified as ANC and UDF supporters. Indeed, Inkatha has been identified by the TRC as the 'dominant perpetrator group' of all organisations in committing human rights violations (with the bulk of these taking place after 1984) in the home-lands (TRC, 1998, vol. 2: 404).

Second, in January 1988, South Africa's military forces in southern Angola (which the government had maintained there since invading in 1975, all the while denying publicly their existence), were outmanoeuvred at Cuito Cuanavale by Cuban troops fighting on the side of the MPLA. Rather than risk complete encirclement, the loss of their heavy equipment and likely defeat, the South African forces retreated south. The Cuban troops had MIG fighters, which were much superior to the French Mirages used by the South Africans, and which gave them air superiority over an area reaching well into South West Africa/Namibia. Recognising that South Africa could no longer extend its military beyond the country's borders without risk of defeat, and that the occupation of Namibia would inevitably become vastly more costly in both money and lives, Botha in August reached an accord to withdraw all South African forces from southern Angola and to begin negotiations for the independence of Namibia (which would likely mean that SWAPO would govern the country).

The combined impact of international sanctions and internal conflict was devastating for the South African economy. Investment in the capital goods necessary to develop a long-term import substitution policy caused, in the short term, the cost of imports to rise by 60 per cent between 1986 and 1987. Unable to borrow further internationally, South Africa spent almost half its foreign exchange reserves in the 14-month period between August 1987 and October 1988 to service existing loans. The value of the rand plummeted, while the price of gold (still South Africa's chief earner of foreign currency) by the end of the 1980s was half what it had been a decade before. Inflation was chronic. The country was far removed from the future pictured in such rosy terms by Botha in January 1984 at the opening of the tricameral parliament when he had predicted 'no foreign debt problem', 'an excellent credit rating', and 'a sound balance of payments . . . to curb inflation'.

Businessmen, who had benefited from the cheap labour policies of the apartheid state, became some of Botha's strongest critics. Even within the Afrikaner business community and the government itself, there was a grow-ing call for new political steps to be taken to alleviate the economic disaster facing the country. In March 1989, the chief economist of the country's largest Afrikaner-owned business, SANLAM, stated publicly that South Africa could not afford to sustain 'a growth rate of more than two percent. . . . Unless we get certain reforms here we won't get foreign capital again. We have to at least show the outside world that we are moving in the right direction.' The same month, Botha's minister of finance stated in parliament that the main question facing the country was whether there could be 'economic survival in the face of an internationally organized assault on the economy'. The answer, he continued, lay in the adoption of 'correct economic measures and political progress' (Price, 1991: 275).

But what was political progress for some in the white community was anathema to others. As a result of the minuscule changes that he had made in the mid-1980s, measures that undercut the views of those who still believed in the attainability of grand apartheid, Botha faced in the latter half of the decade a growing right-wing challenge. In parliamentary by-elections fought in 1985, National Party candidates began losing to right-wing challengers. In May 1987, the Conservative Party led by Andries Treurnicht swamped the **Progressive Federal Party (PFP)** (which in 1984 for the first time in its history had opened party membership to people of all colours) and became the official opposition. In February 1988 Treurnicht, speaking in parliament, proposed a motion of no confidence in the government (a parliamentary manoeuvre in which opposition parties frequently engaged). Botha's reform policies, he argued, had 'not brought about the promised dispensation of peace and love and goodwill' but instead had created 'bitterness . . . in Afrikaner ranks in the spheres of politics, culture and even the church'. The *volk*, in short, was being split apart. Moreover, the reforms had not assuaged black demands for political rights and land. As Treurnicht saw matters, the 'abolition of separateness has given them a foot in the door for Black Power. . . . It is bringing intensified demands for a so-called "open democracy", and means nothing but Black domination in South Africa'. And what did Treurnicht and his party stand for? 'It is resistance to the ambiguity in regard to group areas, to the refusal or inability to take action against non-White intrusion into White residential areas. It is a resistance to the crowding out of Whites on beaches traditionally occupied by Whites and regarded as such.' His supporters and those of other like-minded organisations (such as the **Afrikaner Resistance Movement (AWB, Afrikaner Weerstandsbeweging)**), he continued, had 'one thing in common and that is resistance to the sell-out of the Whites in their own fatherland, and an aspiration to grant the Afrikaner people, and the Whites associated with it, their own fatherland and in that fatherland to be governed by their own people' (Hansard, 1988: cols 36–7, 42).

A survey carried out in 1987 to gauge white feelings about a South Africa governed by black people suggested that fear might lead a majority of voters to support Treurnicht in future elections.

Progressive Federal Party (PFP): Formed in 1977 to represent the views of English-speaking white voters opposed to apartheid. Succeeded by the Democratic Party (DP) in 1989, which in 2000 became the Democratic Alliance (DA) after joining with the New National Party (NNP).

Afrikaner Weerstandsbeweging (AWB): African Resistance Movement established by conservative Afrikaners in 1973 in opposition to what they perceived as government reforms that were undermining Afrikaner culture and political power. Consciously adopted swastika-like emblems on flags and uniforms and attacked both white and black opponents of apartheid.

Table 5.1 Results of a survey to gauge white feelings about a South Africa governed by black people

Question	Percentage answering 'Yes'	
	Afrikaners	*English*
Would blacks discriminate against whites?	91.4	78.2
Would communist policies be implemented?	88.3	67.9
Would black men molest white women?	85.3	60.1
Would white living standards suffer?	82.4	78.9
Would the physical safety of whites decline?	78.5	70.1

Source: Hugo Pierre, 'Towards Darkness and Death: Racial Demonology in South Africa', *Journal of Modern African Studies* 26 no. 4 (1988).

NEGOTIATION

With fighting bringing the country to an impasse, with the black revolution-aries unable to overthrow the white state, and the state unable to eliminate the revolutionaries, Botha contemplated negotiation, but negotiation not in order to compromise or surrender but in order to win. Such a strategy had already been raised at a meeting of the State Security Council late in 1985 when one of those in attendance, General Groenewald, reflecting the con-sensus of the meeting that some form of settlement with anti-apartheid forces was unavoidable in the long term, expressed the strategy thus: 'You can thus only negotiate from a position of power. If we negotiate with the ANC with the purpose of eliminating it, that is acceptable. If we negotiate with the pur-pose of accommodating it, that is unacceptable.' Negotiation could weaken the ANC and destroy its revolutionary potential (TRC, 1998, vol. 2: 703).

Adoption of this strategy lay behind a series of meetings held from May 1988 onwards between a government committee (consisting of the minister of justice, the commissioner of prisons, the director general of prisons, the head of the National Intelligence Service) and Nelson Mandela. But what was meant to be a process of manipulation of Mandela in the hope that he could be turned in some fashion and used against the exiled leaders of the ANC took rather the form of an education of the jailers by the jailee. Mandela, as he has recounted in his autobiography, found that he had to sketch out a history of the ANC because his visitors were 'victims of so much propaganda that it was necessary to straighten them out about certain facts'. Once the preliminaries were over, Mandela and his visitors 'focused on the critical issues: the armed struggle, the ANC's alliance with the Communist Party, the goal of majority rule, and the idea of racial reconciliation'. He stressed, in particular, with regard to their charges that the violence perpetrated by the ANC was a criminal activity, 'that the state was responsible for the violence, and that it is always the oppressor, not the oppressed, who dictates the form of the struggle' (Mandela, 1994: 536–7).

In July 1989, Botha entered the negotiations and even the 'Groot Krokodil' found himself receiving a history lesson from his prisoner. Mandela told the state president that he saw parallels between the 1914 Afrikaner uprising (to protest against South Africa's entry into the First World War on the side of their enemies, the English, and against their old friends, the Germans) and the struggle of Africans. 'From the first, it was not as though we were engaged in tense political arguments but a lively and interesting tutorial.' Botha and the other whites present argued that 'the rebellion had been a quarrel between brothers, whereas my struggle was a revolutionary one'. Mandela countered that the contemporary conflict in South Africa 'could also be seen as a struggle between brothers who happen to be different colors' (Mandela, 1994: 550–1). The president was unconvinced.

A month later Botha was out of office. He had suffered a stroke in January but had continued in office to the increasing dissatisfaction of a growing number of his party members, in particular F.W. de Klerk. In August 1989, Botha resigned in a fit of pique over public criticism by his subordinates, and de Klerk, who had taken over as leader of the National Party in February, replaced him as state president.

De Klerk came to office a largely unknown quantity. He had not been a prominent member of the cabinet. His parliamentary speeches, such as the one quoted at the beginning of this chapter, had marked him as an unremarkable foot soldier of apartheid. Mandela captured the situation best when he wrote that 'To us, Mr. De Klerk was a cipher' (Mandela, 1994: 551).

De Klerk dramatically caught the world's attention. At the opening session of parliament on 2 February 1990, he announced that the banning orders on the ANC, SACP, PAC, and 31 other organisations were to be rescinded. Such steps, he argued, were necessary in order to carry out the process of negotiation that he considered 'the key to reconciliation, peace, and a new and just dispensation' (Hansard, 1990: col. 12). On 11 February, de Klerk released Mandela from prison, finally a free man at the age of 71 after 'ten thousand days of imprisonment'. Mandela was ecstatic. Of the announcement in parliament: 'It was a breathtaking moment, for in one sweeping action he had virtually normalized the situation in South Africa.' Of his own release: 'I felt – even at the age of seventy-one – that my life was beginning anew' (Mandela, 1994: 556–7) [**Doc. 10, pp. 164–6**].

On the day of his release, in a speech given before thousands gathered in Cape Town, Mandela announced that the struggle had to intensify. It would be a struggle, he argued, not just to end apartheid but also to establish democracy, and a key component of that democracy would be 'universal suffrage on a common voters' role in a united democratic and non-racial South Africa'. Such goals, he noted, could only be won by 'disciplined mass action' and, until such time as 'a climate conducive to negotiated settlement could be created', the continuation of Umkhonto we Sizwe's armed struggle. At the end of his speech, he reiterated his readiness to die for his ideals (http://www.anc.org.za/ancdocs/history/mandela/1990/release.html).

Five developments signalled that the struggle to end apartheid and establish democracy would not be an easy one. First, there was the example of the Namibian national election. In order to reduce as much as possible the vote for SWAPO, the South African government budgeted several hundred million rand for covert actions, disrupting election meetings, intimidating voters and assassinating at least one political target, with most of these actions being organised and carried out by members of the CCB. After the election, which SWAPO won, although with a smaller majority than expected, these CCB operatives and other members of the South African security forces returned to South Africa and engaged in further covert actions against the ANC. The example for future elections in South Africa was a disturbing one.

Second, in March 1990, just days before the first official meeting between the ANC and de Klerk's government was to take place, police fired on a crowd of 50,000 ANC supporters, killing 11 and injuring over 400. The Sebokeng massacre took place when panicked police, assisted by armed white civilians, shot without orders and at random in order to prevent the ANC members from marching from the African township of Sebokeng towards white residential areas of Johannesburg.

Third, de Klerk reaffirmed in parliament in mid-April his opposition to majority rule in the form envisaged by Mandela – 'simplistic majority rule on the basis of one man, one vote', de Klerk argued, was 'not suitable for a country such as South Africa because it leads to domination and even suppression of minorities'. He proposed instead a system of 'power-sharing' that would protect the rights of 'minorities' (his code word for whites), including a 'decentralisation of power, devolution of authority, constitutional checks and balances, decision-making by consensus and an independent judiciary'. As envisaged by de Klerk, the result would be a weak central government, with considerable veto power entrenched in the hands of minorities, and immobility the likely result of a constitutionally mandated quest for the chimera of consensus (Hansard, 1990: cols 6528, 6529, 6662).

Fourth, from March 1990 onwards, the AWB and other right-wing white supremacist groups began an orchestrated campaign of shootings and bombings. Targets included primarily members of the ANC, especially those enforcing community boycotts, but also mosques, synagogues, the offices of anti-apartheid newspapers and of black trade unions. In July alone,

48 people were injured and two killed by bomb attacks on black taxi ranks and hotels in the Johannesburg area. Such attacks continued throughout 1990 and beyond without any of the perpetrators being identified and arrested by the police.

Fifth, although de Klerk in May 1990 admitted that the government's policy of promoting independent black homelands had failed and that these 'states' would be reincorporated into South Africa, his administration gave increasing covert assistance to Gatsha Buthelezi and his newly formed national political organisation, the Inkatha Freedom Party (IFP), built on the foundations of the old Inkatha movement. As became publicly known only a year later, de Klerk's government created a secret slush fund to support Inkatha, and encouraged the organisation to disrupt ANC meetings and intimidate Mandela's supporters. Moreover, members of the government's covert forces, such as Eugene de Kock, the head of Vlakplaas, began working on behalf of Inkatha. From mid-1990 onwards violence escalated, especially on the Rand, where over 500 died in August during fighting between township residents and Zulu migrant workers, and in KwaZulu Natal (the latter the only part of South Africa in which a state of emergency remained in force after June 1990) where an average of 100 people a month were killed in politically related incidents. According to the TRC, this 'escalation of violence coincided with the establishment of Inkatha as a national political party, the Inkatha Freedom Party (IFP), in July 1990, and its attempts to develop a political base in the Transvaal' (TRC, 1998, vol. 2: 585). Government security officials also plotted to overthrow the Transkei coup leader, Bantu Holomisa, and replace him with a puppet regime. Although the homeland policy had failed, the South African government still remained intent on trying to keep regional power in the hands of its black collaborators [**Doc. 11, pp. 166–8**].

Mandela concluded that he could not trust de Klerk:

> He did not make any of his reforms with the intention of putting himself out of power. He made them for necessarily the opposite reason: to ensure power for the Afrikaner in a new dispensation. He was not yet prepared to negotiate the end of white rule.
>
> (Mandela, 1994: 578)

Although de Klerk might assert publicly that 'apartheid was dead', as far as Mandela was concerned the government was still committed to upholding and perpetuating white supremacy through divide-and-rule policies that were producing an ever-increasing death rate from political violence: an average of 100 deaths a month in late 1990 continued to rise and reached an average of more than twice that figure by 1993 [**Doc. 12, pp. 168–70**].

De Klerk continued to proclaim his support for reform. A government commission to investigate security force involvement in public killings concluded in November 1990 that while such participation may have taken place there was no proof of the existence of death squads. This conclusion rested in large part on denials by members of the police and the military, including Eugene de Kock, that they had ever engaged in illegal covert activities. De Klerk repealed the main laws underpinning apartheid: the Reservation of Separate Amenities Act was gone in October 1990; the Natives' Land Act, the Group Areas Act and the Population Registration Act were all swept off the law books in February 1991. And, at the end of 1991, together with the ANC and approximately 20 other political organisations, he convened a multi-party conference, known as the **Convention for a Democratic South Africa (CODESA)**, to discuss the process by which South Africa should be transformed.

Convention for a Democratic South Africa (CODESA): Multi-party conference convened in 1991 to determine the process for transformation of South Africa from apartheid to multiracialism. Included representatives from the ANC, the NP, and approximately 20 other political organisations.

Yet de Klerk also had to watch out for the threat from the right. Some of the bombings carried out by the AWB were of the offices of National Party politicians. Members of the Conservative Party denounced de Klerk for failing to protect the political and economic interests of whites. By-elections fought in key electoral districts in late 1991, districts that had been National Party strongholds for decades, resulted in Conservative Party victories and de Klerk believed that in a future general election white voters might well replace the Nationalists with the Conservatives as the governing party in South Africa. He sought to secure his base in part by holding a national referendum of white voters in March 1992. The question asked was whether the voters supported 'the reform process . . . which is aimed at a new constitution through negotiations'. Despite right-wing claims that such a process would lead inevitably to the imposition of a black government on South Africa, whites, likely reassured in part by de Klerk's stated opposition to 'majoritarianism' (which was what 'one-person, one-vote' was labelled), voted 69 per cent in favour of continued negotiation.

As matters stood at the beginning of 1992, de Klerk's government remained in full control of the state, whites assumed that any change in the political structure of the country would be towards some form of power-sharing with no likelihood of a black-ruled majority government, and the security forces publicly and covertly disrupted ANC meetings and shored up the power of homeland rulers such as Gatsha Buthelezi in KwaZulu Natal, Lucas Mangope in Bophuthatswana and Brigadier Oupa Gqozo in Ciskei.

Yet developments in 1992 produced a profound shift in the history of South Africa, away from a perpetuation of divide and rule and firmly towards majority rule. Two events precipitated this sea-change. First, on the night of 17 June, an armed force of Inkatha supporters entered the Vaal township of Boipatong and killed 46 people, most of them women and children. The security forces neither attempted to prevent the massacre, nor took any steps to track down the perpetrators. For Mandela, this was 'the last straw'. 'Mr. de Klerk said nothing . . . and my patience snapped' (Mandela, 1994: 603). Mandela and the ANC sent a memorandum to de Klerk criticising the ongoing negotiation process as nothing more than an attempt by the National Party to embrace 'the shell of a democratic South Africa while seeking to ensure that it is not democratic in content'. The National Party, they argued, prolonged internal conflict by choosing to 'equate majority rule, which is the quintessential hallmark of democracy, with black domination', and by trying to establish 'a white minority veto (often concealed in intricate formulae) . . . [which] continually slid back to white supremacist mechanisms'. Moreover, the continued reliance on security forces that had been 'trained . . . to see the ANC . . . and black people in general as THE ENEMY and "the refusal" of de Klerk to admit that you consciously turn a blind eye to the fact that your government used millions of rands of taxpayers' money to foster' a rivalry between the ANC and Inkatha, undermined the president's reliability as a negotiating partner (http://www.anc.org.za/ancdocs/history/mandela/1992/links/memo920626.html).

The ANC suspended negotiations with de Klerk and, together with the SACP and COSATU, embarked in August on a campaign of mass action. There was a 48-hour strike which brought South Africa to a virtual halt. One hundred thousand people led by Nelson Mandela marched on the Union Buildings (the seat of executive government) in Pretoria. And campaigns were undertaken to bring down the remaining homeland governments.

It was one of the latter attempts that produced the second pivotal event in 1992. On 7 September, 70,000 ANC supporters organised by Chris Hani marched on Bisho, the capital of the Ciskei and headquarters of Brigadier Gqozo. Gqozo was certain that Hani meant 'to oust me at all costs'. He had heard that Hani had spoken of him as 'De Klerk's puppet' and 'kitchen boy'. When the marchers approached Bisho, Gqozo's troops fired on them, killing 29 (http://www.justice.gov.za/trc/hrvtrans/bisho2/gqozo.htm).

Again Mandela condemned de Klerk as the person primarily responsible for the massacre:

Bisho will rank alongside Boipatong on that roll call of infamy that recounts the past two years of F.W. de Klerk's incumbency. . . . The Bisho Massacre should alert all South Africans. De Klerk's continued emphasis on strong regional government, outside of the democratic process and within the context of the homelands, has given a signal to the repressive structures built up over the years by the apartheid regime that they can do what they like to entrench their authoritarian rule.
(http://www.anc.org.za/ancdocs/history/mandela/1992/pr920908.html)

De Klerk's protestations of government non-involvement rang hollow in the face of further evidence of security force participation in the political killings ravaging the country. State financial support of Inkatha was already public knowledge. In July and October a government commission of inquiry headed by an independent-minded jurist, Richard Goldstone, announced that it had discovered evidence of the state's use of covert forces and of the existence of plans by Military Intelligence to destabilise the ANC. His moral authority collapsing, and under increasing attack by right-wing foes denouncing him as a sell-out of the interests of the white community, de Klerk in September 1992 reached a new agreement with Mandela to continue negotiations, this time with the promise that a national election in which all South Africans, black and white, could participate would be held no later than April 1994.

Two quite different types of development underscored de Klerk's and his National Party supporters' recognition that, finally, their hold on power was coming to an end sooner rather than later, and that white supremacy could not be secured through further manipulation of the negotiating process. First, the privatisation of state enterprises accelerated. Whereas after 1948, the NP had brought approximately 57 per cent of the country's fixed assets under state control, with the end of its political control looming the party now became an enthusiastic adherent of state divestment and sale to people in the private sector; in essence a transference into white hands of assets that otherwise would come into the control of a black majority government. Second, from late 1992 onwards, there was a huge increase in the destruction of state records relating to the military, the police and the security apparatus in general. This had already begun at the end of the 1980s with the destruction of most military records relating to South West Africa/Namibia. The National Intelligence Service began a systematic destruction programme in 1991, the South African Police Security Branch followed suit in 1992, and in mid-1993 the cabinet approved guidelines for the wholesale destruction of 'state sensitive' records, including those of the SADF, which expanded the purging of its files. This process of destruction, which included records in the homelands, continued until 1996. The aim, as the TRC determined, 'was to deny a new government access to apartheid secrets through a systematic purging of official memory'; the result was the obliteration of 'swathes of official documentary memory, particularly around the inner workings of the apartheid state's security apparatus . . . [and the removal] from our heritage [of] what may arguably have been the country's richest accumulation of records documenting the struggle against apartheid' (TRC, 1998, vol. 1: 230–6).

Throughout 1993 and early 1994 the National Party, the ANC and other groups negotiated as to the form that political transformation would take.

They agreed on an interim constitution under which South Africa would be ruled by a Government of National Unity. All parties that got more than 5 per cent of the vote in the 1994 election would have representation in the cabinet, any party securing more than 80 seats would be entitled to a deputy presidency, no party would have the right of veto, but any new constitution would have to be supported by at least 66 per cent of parliament's members. Nine new provinces were to be created to replace the old provinces and homelands, and these regional bodies would have their own governing bodies – not exactly majority rule, but not power-sharing either.

As the ANC and the National Party negotiated a political transition, their foes, who refused to participate in the negotiations, engaged in actions that either undermined their own credibility or caused their self-destruction. Buthelezi and Inkatha made claims to national leadership of Africans, yet neither the man nor the movement secured support beyond the regional base of KwaZulu Natal. Even the latter was threatened by further evidence disclosed of the role of Inkatha in political killings (doubling in number from the end of 1992 through to mid-1994) and of continued receipt of support (financial and personnel) from 'third force' government units. The PAC, in the form of its armed wing, APLA, tried to gain popular support with its slogan of 'one settler, one bullet', but while it had a considerable and growing following among young people impatient with the slow pace of change, it also came under considerable criticism within the country and internationally when several of its supporters, on 25 August 1993, beat to death a young American student, Amy Biehl, who had been working with blacks in South Africa to end apartheid.

To the right of de Klerk, a range of organisations plotted to resist the end of white political supremacy. A group of former military and police officers opposed to black majority rule established in May 1993 a 'Committee of Generals'. Similar organisations included the Afrikaner Volksfront (People's Front), the Freedom Alliance and the Freedom Front (the Volksfront renamed). The Freedom Front was led by Constand Viljoen, chief of the armed forces throughout most of the 1980s and early 1990s, who in testimony given to the TRC in 1997 stated that he had planned in 1994 to establish by force a volkstaat (people's state), in essence a white state by coup d'état. The AWB, under the leadership of Eugene Terre'Blanche, continued its bombing campaign and added assassination, killing, on 10 April 1993, the leader of Umkhonto we Sizwe, Chris Hani, gunned down at his home in Johannesburg. Support for the AWB was limited by the incompetent and thuggish behaviour of its members and its leader. Hani's assassins were quickly and easily identified by one of his neighbours. An attempt by Terre'Blanche to derail the negotiation process by storming the hall where the talks were being held was captured by television crews and conjured up images of Nazi thugs,

especially since the AWB consciously used Swastika-like emblems on its uniforms and flags.

   But the real collapse of the white right as a serious threat to political transformation came in March 1994 in a vain attempt to shore up the leadership
of Lucas Mangope in Bophuthatswana and thereby affirm the persistence
of grand apartheid. Homeland troops who favoured the ANC had overthrown Mangope earlier that month and imprisoned him. Constand Viljoen
planned with other South African military and police officers to invade
Bophuthatswana and reinstate Mangope and to do so without the assistance
of the AWB 'since Mangope [had] stated that they would not be politically
acceptable to his own forces' (TRC, 1998, vol. 2: 664). But before Viljoen
could act, Terre'Blanche led 600 of his followers on a raid into the homeland
on 10 March. Driving erratically around Bophuthatswana, Terre'Blanche and
his supporters shot randomly at any Africans they assumed to be ANC supporters. Their expedition ended in tragic farce at a Bophuthatswana army
roadblock guarded by black soldiers opposed to Mangope and appalled
by the spree of killings in which the AWB members had engaged. Still and
television cameras caught the scene as the soldiers shot into a white
Mercedes Benz driven by AWB members and, when one of the wounded
pleaded for assistance, the cameras recorded his death as the soldiers fired
again. The image broadcast throughout South Africa and worldwide was one
of white amateur incompetence when faced by black professional soldiers,
of the unlikelihood of mercy for those who persisted in fighting for white
supremacy, and of the inability of the right wing to mount a coup even in a
homeland. After that event, the security establishment in South Africa gave
up its ideas of overthrowing the state and ceased working with organisations
like the AWB (which continued with plans for an armed takeover of
the Transvaal and the Orange Free State and the creation of a new
Boererepubliek). In the aftermath of the Bophuthatswana debacle, Inkatha, the
Conservative Party and most other groups which had stated their intention
to boycott the April election announced their readiness to participate and
campaign for votes.

   Violence continued right up to the holding of the national election on four
days beginning 26 April. That same month eight employees of a company
distributing informational pamphlets regarding voting procedures were tortured and murdered on the orders of an Inkatha supporter; at the supporter's
murder trial, Inkatha paid the costs of his defence. On the election days,
members of the AWB shot at minibus taxis on the Rand, raided police
stations to get weapons for the 'revolution' and sought in general to disrupt
voting.

   But it was all without success. During the four days of polling more than
19 million South Africans, roughly 91 per cent of registered voters, cast their

ballots, most for the first time, and elected South Africa's first democratic government. Reflecting the divides created by half a century of apartheid, and an even longer experience with racial discrimination, most of the votes were cast along 'race' lines. Africans voted overwhelmingly for the ANC, except in KwaZulu Natal where Inkatha squeaked ahead. Indeed, largely as a result of the unexpectedly strong showing of Inkatha (10.5 per cent of the national vote), the ANC fell short of the 66 per cent of the votes (it received 62.6 per cent) needed to be able to change unilaterally the interim constitution, a result much like that achieved by the South African government in 1989 when its interference had prevented SWAPO from getting a two-thirds majority. The NP won the second largest number of votes nationally (20.4 per cent), sufficient to ensure that F.W. de Klerk became a deputy president in the interim Government of National Unity, alongside Thabo Mbeki of the ANC. Right-wing white parties got less than two per cent of the vote, the PAC barely one per cent. Apartheid was formally at an end. White supremacy had lost its control of the state.

On 9 May 1994, the National Assembly unanimously elected Nelson Mandela president of South Africa. Fourteen thousand people had been killed in politically related incidents between 1990 and 1994, a death rate far higher than that in any period in the country's twentieth-century history.

But freedom had been won. In the words of Nelson Mandela, spoken at his inauguration as the first leader elected by a majority of South Africans:

> The time for the healing of the wounds has come. The moment to bridge the chasms that divide us has come. The time to build is upon us. We have, at last, achieved our political emancipation. We pledge ourselves to liberate all our people from the continuing bondage of poverty, deprivation, suffering, gender, and other discrimination. . . . We enter into a covenant that we shall build the society in which all South Africans, both black and white, will be able to walk tall, without any fear in their hearts, assured of their inalienable right to human dignity – rainbow nation at peace with itself and the world. . . .
>
> We dedicate this day to all the heroes and heroines in this country and the rest of the world who sacrificed in many ways and surrendered their lives so that we could be free. Their dreams have become reality. Freedom is their reward.
>
> (http://www.anc.org.za/ancdocs/history/mandela/1994/inaugpta.html)
>
> [**Doc. 13, pp. 170–2**]

Part 3

ASSESSMENT

6

The legacy of apartheid

The most remarkable feature of South Africa after the bitter struggles that had engulfed the country for a decade since P.W. Botha's hollow claims of reform in 1984 was the peaceful transition after 1994 from apartheid structures of white minority government to majority rule. The politically motivated killings of the early 1990s declined precipitously after the election: 1,600 deaths in 1994, half that number in 1995, and a continuing fall thereafter. The Government of National Unity established under the terms of the 1994 electoral process included in the cabinet representatives of the ANC, the National Party and Inkatha, thereby making all appear part of the process of initiating political, economic and social change in the country. Moreover, when Nelson Mandela announced in February 1995 that he would not stand again in 1999 for re-election as president, there was little concern expressed that the transition would be anything but peaceful.

The most significant achievement of the Government of National Unity was the passage, in December 1996, of a new constitution. Unlike its forebears of 1910 and 1983, which had been based fundamentally on principles of racial separation and inequality, the new constitution sought, in the words of its preamble, to 'heal the divisions of the past and establish a society based on democratic values, social justice and fundamental human rights' and in which 'government is based on the will of the people and every citizen is equally protected by law'. The most important part of the new constitution was a bill of rights that recognised the equality of every person before the law, and prohibited the state from discriminating on any grounds, 'including race, gender, sex, pregnancy, marital status, ethnic or social origin, colour, sexual orientation, age, disability, religion, conscience, belief, culture, language and birth'. The framers of the bill of rights specified certain features of apartheid that would never again be allowed to be practised. Expressly prohibited was any detention without trial, any torture, any searching and seizing of homes and property without due cause, any limitation on the freedom of movement either within South Africa or outside, any prohibition of people living wherever they chose in the country, and any arbitrary eviction from one's home and its demolition. The bill also committed the state to promoting equality, including implementing legislative measures 'to protect or advance persons, or categories of persons, disadvantaged by unfair discrimination'. Land and housing were especially important. The bill of rights required the state either to return property or to provide some other form of 'equitable redress' to any person or community who, after 19 June 1913 (the Natives' Land Act) had been 'dispossessed of property . . . as a result of past racially discriminatory laws or practices'. The state was additionally required, 'within its available resources', to ensure that every South African had 'access to adequate housing' (http://www.info.gov.za/documents/constitution/1996/index.htm).

Since that time, the political scene in post-apartheid South Africa has been remarkably stable. National elections in 2004 and 2009 proceeded peacefully and efficiently with the ANC dominating the returns, winning nearly 70 per cent of the vote in 2004, and just under 66 per cent in 2009. The **Democratic Alliance**, the new official opposition drawing its support from white and Coloured voters in the Cape, got just over 12 per cent in the 2004 election and just over 16 per cent in that of 2009. No other party got more than 7.5 per cent of the vote in either election, with the Freedom Front and AZAPO each getting less than 1 per cent of the vote in both elections. The New National Party, successor to de Klerk's and Botha's and Vorster's and Verwoerd's and Malan's National Party, architect of apartheid and governing party for over 40 years, won just 1.65 per cent of the vote in 2004 and voted to disband itself the following year.

At a fundamental level, however, profound divisions still exist between those who established and managed the apartheid state and those who brought about its overthrow. These divisions were best exemplified when, under the terms of the optimistically named 1995 Promotion of National Unity and Reconciliation Act, the South African government established a formal body, the **Truth and Reconciliation Commission (TRC)**, to investigate the sufferings of ordinary people under apartheid and to hear testimony from former agents of the state seeking amnesty for crimes that they had committed. During the two and a half years that it held hearings, over 22,000 people, most but not all of them black, appeared before the TRC and told of what had happened to them – of being beaten and tortured and raped, of being driven from their homes and imprisoned without trial, of being blinded and crippled and maimed. In the short term, these people were taking advantage of an unprecedented opportunity to tell the story of their lives in public and to make known their suffering during the decades of apartheid. The thousands of pages of their testimonies, replete with the details of their experiences, bear witness to the enormity of suffering (http://www.doj.gov.za/trc/index.html).

Democratic Alliance (DA): Formed in 2000 with the brief alliance of the Democratic Party (DP), successor to the PFP, and the New National Party (NNP), successor to the National Party (NP). Has succeeded in winning the votes of white and coloured voters in the Cape Province.

Truth and Reconciliation Commission (TRC): Established in 1995 under the Promotion of National Unity and Reconciliation Act. Charged to investigate the sufferings of ordinary people under apartheid and to hear testimony from former agents of the state seeking amnesty for the crimes they had committed. Held hearings for two and a half years and heard testimony of over 29,000 people.

Another 7,000 or so people appeared before the commissioners to request amnesty. Under the terms of its enabling legislation, the TRC could grant amnesty to those who could demonstrate that whatever actions they had undertaken, including illegal acts such as kidnapping and murder, were done with a political rather than personal aim in mind, and so long as the commissioners believed that the applicant had made a full disclosure of his (and the applicants were all men) actions.

Such applicants included the confessed murderer Eugene de Kock, the assassin Craig Williamson, and the bomb plotter and former minister of law and order Adriaan Vlok, each of whom argued that whatever he had done it had been in the interests of protecting the state. Their testimony, detailed as to the ways in which opponents of the National Party government had been abducted, tortured and murdered throughout the 1980s and early 1990s, presented publicly for the first time overwhelming evidence of the involvement of the state security apparatus in covert and illegal actions against supporters of the ANC and other anti-apartheid groups.

These deep wounds continued to resonate within South Africa, erupting dramatically in early 2010 with events surrounding two politically controversial individuals, Julius Malema, the newly elected leader of the ANC Youth League, and Eugene Terre'Blanche, founder of the white supremacist Afrikaner Weerstandbeweging (AWB). Malema, born in 1981 and thus only 8 years old when Mandela was released from prison in 1990, garnered notoriety in 2010 at ANC rallies for singing 'dubul'ibhunu', 'kill the boer, kill the farmer', first sung in 1993 following the murder of Chris Hani. Malema's public use of this song took on particular significance because of his role as a public firebrand and a supporter of Robert Mugabe, whose confiscation of the land of white farmers in Zimbabwe has resulted in the deaths of many of those farmers. Afrikaners, unnerved by the resurrection of political violence implicit in the song, successfully petitioned the government to outlaw singing it in public. Just as many Africans were coming to Malema's defence and the issue began to incite heated debate, Eugene Terre'Blanche, the personification of 'boer' nationalism, was brutally murdered in his bed on 4 April 2010, clubbed and knifed to death by two African farm workers. His murder produced an outpouring of anger from his supporters who denounced the government of President Jacob Zuma (elected 2009) and called, as they had under Terre'Blanche, for the creation of a separate white state. They took to flying the AWB flag, designed originally to mimic Nazi symbolism. While Malema's public stance resonates with Africans disappointed in the aftermath of apartheid, Terre'Blanche's death reignited white fears that they were endangered in a democratic South Africa. In 2010, it was clear that the wounds left by apartheid are far from healed.

Just as in politics, apartheid continues to cast a long shadow on South Africa's social and economic transformation. Initially, the leaders of the ANC were not ready to implement the economic and social revolution that their critics had always accused them of favouring. Indeed, *The Economist* noted favourably in 2002 that, since 1994, the ANC-led government had followed 'an impressive seven years of consolidating public finances and pursuing a policy of fiscal restraint against populist pressure' (Economist Intelligence Unit, 2002: 20). In the first decade after 1994 there was a continuation of the privatisation of state corporations begun by de Klerk, limited spending on compensating victims of past discrimination, and what critics of the government in the trade union movement (COSATU) and on the left (SACP) called a general 'pro-business' approach to economic planning. And as a result, foreign investment in the country expanded enormously, especially from 2005 onward, with the highest levels of investment to date reached in 2008. South Africa's Gross Domestic Product (GDP), the total market value of goods and services produced in a given year and a key indicator of economic prosperity, rose from an average of 2 per cent increase per year in the period 1997–2001, half the world's average, to a 5 per cent increase annually in 2004–2007. Unfortunately, most of this growth has been built on the same foundations that supported apartheid. As the International Monetary Fund noted in a 2009 report, South Africa continues 'to face formidable medium-term structural challenges largely reflecting its apartheid legacy' (http://www.imf.org/external/pubs/ft/scr/2009/cr09273.pdf: 6). In particular, profits continue to be generated through the use of exploited and under-educated African labour. The mining industry continues to rely on migrant labour, and, as a result of decreasing gold production within South Africa and a greater investment in gold mines elsewhere (in Africa, Australia, and the United States) made possible by the end of international anti-apartheid measures, now employs slightly over half as many men in its mines as it did a decade ago.

Not surprisingly, the prime beneficiaries of these trends are whites (who still earn on average five times as much as blacks), and a small but growing elite class within the African, Coloured and Indian communities. More than a decade after the end of apartheid, 83 per cent of whites were in the top 20 per cent of the population measured by household income, compared with 7.9 per cent of Africans, 25.6 per cent of Coloureds, and 50 per cent of Indians. Within the top quintile whites comprised 81 per cent of the highest income earners, Africans 10 per cent, Indians 5 per cent, and Coloureds 4 per cent. Thus income inequality, always cited by critics of apartheid as one of the most important indicators of the effects of white supremacy, remains among the highest in the world in post-apartheid South Africa despite massive economic expansion.

More devastating, unemployment among Africans in general continues to be a huge problem. Of the 24.4 million Africans, men and women, of working age (15–64 years) in the first quarter of 2010, 12.5 million were officially considered economically active, and of those 29.7 per cent were listed as unemployed. While an extraordinarily high unemployment rate by world standards, that figure pales when it is realised that the remaining 11.9 million working age Africans were defined as either not part of the formal economy or discouraged work seekers, in other words, 'not economically active'. Many of the unemployed and not economically active in 2010 were young Africans, 15–24 year olds who found themselves without jobs at a higher rate a decade and a half after apartheid ended than in the mid-1990s. Reflecting the racial stratification left by apartheid, unemployment figures in 2010 were much lower among Coloureds, Asians and whites at 21.8, 9.2 and 6.1 per cent respectively. While there has been some deracialisation of the top 20 per cent of income earners, due to the opening up of management jobs for blacks in the public and private sector, over half of African households still exist at or below the poverty line, and Africans, though 80 per cent of the population, constitute 93.3 per cent of the poor compared with the 0.1 per cent of whites comprising South Africa's 'poor individuals' (Table 6.1). Moreover, according to the Human Sciences Research Council (HSRC), 'poor households have sunk deeper into poverty since 1996' (www.sarpn.org.za/documents/. . ./ P1096-Fact_Sheet_No_1_Poverty.pdf).

The continuing distortion of economic growth has limited government attempts to equalise living conditions for the majority of the population. In particular, the government has not been able to rescue the rural areas where millions of Africans were trapped in 'homelands' without the legal right to leave or the economic means to survive. These areas remain destitute.

Table 6.1 Poverty rate, population share and poverty share, by population group

Group	Poverty rate of individuals (%)	Percentage shares of	
		Population	Poor individuals
Blacks	54.8	80.1	93.3
Coloureds	34.2	8.7	6.3
Indians	7.1	2.5	0.4
Whites	0.4	8.6	0.1
All	47.1	100.0	100.0

Source: Paula Armstrong, Bongisa Lekezwa, and Franz Krige Siebrits, and 'Poverty in South Africa: A Profile Based on Recent Household Surveys', Stellenbosch Economic Working Papers, 04/2008, p. 12 (www.ekon.sun.ac.za/wpapers/2008/wp042008/wp-04-2008.pdf)

Between 1994 and 2006, the government reduced the number of people lacking access to clean water from 40 per cent of the population to 19 per cent, but most of the latter lived in the former homelands where by 2010 more than half the people still remain without access to clean water and to adequate sanitation facilities. Between 1994 and 2003, nearly four million households, nearly all of them African, were connected to the national electricity grid, but more than half the people in rural areas remain in 2010 without access, and national electrical generation is inadequate to meet household and industrial needs with the result that there is a constant threat of country-wide blackouts. One and a quarter million new homes, often of a style known as Mandela houses, were constructed to give poor people access to reasonable accommodation rather than the shacks and ghettos of apartheid South Africa, but the pace of African urbanisation exceeds supply and 'informal settlements' – squatter camps, slums, shanty towns – have continued to grow and surround all the major cities. Land restitution has proceeded slowly. Whereas in 1994, Mandela's government announced that it intended to have 30 per cent of the land owned by whites at that time (86 per cent of the arable land in the country) transferred (by means of redistribution, restitution and tenure reform) into African hands within five years, by 2008 the figure achieved was only 5 per cent and the target date had been moved back to 2014, though even that is now seen as an unachievable deadline.

Not surprisingly, unequal development between rural and urban areas drove an increasing number of Africans to the cities. Better employment opportunities and government policies favouring large-scale commercial agriculture (almost exclusively white-owned), led more Africans (nearly 2.5 million of them, 1 million of them evicted) to leave the rural areas in the first decade after 1994 than had done so in the decade preceding the election of Mandela. Part of the attraction of the cities lay also in new educational opportunities. With the formerly white universities like those of Pretoria, Cape Town and the Witwatersrand (Johannesburg) open to students irrespective of race, the numbers of African university students doubled during the 1990s, and those enrolled in technical colleges quintupled. However, the drop-out rate of first year African university students ranges around 40 per cent, largely because of the high cost of education. A Supreme Court decision in 1996 required that all public schools be opened to students irrespective of race, in contradiction of attempts by rural white communities to keep their schools segregated in practice, if no longer in theory. But of the approximately 25,000 public elementary and high schools in South Africa in 2009, 79 per cent had no library, 77 per cent had no computers, and 85 per cent had no laboratories. And the quality of education remains racially stratified: among African high school students only 48 per cent graduate; among white, 95 per cent.

The flight of increasing numbers of Africans into the cities in an often unsuccessful search for housing and jobs (the unemployment rate in Johannesburg, for example, approaches 40 per cent), has produced a high rate of crime. This has been exacerbated by the ready availability of guns, often high powered military weapons such as AK 47s, resulting from the arming of the white population under apartheid and the importation of huge numbers of weapons from the former war zones of Angola, Mozambique, and other parts of southern Africa. Still, despite constant references in the press to the dangers of living in or visiting South Africa, the overall number of violent crimes post-1994 has declined as police have focused their attention on protecting the general population rather than just whites as had been the case under apartheid. The murder rate, for example, has dropped from 68 individuals killed per 100,000 population in 1994, to 37 per 100,000 in 2008–9.

The exception to the general decline in violence has been growing xenophobia, expressed through riots and killings in 2008 and 2009, against African job seekers from other parts of Africa. They have been drawn to South Africa by its relatively stronger economy compared with those of the Congo, Mozambique, Nigeria and Zimbabwe. They have benefitted also in the South African job market by their generally better educational qualifications than those left uneducated in South Africa during the apartheid era. Elementary schoolteachers from Zimbabwe, for example, can find it more financially advantageous to work at the bottom of the food chain as cooks, cleaners, and gardeners in South Africa, and to remit home to their families more than they could earn by working in their profession. Such people are perceived by unemployed black South Africans as taking jobs that should be theirs and violence has been the result.

The most serious threat to the social and economic well-being of South Africans, however, is HIV/Aids. Whereas in 1992 there were just 1,352 cases of the disease, by 2001 the number infected had risen to 5,000,000, with an annual death rate of 360,000 and expanding rapidly, and approximately 660,000 children under the age of 15 orphaned by the death of one or both parents. In 2000–3 HIV/Aids accounted for 57 per cent of the deaths of all children aged five and under, and 53 per cent of all deaths in South Africa. Average life expectancy dropped from 62 years in 1990 to 50 years in 2007 and continues to decline. Much of the blame for these high rates of infection and mortality were placed on President Mbeki, especially because of his claim that HIV and Aids were not related and that HIV was a product above all of poverty, a line of argument that he used to defend his government's refusal (until forced to change by court decisions in 2002) to pay for antiretroviral drugs for HIV/Aids sufferers. What the critics often fail to take into account, however, is the extent to which the apartheid migrant labour system with its constant movement of people throughout southern Africa, has led to the whole region, not just South Africa, having the highest rates of infection in the world.

More recent developments have led to a levelling off of HIV/Aids infection rates, though the impact of the disease on South Africa remains enormous. Whereas in 2003 only 2 per cent of people infected had access to retrovirals, by 2008 44 per cent had access. Twice as many people reported using condoms in 2008 as had in 2002. In 2008 South Africa had 5.7 million people living with HIV/Aids, more than any other country in the world, but close to the number reported for 2001 (Figure 6.1). The impact falls disproportionately on women and children. In 2008, 33 per cent of women aged 25–29 tested positive, compared with 15.7 per cent among men in the same age range (though the rate rises to 25.8 among men aged 30–34). In 2008, there were more than twice as many Aids orphans – 1.4 million – as there had been in 2001. Such statistics indicate the huge impact of HIV/Aids on family structures, as well as upon the economy by devastating the workforce and putting an enormous strain on the provision of social services (http://www.unaids.org/en/CountryResponses/Countries/south_africa.asp).

Many of the marks of this history remain just below the surface, obscured from the vision of most South African whites who continue to choose, as they did under apartheid, not to visit the urban townships or travel in the homelands, and who now mostly avoid the monuments to apartheid such as Robben Island and the Apartheid Museum in Johannesburg. Foreign visitors

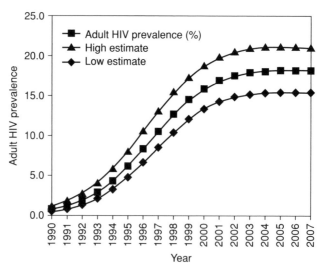

Figure 6.1 Estimated adult HIV (15–49) prevalence %, 1990–2007
Source: UNAIDS, WHO epidemiological fact sheet on HIV and Aids 2008,
http://apps.who.int/globalatlas/predefinedReports/EFS2008/full/EFS2008_ZA.pdf

to South Africa in 2010 see a modern country with advanced highway systems, shopping malls that rival the mega complexes in North America, electric lights and rows of modern homes and apartment buildings in cities such as Cape Town, Johannesburg, Durban, and Pretoria, experiences that make many of them think that they are 'not really' in Africa. When they venture into the countryside, they are often shown an 'authentic' African bush complete with quaint huts and game reserves.

One of the most popular tourist sites in South Africa, the Sun City Resort complex in the North West province, two hour's drive west of Johannesburg, provides such an experience, but masks the very essence of the legacy of apartheid that lives on in South Africa.

Sun City is advertised as the resurrection of a fantastic African kingdom where visitors can have their 'total experience of Africa'. At the centre of the Sun City complex of hotels and golf courses is the sumptuous and quite remarkable Palace of the Lost City:

> The Palace of the Lost City is an extraordinary fantasy stemming from a North African legend. The legend tells us that a tribe from an ancient civilization of Africa brought their proud traditions of mighty architecture, luxurious hospitality and love of nature to an ancient volcanic crater that they called the Valley of the Sun in South Africa. Here they built a palace which was destroyed by an earthquake. Hence the name The Palace of the Lost City. Today, the legend has come to life again and the Palace has been rebuilt in the magnificent surrounds of South Africa.
>
> (http://www.sun-city-south-africa.com/palace.asp)

Sun City also sits next to a beautiful reserve where visitors to the resort can view game from jeeps on a convenient morning or afternoon safari, snapping pictures of elephants, giraffes, zebra, and the occasional lion or leopard. The Pilanesberg Game Reserve, so goes the advertising, is a place where, 'Over time, wind and water have carved a spectacular landscape with rocky outcrops, open grasslands, wooded valleys and thickets' (http://www.pilanesberg-game-reserve.co.za/).

What appears to be untouched by time, save the claim to the African resurrection of the Palace (and that story has its origins in H. Rider Haggard's 1885 novel *King Solomon's Mines* and not in any North African legend), is in fact land which was taken from African farmers less than 40 years ago. Following the conquest of the Tswana in the nineteenth century, the local BaKgatla clan were overrun by Boer farmers (including Transvaal President Paul Kruger) and turned into indentured labourers on what had been their own farms. By the early twentieth century, with the land played out and the Boer farmers moving to more productive land, the area was deemed a 'Native

Reserve', and later one of the infamous 'homelands', where growing numbers of Africans were crowded on overworked land and pushed to starvation. By 1976, when the area was designated as 'Bophuthatswana', one of the homelands, it had lost its value other than as a dumping ground for Africans. That is when the energetic hotel entrepreneur Sol Kerzner first envisaged the area – close enough to Johannesburg to draw tourists and remote enough to avoid the ongoing upheavals against the government – as a site for his 'Lost City'. In 1976, Kerzner began negotiating with Lucas Mangope, premier of the Bophuthatswana homeland, to build a hotel complex and adjoining game park just outside South Africa and therefore not subject to the worldwide condemnation and growing call for sanctions against apartheid. When the deal was made, the poverty-stricken farmers were moved off the land to make way for the giraffes, elephants, casinos, and golf courses. Today it is relatively easy to see the taller game such as elephants and giraffe because none of the trees, allowed to grow only since 1979 when the farmers were removed, are more than about 20 feet high.

Few connect this bucolic vista to the world beyond, other than as a place of escape from the pressures of modern day life, but the vision of the visitor (practically all of whom are white) needs to stretch, beyond the park, beyond Sun City, beyond the surrounding North West province (formerly Bophuthatswana), to the horizon and beyond to encompass Johannesburg and the rest of South Africa as one entangled whole. In 2010, as in 1994, the white man is no longer *baas*, but the relics of apartheid remain, now emerging more clearly than they appeared during the heady years immediately after the fall of white supremacy.

Part 4

DOCUMENTS

Document 1   MANIFESTO OF THE ANC YOUTH LEAGUE, 1944

The ANC Youth League was founded in 1944 by Anton Lembede, Peter Mda,
Nelson Mandela, Walter Sisulu and Oliver Tambo, and in March of that year
issued a manifesto calling on members of the ANC to take stronger measures
to challenge white rule in South Africa. By the end of the 1940s, these young
men (with the exception of Lembede who died in 1947) had taken on leader-
ship roles in the ANC and were developing it into a mass movement for African
nationalism.

Statement of policy

South Africa has a complex problem. Stated briefly it is: The contact of
the White race with the Black has resulted in the emergence of a set of
conflicting living conditions and outlooks on life which seriously hamper
South Africa's progress to nationhood.

The White race, possessing superior military strength and at present
having superior organising skill has arrogated to itself the ownership of the
land and invested itself with authority and the right to regard South Africa
as a White man's country. This has meant that the African, who owned the
land before the advent of the Whites, has been deprived of all security
which may guarantee him an independent pursuit of destiny or ensure his
leading a free and unhampered life. He has been defeated in the field of
battle but refuses to accept this as meaning that he must be oppressed, just
to enable the White man to further dominate him.

The African regards Civilisation as the common heritage of all Mankind
and claims as full a right to make his contribution to its advancement and to
live free as any White South African: further, he claims the right to all sources
and agencies to enjoy rights and fulfil duties which will place him on a foot-
ing of equality with every other South African racial group.

The majority of White men regard it as the destiny of the White race
to dominate the man of colour. The harshness of their domination, however, is rousing in the African feelings of hatred of everything that bars
his way to full and free citizenship and these feelings can no longer be
suppressed.

In South Africa, the conflict has emerged as one of race on the one side
and one of ideals on the other. The White man regards the Universe as a
gigantic machine hurtling through time and space to its final destruction:
individuals in it are but tiny organisms with private lives that lead to private
deaths: personal power, success and fame are the absolute measures of
values; the things to live for. This outlook on life divides the Universe into a
host of individual little entities which cannot help being in constant conflict
thereby hastening the approach of the hour of their final destruction.

The African, on his side, regards the Universe as one composite whole; an organic entity, progressively driving towards greater harmony and unity whose individual parts exist merely as interdependent aspects of one whole realising their fullest life in the corporate life where communal contentment is the absolute measure of values. His philosophy of life strives towards unity and aggregation; towards greater social responsibility.

These divergences are not simplified by the fact that the two major races are on two different planes of achievement in the Civilisation of the West. This is taken advantage of to 'civilise' the African with a view to making him a perpetual minor. This obstruction of his progress is disguised as letting him 'develop along his own lines'. He is, however, suspicious of any 'lines' of development imposed on him from above and elects to develop along what the Natives' Representative Council recently called the 'lines of his own choosing'.

In practice these divergences and conflicts work to the disadvantage of the African. South Africa's two million Whites are highly organised and are bound together by firm ties. They view South African problems through the perspective of Race destiny; that is the belief that the White race is the destined ruler and leader of the world for all time. This has made it imperative for the African to view his problems and those of his country through the perspective of Race. Viewing problems from the angle of Race destiny, the White man acts as one group in relations between Black and White. Small minorities view South African problems through the perspective of Human destiny. These number among their ranks the few Whites who value Man as Man and as above Colour. Yet these are so few that their influence on national policies is but little felt.

The advantages on the side of the Whites enable two million White men to control and dominate with ease eight million Africans and to own 87 per cent of the land while the Africans scrape a meagre existence on the remaining 13 per cent. The White man means to hold to these gains at all costs and to consolidate his position, has segregated the African in the State, the Church, in Industry, Commerce etc., in all these relegating him to an inferior position where, it is believed, the African will never menace White domination.

Trusteeship

To mislead the world and make it believe that the White man in South Africa is helping the African on the road to civilised life, the White man has arrogated to himself the title and role of Trustee for the African people.

The effects of Trusteeship alone have made the African realise that Trusteeship has meant, as it still means, the consolidation by the White man of his position at the expense of the African people, so that by the time national awakening opens the eyes of the African people to the bluff they live under, White domination should be secure and unassailable. . . .

But Africans reject the theory that because he is non-White and because he is a conquered race, he must be exterminated. He demands the right to be a free citizen in the South African democracy; the right to an unhampered pursuit of his national destiny and the freedom to make his legitimate contribution to human advancement. . . .

Loss of faith in trusteeship

These conditions have made the African lose all faith in all talk of Trusteeship. HE NOW ELECTS TO DETERMINE HIS FUTURE BY HIS OWN EFFORTS. He has realised that to trust to the mere good grace of the White man will not free him, as no nation can free an oppressed group other than that group itself.

Self-determination is the philosophy of life which will save him from the disaster he clearly sees on his way – disaster to which Discrimination, Segregation, Pass Laws and Trusteeship are all ruthlessly and inevitably driving him.

The African is aware of the magnitude of the task before him, but has learnt that promises, no matter from what high source, are merely palliatives intended to drum him into yielding to more oppression. He has made up his mind to sweat for his freedom; determine his destiny himself and THROUGH HIS AFRICAN NATIONAL CONGRESS IS BUILDING A STRONG NATIONAL UNITY FRONT WHICH WILL BE HIS SUREST GUARANTEE OF VICTORY OVER OPPRESSION.

Source: ANC Youth League Manifesto, March 1944, available at http://www.anc.org.za/ancdocs/history/ancylman.html.

Document 2   VERWOERD EXPLAINS APARTHEID, 1950

Hendrik Verwoerd, the minister of native affairs in the first National Party government, met with African members of the Native Representative Council in December 1950 and addressed them on the theory and practice of apartheid.

Next, I wish to accede to the wish which, I understand, has long been felt by members of this council, namely that a member of the Government should explain the main features of what is implied by the policy of Apartheid.

Within the compass of an address I have, naturally, to confine myself to the fundamentals of the Apartheid policy and to the main steps following logically from the policy. . . .

As a premise, the question may be put: Must Bantu and European in future develop as intermixed communities, or as communities separated from one another in so far as this is practically possible? If the reply is 'intermingled communities', then the following must be understood. There will be competition and conflict everywhere. So long as the points of contact are still comparatively few, as is the case now, friction and conflict will be few and less evident. The more this intermixing develops, however, the stronger the conflict will become. In such conflict, the Europeans will, at least for a long time, hold the stronger position, and the Bantu be the defeated party in every phase of the struggle. This must cause to rise in him an increasing sense of resentment and revenge. Neither for the European, nor for the Bantu, can this, namely increasing tension and conflict, be an ideal future, because the intermixed development involves disadvantage to both.

Perhaps, in such an eventuality, it is best frankly to face the situation which must arise in the political sphere. In the event of an intermixed development, the Bantu will undoubtedly desire a share in the government of the intermixed country. He will, in due course, not be satisfied with a limited share in the form of communal representation, but will desire full participation in the country's government on the basis of an equal franchise. For the sake of simplicity, I shall not enlarge here on the fact that, simultaneously with the development of this demand, he will desire the same in the social, economic and other spheres of life, involving in due course, intermixed residence, intermixed labour, intermixed living, and, eventually, a miscegenated population – in spite of the well-known pride of both the Bantu and the European in their respective purity of descent. It follows logically, therefore, that, in an intermixed country, the Bantu must, in the political sphere, have as their object equal franchise with the European.

Now examine the same question from the European's point of view. A section of the Europeans, consisting of both Afrikaans- and English-speaking peoples, says equally clearly that, in regard to the above standpoint, the European must continue to dominate what will be the European part of South Africa. It should be noted that, notwithstanding false representations, these Europeans do not demand domination over the whole of South Africa, that is to say, over the Native territories according as the Bantu outgrow the need for their trusteeship. Because that section of the European population states its case very clearly, it must not be accepted, however, that the other section of the European population will support the above possible future demand of the Bantu. That section of the European population (English as well as Afrikaans) which is prepared to grant representation to the Bantu in the country's government does not wish to grant anything beyond communal representation, and that on a strictly limited basis. They do not yet realize that a balance of power may thereby be given to the non-European with which an attempt may later be made to secure full and equal franchise on the same voters' roll. The moment they realize that, or the moment when the attempt is made, this latter section of the European population will also throw in its weight with the first section in the interests of European supremacy in the European portion of the country. This appears clearly from its proposition that, in its belief on the basis of an inherent superiority, or greater knowledge, or whatever it may be, the European must remain master and leader. The section is, therefore, also a protagonist of separate residential areas, and of what it calls separation.

My point is this that, if mixed development is to be the policy of the future in South Africa, it will lead to the most terrific clash of interests imaginable. The endeavours and desires of the Bantu and the endeavours and objectives of all Europeans will be antagonistic. Such a clash can only bring unhappiness and misery to both. Both Bantu and European must, therefore, consider in good time how this misery can be averted from themselves and from their descendants. They must find a plan to provide the two population groups with opportunities for the full development of their respective powers and ambitions without coming into conflict.

The only possible way out is the second alternative, namely, that both adopt a development divorced from each other. That is all that the word apartheid means. Any word can be poisoned by attaching a false meaning to it. That has happened to this word. The Bantu have been made to believe that it means oppression, or even that the Native territories are to be taken away from them. In reality, however, exactly the opposite is intended with the policy of apartheid. To avoid the above-mentioned unpleasant and dangerous future for both sections of the population, the present Government adopts the attitude that it concedes and wishes to give to others precisely what it demands for itself. It believes in the supremacy (*baasskap*) of the European in his sphere but, then, it also believes equally in the supremacy (*baasskap*) of the Bantu in his own sphere. For the European child it wishes to create all the possible opportunities for its own development, prosperity and national service in its own sphere; but for the Bantu it also wishes to create all the opportunities for the realization of ambitions and the rendering of service to *their* own people. There is thus no policy of oppression here, but one of creating a situation which has never existed for the Bantu; namely, that, taking into consideration their languages, traditions, history and different national communities, they may pass through a development of their own. That opportunity arises for them as soon as such a division is brought into being between them and the Europeans that they need not be the imitators and henchmen of the latter.

The next question, then, is how the division is to be brought about so as to allow the European and the Bantu to pass through a development of their own, in accordance with their own traditions, under their own leaders in every sphere of life. . . .

The realities of today are that a little over one-third of the Bantu resides, or still has its roots, in what are unambiguously termed Native territories. A little over a third lives in the countryside and on the farms of Europeans. A little less than a third lives and works in the cities, of whom a section have been detribalized and urbanized. The apartheid policy takes this reality into account.

Obviously, in order to grant equal opportunities to the Bantu, both in their interests as well as those of the Europeans, its starting-point is the Native territories. For the present, these territories cannot provide the desired opportunities for living and development to their inhabitants and their children, let alone to more people. Due to neglect of their soil and over-population by man and cattle, large numbers are even now being continu-ously forced to go and seek a living under the protection of the European and his industries. In these circumstances it cannot be expected that the Bantu community will so provide for itself and so progress as to allow ambitious and developed young people to be taken up by their own people in their own national service out of their own funds. According as a flourishing commu-nity arises in such territories, however, the need will develop for teachers, dealers, clerks, artisans, agricultural experts, leaders of local and general governing bodies of their own. In other words, the whole superstructure of administrative and professional people arising in every prosperous commu-nity will then become necessary. Our first aim as a Government is, therefore, to lay the foundation of a prosperous producing community through soil reclamation and conservation methods and through the systematic establish-ment in the Native territories of Bantu farming on an economic basis.

The limited territories are, however, as little able to carry the whole of the Bantu population of the reserves of the present and the future – if all were to be farmers – as the European area would be able to carry all the Europeans if they were all to be farmers, or as England would be able to carry its whole population if all of them had to be landowners, farmers and cattle breeders. Consequently, the systematic building up of the Native territories aims at a development precisely as in all prosperous countries. Side by side with agri-cultural development must also come an urban development founded on industrial growth. The future Bantu towns and cities in the reserves may arise partly in conjunction with Bantu industries of their own in those reserves. In their establishment Europeans must be prepared to help with money and knowledge, in the consciousness that such industries must, as soon as is possible, wholly pass over into the hands of the Bantu.

On account of the backlog, it is conceivable, however, that such industries may not develop sufficiently rapidly to meet adequately the needs of the

Bantu requiring work. The European industrialist will, therefore, have to be encouraged to establish industries within the European areas near such towns and cities. Bantu working in those industries will then be able to live within their own territories, where they have their own schools, their own traders, and where they govern themselves. Indeed, the kernel of the apartheid policy is that, as the Bantu no longer need the European, the latter must wholly withdraw from the Native territories.

What length of time it will take the Bantu in the reserves to advance to that stage of self-sufficiency and self-government will depend on his own industry and preparedness to grasp this opportunity offered by the apartheid policy for self-development and service to his own nation. This development of the reserves will not, however, mean that all Natives from the cities or European countryside will be able, or wish, to trek to them. In the countryside there has, up to the present, not been a clash of social interests. The endeavour, at any rate for the time being, must be to grant the Bantu in town locations as much self-government as is practicable under the guardianship of the town councils, and to let tribal control of farm Natives function effectively. There the residential and working conditions will also have to enjoy special attention so that the Bantu community finding a livelihood as farm labourers may also be prosperous and happy. Here the problem is rather how to create better relationships, greater stability, correct training and good working conditions. Apart from the removal of black spots (like the removal of white spots in the Native areas), the policy of apartheid is for the time being, not so much an issue at this juncture, except if mechanization of farming should later cause a decrease in non-European labourers.

Finally, there are the implications of the apartheid policy in respect of European cities. The primary requirement of this policy is well known, namely, that not only must there be separation between European and non-European residential areas, but also that the different non-European groups, such as the Bantu, the Coloured, and the Indian, shall live in their own residential areas. Although considerable numbers of Bantu who are still rooted in the reserves may conceivably return thither, particularly according as urban and industrial development take place, or even many urbanized Bantu may proceed thence because of the opportunities to exercise their talents as artisans, traders, clerks or professionals, or to realize their political ambitions – large numbers will undoubtedly still remain behind in the big cities. For a long time to come, this will probably continue to be the case.

For these Bantu also the apartheid policy and separate residential areas have great significance. The objective is, namely, to give them the greatest possible measure of self-government in such areas according to the degree in which local authorities, who construct these towns, can fall into line. In due course, too, depending on the ability of the Bantu community, all the work there will have to be done by their own people, as was described in connection with the reserves. Even within a European area, therefore, the Bantu communities would not be separated for the former to oppress them, but to form their own communities within which they may pursue a full life of work and service.

In view of all this, it will be appreciated why the apartheid policy also takes an interest in suitable education for the Bantu. This, in fact, brings in its train the need for sufficiently competent Bantu in many spheres. The only and obvious reservation is that the Bantu will have to place his development and his knowledge exclusively at the service of his own people.

Co-operation in implementing the apartheid policy as described here is one of the greatest services the present leader of the Bantu population can render his people. Instead of striving after vague chimeras and trying to equal the European in an intermingled community with confused ideals and inevitable conflict, he can be a national figure helping to lead his own people along the road of peace and prosperity. He can help to give the children and educated men and women of his people an opportunity to find employment or fully to realize their ambitions within their own sphere or, where this is not possible, as within the Europeans' sphere, employment and service within segregated areas of their own.

I trust that every Bantu will forget the misunderstandings of the past and choose not the road leading to conflict, but that which leads to peace and happiness for both the separate communities. Are the present leaders of the Bantu, under the influence of Communist agitators, going to seek a form of equality which they will not get? For in the long run they will come up against the whole of the European community, as well as the large section of their own compatriots who prefer the many advantages of self-government within a community of their own. I cannot believe that they will. Nobody can reject a form of independence, obtainable with everybody's co-operation, in favour of a futile striving after that which promises to be not freedom but downfall.

Source: A.N. Pelzer, ed. (1966) *Verwoerd Speaks: Speeches 1948–1966*. Johannesburg: APB Publishers, pp. 23–9.

MANDELA SPEAKS ON THE NEED TO CHALLENGE APARTHEID, 1953 **Document 3**

Because Nelson Mandela had been served with a banning order early in 1953 that prevented him from speaking in public, his speech as president to the annual meeting of the Transvaal branch of the ANC later that year had to be read on his behalf. In his speech, Mandela wrote of the need to organise in new ways to meet government repression. He stressed in particular the importance of developing a programme of mass action, and he linked the struggles of people in South Africa with those of colonised people elsewhere in the world, quoting in the final two paragraphs Jawaharlal Nehru, the first president of independent India.

Since 1912 and year after year thereafter, in their homes and local areas, in provincial and national gatherings, on trains and buses, in the factories and on the farms, in cities, villages, shanty towns, schools and prisons, the African people have discussed the shameful misdeeds of those who rule the country. Year after year, they have raised their voices in condemnation of the grinding poverty of the people, the low wages, the acute shortage of land, the inhuman exploitation and the whole policy of white domination. But instead of more freedom, repression began to grow in volume and intensity and it seemed that all their sacrifices would end up in smoke and dust. Today the entire country knows that their labours were not in vain for a new spirit and new ideas have gripped our people. Today the people speak the language of action: there is a mighty awakening among the men and women of our country and the year 1952 stands out as the year of this upsurge of national consciousness.

In June, 1952, the AFRICAN NATIONAL CONGRESS and the SOUTH AFRICAN INDIAN CONGRESS, bearing in mind their responsibility as the representatives of the downtrodden and oppressed people of South Africa, took the plunge and launched the Campaign for the Defiance of the Unjust Laws. Starting off in Port Elizabeth in the early hours of June 26 and with only thirty-three defiers in action and then in Johannesburg in the afternoon of the same day with one hundred and six defiers, it spread throughout the country like wild fire. Factory and office workers, doctors, lawyers, teachers, students and the clergy; Africans, Coloureds, Indians and Europeans, old and young, all rallied to the national call and defied the pass laws and the curfew and the railway apartheid regulations. At the end of the year, more than 8,000 people of all races had defied. The Campaign called for immediate and heavy sacrifices. Workers lost their jobs, chiefs and teachers were expelled from the service, doctors, lawyers and businessmen gave up their practices and businesses and elected to go to jail. Defiance was a step of great political significance. It released strong social forces which affected thousands of our countrymen. It was an effective way of getting the masses to function politic- ally; a powerful method of voicing our indignation against the reactionary policies of the Government. It was one of the best ways of exerting pressure on the Government and extremely dangerous to the stability and security of the State. It inspired and aroused our people from a servile community of yesmen to a militant and uncompromising band of comrades-in-arms. The entire country was transformed into battle zones where the forces of liberation were locked up in immortal conflict against those of reaction and evil. Our flag flew in every battlefield and thousands of our countrymen rallied around it. We held the initiative and the forces of freedom were advancing on all fronts. . . .

The government launched its reactionary offensive and struck at us. Between July last year and August this year forty-seven leading members from both Congresses in Johannesburg, Port Elizabeth and Kimberley were arrested, tried and convicted for launching the Defiance Campaign and given suspended sentences ranging from three months to two years on condition that they did not again participate in the defiance of the unjust laws. In November last year, a proclamation was passed which prohibited meetings of more than ten Africans and made it an offence for any person to call upon an African to defy. Contravention of this proclamation carried a penalty of three years or of a fine of three hundred pounds. In March this year the Government passed the so-called Public Safety Act which empowered it to declare a state of emergency and to create conditions which would permit of the most ruthless and pitiless methods of suppressing our movement. Almost simultaneously, the Criminal Laws Amendment Act was passed which provided heavy penalties for those convicted of Defiance offences. This Act also made provision for the whipping of defiers including women. . . . The Government also made extensive use of the Suppression of Communism Act. . . . In December last year, the Secretary-General, Mr. W.M. Sisulu, and I were banned from attending gatherings and confined to Johannesburg for six months. Early this year, the President-General, Chief Luthuli, whilst in the midst of a national tour which he was prosecuting with remarkable energy and devotion, was prohibited for a period of twelve months from attending public gatherings and from visiting Durban, Johannesburg, Cape Town, Port Elizabeth and many other centres. . . .

The Congresses realised that these measures created a new situation which did not prevail when the Campaign was launched in June 1952. The tide of defiance was bound to recede and we were forced to pause and to take stock of the new situation. We had to analyse the dangers that faced us, formulate plans to overcome them and evolve new plans of political struggle. A political movement must keep in touch with reality and the prevailing conditions. Long speeches, the shaking of fists, the banging of tables and strongly worded resolutions out of touch with the objective conditions do not bring about mass action and can do a great deal of harm to the organisation and the struggle we serve. The masses had to be prepared and made ready for new forms of political struggle. . . . The old methods of bringing about mass action through public mass meetings, press statements and leaflets calling upon the people to go to action have become extremely dangerous and difficult to use effectively. The authorities will not easily permit a meeting called under the auspices of the A.N.C., few newspapers will publish statements openly criticising the policies of the Government and there is hardly a single printing press which will agree to print leaflets calling upon workers to embark on industrial action for fear of prosecution under the Suppression of Communism Act and similar measures. . . .

Meanwhile the living conditions of the people, already extremely difficult, are steadily worsening and becoming unbearable. The purchasing power of the masses is progressively declining and the cost of living is rocketing. Bread is now dearer than it was two months ago. The cost of milk, meat and vegetables is beyond the pockets of the average family and many of our people cannot afford them. The people are too poor to have enough food to feed their families and children. They cannot afford sufficient clothing, housing and medical care. They are denied the right to security in the event of unemployment, sickness, disability, old age and where these exist, they are of an extremely inferior and useless nature. Because of lack of proper medical amenities our people are ravaged by such dreaded diseases as tuberculosis, venereal disease, leprosy, pelagra, and infantile mortality is very high. The recent state budget made provision for the increase of the cost-of-living allowances for Europeans and not a word was said about the poorest and most hard-hit section of the population – the African people. The insane policies of the Government which have brought about an explosive situation in the country have definitely scared away foreign capital from South Africa and the financial crisis through which the country is now passing is forcing many industrial and business concerns to close down, to retrench their staffs and unemployment is growing every day. The farm labourers are in a particularly dire plight. . . . You will recall how human beings, wearing only sacks with holes for their heads and arms, never given enough food to eat, slept on cement floors on cold nights with only their sacks to cover their shivering bodies. You will remember how they are woken up as early as 4 a.m. and taken to work on the fields with the indunas sjamboking [whipping] those who tried to straighten their backs, who felt weak and dropped down because of hunger and sheer exhaustion. You will also recall the story of human beings toiling pathetically from the early hours of the morning till sunset, fed only on mealie [corn] meal served on filthy sacks spread on the ground and eating with their dirty hands. People falling ill and never once being given medical attention. You will also recall the revolting story of a farmer who was convicted for tying a labourer by his feet from a tree and had him flogged to death, pouring boiling water into his mouth whenever he cried for water. These things which have long vanished from many parts of the world still flourish in S.A. today. None will deny that they constitute a serious challenge to Congress and we are in duty bound to find an effective remedy for these obnoxious practices.

The Government has introduced in Parliament the Native Labour (Settlement of Disputes) Bill and the Bantu Education Bill. Speaking on the Labour Bill, the Minister of Labour, Ben Schoeman, openly stated that the aim of this wicked measure is to bleed African trade unions to death. By forbidding strikes and lockouts it deprives Africans of the one weapon the workers have to improve their position. . . . The Minister of Native Affairs, Verwoerd, has also been brutally clear in explaining the objects of the Bantu Education Bill. According to him the aim of this law is to teach our children that Africans are inferior to Europeans. African education would be taken out of the hands of people who taught equality between black and white. When this Bill becomes law, it will not be the parents but the Department of Native Affairs which will decide whether an African child should receive higher or other education. It might well be that the children of those who criticise the Government and who fight its policies will almost certainly be taught how to drill rocks in the mines and how to plough potatoes on the farms of Bethal. High education might well be the privilege of those children whose families have a tradition of collaboration with the ruling circles.

The attitude of the Congress on these bills is very clear and unequivocal. Congress totally rejects both bills without reservation. The last provincial Conference strongly condemned the then proposed Labour Bill as a measure designed to rob the African workers of the universal right of free trade union-ism and to undermine and destroy the existing African trade unions. Conference further called upon the African workers to boycott and defy the application of this sinister scheme which was calculated to further the exploitation of the African worker. To accept a measure of this nature even in a qualified manner would be a betrayal of the toiling masses. At a time when every genuine Congressite should fight unreservedly for the recognition of African trade unions and the realisation of the principle that everyone has the right to form and to join trade unions for the protection of his interests, we declare our firm belief in the principles enunciated in the Universal Declaration of Human Rights that everyone has the right to education; that education shall be directed to the full development of human personality and to the strengthening of respect for human rights and fundamental freedoms. It shall promote understanding, tolerance and friendship among the nations, racial or religious groups and shall further the activities of the United Nations for the maintenance of peace. That parents have the right to choose the kind of education that shall be given to their children.

The cumulative effect of all these measures is to prop up and perpetuate the artificial and decaying policy of the supremacy of the white men. The attitude of the Government to us is that: 'Let's beat them down with guns and batons and trample them under our feet. We must be ready to drown the whole country in blood if only there is the slightest chance of preserving white supremacy.'

But there is nothing inherently superior about the *herrenvolk* idea of the supremacy of the whites. In China, India, Indonesia and Korea, American, British, Dutch and French Imperialism, based on the concept of the supremacy of Europeans over Asians, has been completely and perfectly exploded. In Malaya and Indo-China British and French imperialisms are being shaken to their foundations by powerful and revolutionary national liberation movements. In Africa, there are approximately 190,000,000 Africans as against 4,000,000 Europeans. The entire continent is seething with discontent and already there are powerful revolutionary eruptions in the Gold Coast, Nigeria, Tunisia, Kenya, the Rhodesias and South Africa. The oppressed people and the oppressors are at loggerheads. *The day of reckoning* between the forces of freedom and those of reaction is not very far off. I have not the slightest doubt that when that day comes truth and justice will prevail.

The intensification of repressions and the extensive use of the bans is designed to immobilise every active worker and to check the national libera-tion movement. But gone forever are the days when harsh and wicked laws provided the oppressors with years of peace and quiet. The racial policies of the Government have pricked the conscience of all men of good will and have aroused their deepest indignation. The feelings of the oppressed people have never been more bitter. If the ruling circles seek to maintain their position by such inhuman methods then a clash between the forces of free-dom and those of reaction is certain. The grave plight of the people compels them to resist to the death the stinking policies of the gangsters that rule our country. . . .

From now on the activity of Congressites must not be confined to speeches and resolutions. Their activities must find expression in wide-scale work among the masses, work which will enable them to make the greatest possible contact with the working people. You must protect and defend your trade unions. If you are not allowed to have your meetings publicly, then you must hold them over your machines in the factories, on the trains and buses as you travel home. You must have them in your villages and shantytowns. You must make every home, every shack and every mud struc-ture where our people live, a branch of the trade union movement and *never surrender*.

You must defend the right of African parents to decide the kind of educa-tion that shall be given to their children. Teach the children that Africans are not one iota inferior to Europeans. Establish your own community schools where the right kind of education will be given to our children. If it becomes dangerous or impossible to have these alternative schools, then again you must make every home, every shack or rickety structure a centre of learning for our children. Never surrender to the inhuman and barbaric theories of Verwoerd.

The decision to defy the unjust laws enabled Congress to develop considerably wider contacts between itself and the masses and the urge to join Congress grew day by day. But due to the fact that the local branches did not exercise proper control and supervision, the admission of new members was not carried out satisfactorily. No careful examination was made of their past history and political characteristics. As a result of this, there were many shady characters ranging from political clowns, place-seekers, splitters, saboteurs, agents-provocateurs to informers and even policemen, who infiltrated into the ranks of Congress. One need only refer to the Johannesburg trial of Dr. Moroka and nineteen others, where a member of Congress who actually worked at the National Headquarters turned out to be a detective-sergeant on special duty. . . . Here in South Africa, as in many parts of the world, a revolution is maturing: it is the profound desire, the determination and the urge of the overwhelming majority of the country to destroy for ever the shackles of oppression that condemn them to servitude and slavery. To overthrow oppression has been sanctioned by humanity and is the highest aspiration of every free man. If elements in our organisation seek to impede the realisation of this lofty purpose then these people have placed themselves outside the organisation and must be put out of action before they do more harm. To do otherwise would be a crime and a serious neglect of duty. We must rid ourselves of such elements and give our organisation the striking power of a real militant mass organisation.

Kotane, Marks, Bopape, Tloome and I have been banned from attending gatherings and we cannot join and counsel with you on the serious problems that are facing our country. We have been banned because we champion the freedom of the oppressed people of our country and because we have consistently fought against the policy of racial discrimination in favour of a policy which accords fundamental human rights to all, irrespective of race, colour, sex or language. We are exiled from our own people for we have uncompromisingly resisted the efforts of imperialist America and her satellites to drag the world into the rule of violence and brutal force, into the rule of the napalm, hydrogen and the cobalt bombs where millions of people will be wiped out to satisfy the criminal and greedy appetites of the imperial powers. We have been gagged because we have emphatically and openly condemned the criminal attacks by the imperialists against the people of Malaya, Vietnam, Indonesia, Tunisia and Tanganyika and called upon our people to identify themselves unreservedly with the cause of world peace and to fight against the war policies of America and her satellites. We are being shadowed, hounded and trailed because we fearlessly voiced our horror and indignation at the slaughter of the people of Korea and Kenya. The massacre of the Kenya people by Britain has aroused world-wide indignation and protest. Children are being burnt alive, women are raped, tortured, whipped and boiling water poured on their breasts to force confessions from them that Jomo Kenyatta had administered the Mau Mau oath to them. Men are being castrated and shot dead. In the Kikuyu country there are some villages in which the population has been completely wiped out. We are prisoners in our own country because we dared to raise our voices against these horrible atrocities and because we expressed our solidarity with the cause of the Kenya people.

You can see that 'there is no easy walk to freedom anywhere, and many of us will have to pass through the valley of the shadow (of death) again and again before we reach the mountain tops of our desires'.

'Dangers and difficulties have not deterred us in the past, they will not frighten us now. But we must be prepared for them like men in business who do not waste energy in vain talk and idle action. The way of preparation (for action) lies in our rooting out all impurity and indiscipline from our organisation and making it the bright and shining instrument that will cleave its way to (Africa's) freedom.'

Source: 'No Easy Walk to Freedom', Presidential address by Nelson Mandela to the ANC (Transvaal branch), 21 September 1953, available at http://db.nelsonmandela. org/speeches/pub_view.asp?pg=item&ItemID=NMS003&txtstr=no%20easy% 20walk.

Document 4   THE FREEDOM CHARTER, 1955

On 26 June 1955, opponents of apartheid who had gathered together at the Congress of the People adopted unanimously a 'Freedom Charter' that expressed their opposition to the oppression and divisiveness of apartheid, and stressed their commitment to work for a South Africa in which all of its residents were viewed as full and equal citizens in all spheres of life.

Preamble

We, the people of South Africa, declare for all our country and the world to know:

That South Africa belongs to all who live in it, black and white, and that no government can justly claim authority unless it is based on the will of the people;

That our people have been robbed of their birthright to land, liberty and peace by a form of government founded on injustice and inequality;

That our country will never be prosperous or free until all our people live in brotherhood, enjoying equal rights and opportunities;

That only a democratic state, based on the will of the people, can secure to all their birthright without distinction of colour, race, sex or belief;

And therefore, we the people of South Africa, black and white, together – equals, countrymen and brothers – adopt this FREEDOM CHARTER. And we pledge ourselves to strive together, sparing nothing of our strength and courage, until the democratic changes here set out have been won.

The people shall govern!

Every man and woman shall have the right to vote for and stand as a candidate for all bodies which make laws;

All the people shall be entitled to take part in the administration of the country;

The rights of the people shall be the same regardless of race, colour or sex;

All bodies of minority rule, advisory boards, councils and authorities shall be replaced by democratic organs of self-government.

All national groups shall have equal rights!

There shall be equal status in the bodies of the state, in the courts and in the schools for all national groups and races;

All national groups shall be protected by law against insults to their race and national pride;

All people shall have equal rights to use their own language and to develop their own folk culture and customs;

The preaching and practice of national, race or colour discrimination and contempt shall be a punishable crime;

All apartheid laws and practices shall be set aside.

The people shall share in the country's wealth!

The national wealth of our country, the heritage of all South Africans, shall be restored to the people;

The mineral wealth beneath the soil, the banks and monopoly industry shall be transferred to the ownership of the people as a whole;

All other industries and trades shall be controlled to assist the well-being of the people;

All people shall have equal rights to trade where they choose, to manufacture and to enter all trades, crafts and professions.

The land shall be shared among those who work it!

Restriction of land ownership on a racial basis shall be ended, and all the land re-divided among those who work it, to banish famine and land hunger;

The state shall help the peasants with implements, seed, tractors and dams to save the soil and assist the tillers;

Freedom of movement shall be guaranteed to all who work on the land;

All shall have the right to occupy land wherever they choose;

People shall not be robbed of their cattle, and forced labour and farm prisons shall be abolished.

All shall be equal before the law!

No one shall be imprisoned, deported or restricted without fair trial;

No one shall be condemned by the order of any Government official;

The courts shall be representative of all the people;

Imprisonment shall be only for serious crimes against the people, and shall aim at re-education, not vengeance;

The police force and army shall be open to all on an equal basis and shall be the helpers and protectors of the people;

All laws which discriminate on the grounds of race, colour or belief shall be repealed.

All shall enjoy human rights!

The law shall guarantee to all their right to speak, to organise, to meet together, to publish, to preach, to worship and to educate their children;

The privacy of the house from police raids shall be protected by law;

All shall be free to travel without restriction from countryside to town, from province to province, and from South Africa abroad;

Pass laws, permits and all other laws restricting these freedoms shall be abolished.

There shall be work and security!

All who work shall be free to form trade unions, to elect their officers and to make wage agreements with their employers;

The state shall recognise the right and duty of all to work, and to draw full, unemployment benefits;

Men and women of all races shall receive equal pay for equal work;

There shall be a forty-hour working week, a national minimum wage, paid annual leave, and sick leave for all workers, and maternity leave on full pay for all working mothers;

Miners, domestic workers, farm workers and civil servants shall have the same rights as all others who work;

Child labour, compound labour, the tot system [whereby workers were paid in alcohol rather than cash] and contract labour shall be abolished.

The doors of learning and of culture shall be opened!

The government shall discover, develop and encourage national talent for the enhancement of our cultural life;

All the cultural treasures of mankind shall be open to all, by free exchange of books, ideas and contact with other lands;

The aim of education shall be to teach the youth to love their people and their culture, to honour human brotherhood, liberty and peace;

Education shall be free, compulsory, universal and equal for all children;

Higher education and technical training shall be opened to all by means of state allowances and scholarships awarded on the basis of merit;

Adult illiteracy shall be ended by a mass state education plan;

Teachers shall have all the rights of other citizens;

The colour bar in cultural life, in sport and in education shall be abolished.

There shall be houses, security and comfort!

All people shall have the right to live where they choose, to be decently housed, and to bring up their families in comfort and security;

Unused housing space to be made available to the people;

Rent and prices shall be lowered, food plentiful and no one shall go hungry;

A preventive health scheme shall be run by the state;

Free medical care and hospitalisation shall be provided for all, with special care for mothers and young children;

Slums shall be demolished and new suburbs built where all shall have transport, roads, lighting, playing fields, crêches and social centres;

The aged, the orphans, the disabled and the sick shall be cared for by the state;

Rest, leisure and recreation shall be the right of all;

Fenced locations and ghettos shall be abolished, and laws which break up families shall be repealed.

There shall be peace and friendship!

South Africa shall be a fully independent state, which respects the rights and sovereignty of all nations;

South Africa shall strive to maintain world peace and the settlement of all international disputes by negotiation – not war;

Peace and friendship among all our people shall be secured by upholding the equal rights, opportunities and status of all;

The people of the protectorates – Basutoland, Bechuanaland and Swaziland – shall be free to decide for themselves their own future;

The right of all the peoples of Africa to independence and self-government shall be recognised, and shall be the basis of close cooperation.

Let all who love their people and their country now say, as we say here: 'THESE FREEDOMS WE WILL FIGHT FOR, SIDE BY SIDE, THROUGH-OUT OUR LIVES, UNTIL WE HAVE WON OUR LIBERTY.'

Source: The Freedom Charter, available at http://www.anc.org.za/show.php?include=docs/misc/1955/charter.html.

Document 5   FRANCES BAARD DESCRIBES HOW WOMEN ORGANISED TO PROTEST THE PASS LAWS, 1956

Frances Baard, born in 1901 in Kimberley, worked as a domestic servant and teacher before becoming active in the ANC. She helped organise the 1952 Defiance Campaign, and helped in drafting the 1955 Freedom Charter. Here she describes how she and other women pooled resources to pay for their march on Pretoria in 1956.

[I]n October [1955] many women in the Transvaal went to the Union Buildings to protest to Strijdom, the prime minister, that we didn't want these passes. That was a very strong protest, 2,000 women of all races at the Union Buildings. In Port Elizabeth we had a meeting of the women to support the Transvaal women in this thing.

This protest to the Union Buildings was so good that the next year the Federation decided that we should do it again but this time we would send thousands of women from all over South Africa, black and white, to tell Strijdom the same thing. So each of us in her own place had to organize the women for this protest. We only had a few months to prepare for this but we wanted to send many, many women so that Strijdom would know that we really meant what we were saying. The first thing that we did in Port Elizabeth after the decision had been made was to call a meeting of all the women. We told them what had been decided and that we are going to the Union Buildings to protest, and that we will have to work very hard to do this.

We went from branch to branch organizing the women. Florence Matomela and I used to organize together for most of the campaigns, and we worked together on this one too. She would take one section of the location, and I would take another, and we would each work in that portion.

But now the other thing was we had to raise the money to take the women to Pretoria, and so in Port Elizabeth we divided ourselves into clubs. We divided into about 10 women in one club, 10, 10, 10 and a certain club had to bring a certain amount of money. The women made tea parties, concerts and bazaars, and they sold oranges or anything, until we managed to get a lot of money for the trip. The women even said that if we had to, we would sell our furniture to get to Pretoria! But we managed to get the money without that. Then we went to the railway station and asked them how much it would cost for a whole coach to Johannesburg. It cost us I think about 700 pounds for that coach, and that would take about 70 women. But there were many women who wanted to go and so we had to vote, this one must go, and this one, and this one, until we had chosen those women who were to go from Port Elizabeth to represent us.

But before we went to Pretoria we got all the women who couldn't go to sign petitions to say that they also didn't want these passes. Every woman who was on that train took those petitions with her to give to Strijdom.

It is two days by train from Port Elizabeth to Pretoria. Two days on the train sitting in the railway carriage, singing all the way. First we went to Johannesburg and we slept the night in Soweto, and then the next day, it was August 9th, we went to Pretoria. Some took buses, some trains, some taxis, anything to get to Pretoria. Some people were volunteers who were to look after everyone and make sure that everything went smoothly. They had to see that the women got to the Union Buildings, either by bus or on foot. They told the women walking not to walk like it is a procession because otherwise the police would have stopped them before they got there. We had to walk like we were all going somewhere by ourselves, not like we were a group. Then we all walked into the yard of the Union Buildings and we waited there for all the women coming from other places: Lady Selborne, and all through the Transvaal, and through the Cape and so on. We all had those protest forms with us and there were some extra ones for those who hadn't brought them. We waited until all the women were gathered there. It was about 20,000 of us altogether!

Then we went up into the place there in front of the buildings, what they call the amphitheatre. It took a long time, maybe nearly two hours or more for all the women to walk up the steps to that place. Some of us had been chosen, Lillian [Ngoyi], Helen [Joseph], Rahima Moosa, myself and some others, eight of us, we took all those petitions that had been signed, piles and piles of them, and we marched up to Strijdom's office to give them to him. The secretary told us that Strijdom was not there and that we were not allowed in anyway because we were black and white together. They said he was not there, just like that. But we knew that he was just too scared to see us! We walked past the secretary and into his office and we put those pamphlets on his desk, and on the floor, and the room was full of them. You know, they say Strijdom never even looked at those petitions; the special branch just took them away!

Then we walked outside again and joined the other women who were waiting in the amphitheatre. All the women were quiet. 20,000 women standing there, some with their babies on their backs, and so quiet, no noise at all, just waiting. What a sight, so quiet, and so much colour, many women in green, gold and black, and the Indian women in their bright saris! Then Lillian started to speak. She told everyone that the prime minister was not there and that he was too scared to see us but that we left the petitions there for him to see. Then we stood in silence for half an hour. Everyone stood with his or her hands raised in the salute, silent – and even the babies hardly cried. For half an hour we stood there in the sun. And not a sound, just the clock striking. Then Lillian started to sing and we all sang with her. I'll never forget the song we sang then. It was a song especially written for that occasion. A woman wrote it from the Free State. It went:

'*Wena Strijdom, wa'thinthabafazi, wathint'imbokotho uzokufa!*' That means: 'You Strijdom, you have touched the women, you have struck against rock, you will die.' Of course he did die, not long after that.

Source: Frances Baard (1986), *My Spirit is not Banned (as told by Frances Baard to Barbie Schreiner)*, Harare, Zimbabwe: Zimbabwe Publishing House, accessible at http://www.anc.org.za/ancdocs/pubs/umrabulo/umrabulo19/baard.html.

Document 6   STEPHEN BIKO EXPLAINS 'BLACK CONSCIOUSNESS', 1971

Stephen Biko here discusses with members of SASO what he believes are the basic tenets of the philosophy of black consciousness to which he adheres. Note his stress on such themes as positive action, especially the example of the first leader of independent Ghana, Kwame Nkrumah, that adhering to black consciousness did not mean hating whites, and the importance of ideas emanating from African-American leaders in the United States.

What are we talking about?
Here we are primarily concerned with SASO and its work. We talk glibly of 'Black Consciousness' and yet we show that we hardly understand what we are talking about. In this regard it is essential for us to realise a few basic facts about 'Black Consciousness'.

'Black Consciousness' is essentially a slogan directing us away from the traditional political big talk to a new approach. This is an inward-looking movement calculated to make us look at ourselves and see ourselves, not in terms of what we have been taught through the absolute values of white society, but with new eyes. It is a call upon us to see the innate value in us, in our institutions, in our traditional outlook to life and in our own worth as people. The call of 'Black Consciousness' is by no means a slogan driving people to think in a certain way politically. Rather it is a social slogan directed at each member of the black community calling upon him to discard the false mantle that he has been forced to wear for so many years and to think in terms of himself as he should. In this regard therefore Black Consciousness is a way of life that must permeate through the society and be adopted by all. The logic behind it is that if you see yourself as a person in your own right there are certain basic questions that you must ask about the conditions under which you live. To get to this stage there are three basic steps that have to be followed.

(i)   We have to understand thoroughly what we are talking about and to impart it in the right context. This becomes especially necessary in a country like ours where such an approach lends itself easily to misinterpretation. For this reason we have made provision for a historical study of the theory of 'black power' in this formation school.

(ii) We have to create channels for the adoption of the same approach by the black community at large. Here, again, one has to be realistic. An approach of this nature, to be successful, has to be adopted by as large a fraction of the population as possible in order to be effective. Whilst the student community may be instrumental in carrying the idea across to the people and remaining the force behind it, the approach will remain ineffective unless it gains grassroots support. This is why it is necessary to create easily acceptable slogans and follow these up with in-depth explanations. Secondary institutions built up from members of the community and operating amongst the community have to be encouraged and these must be run by people who themselves understand what is involved in these institutions and in the approach we are adopting. One can expand and give many examples of such institutions but we expect this to come out of discussions at this formation school. Let it suffice to say that such institutions must cover all fields of activity of the black community – educational, social, economic, religious, etc.

(iii) People have to be taught to see the advantages of group action. Here one wonders whether a second look should not be taken at the government-instituted bodies like Urban Bantu Councils and bantustans. It is a universal fact that you cannot politicise people and hope to limit their natural and legitimate aspirations. If the people demand something and get it because they have an Urban Bantu Council or 'territorial authority' to talk for them, then they shall begin to realise the power they wield as a group. Political modernisation of the black people may well find good expression in these institutions which at present are repugnant to us. In contrasting the approach adopted in the United States by the black people and our own approach here, it will be interesting to know what this formation school thinks of the various 'territorial authorities' in our various 'own areas'.

There are some dangers that we have to guard against as we make progress in the direction we are pursuing. The first and foremost is that we must not make the mistake of wishing to get into the white man's boots. Traditional indigenous values tell us of a society where poverty was foreign and extreme richness unknown except for the rulers of our society. Sharing was at the heart of our culture. A system that tends to exploit *many* and favour a few is as foreign to us as hair which is not kinky or a skin which is not dark. Where poverty reigned, it affected the whole community simply because of weather conditions beyond our control. Hence even in our aspirations basic truth will find expression. We must guard against the danger of creating a black middle class whose blackness will only be literally skin-deep. . . .

Secondly we must not be limited in our outlook. There is a mile of difference between preaching Black Consciousness and preaching hatred of white. Telling people to hate whites is an outward and reactionary type of preaching which, though understandable, is undesirable and self-destructive. It makes one think in negative terms and preoccupies one with peripheral issues. In a society like ours it is a 'positive feed-forward' approach that leads one into a vicious circle and ultimately to self-destruction through ill-advised and impetuous action. In fact it is usually an extreme form of inferiority complex where the sufferer has lost hope of 'making it' because of conditions imposed upon him. His actual aspirations are to be like the white man and the hatred arises out of frustration.

On the other hand Black Consciousness is an inward-looking process. It takes cognisance of one's dignity and leads to positive action. It makes you seek to assert yourself and to rise to majestic heights as determined by you. No doubt you resent all forces that seek to thwart your progress but you meet them with strength, resilience and determination because in your heart of hearts you are convinced you will get where you want to get to. In the end you are a much more worthy victor because you do not seek to revenge but to implement the truth for which you have stood all along during your struggle. You were no less angry than the man who hated whites but your anger was channelled to positive action. Because you had a vision detached from the situation you worked hard regardless of immediate setbacks. White hatred leads to precipitate and short-run methods whereas we are involved in an essentially long-term struggle where cool-headedness must take precedence over everything else.

The third point is that we must not make the mistake of trying to cat-egorise whites. Essentially all whites are the same and must be viewed with suspicion. This may apparently sound contradictory to what I have been say-ing but it is not in actual fact. A study of the history of South Africa shows that at almost all times whites have been involved in black struggles and in almost all instances led to the death or confusion of what they were involved in. This may not have been calculated sometimes but it arises out of genuine differences in approach and commitments. That blacks are deciding to go it alone is not an accident but a result of years of history behind black–white co-operation. Black–white co-operation in this country leads to limitations being imposed on the programme adopted. We must by all means encourage 'sympathetic whites' to stand firm in their fight but this must be away from us. In many ways this is dealt with adequately in an article that appears in the August *SASO Newsletter*, 'Black Souls in White Skins'. The fact that 'sym-pathetic whites' have in the past made themselves the traditional pace-setters in the black man's struggle has led to the black man's taking a backseat in a struggle essentially his own. Hence excluding whites tends to activate black people and in the ultimate analysis gives proper direction to whatever is being done. This is a fact that overseas observers visiting the country find hard to accept but it remains very true. Racial prejudice in this country has gone beyond all proportions and has subconsciously affected the minds of some of the most well-known liberals. . . .

Whither are we going?

At all costs we must make sure that we are marching to the same tune as the rest of the community. At no stage must we view ourselves as a group endowed with special characteristics. Whilst we may be playing the tune, it is the rhythmic beating of the community's boots that spurs us to march on and at no stage should that rhythm be disturbed. As the group grows larger and more boots join the rhythmic march, let us not allow the beating of the boots to drown the pure tones of our tune, for the tune is necessary and essential to the rhythm.

Source: Hendrik van der Merwe *et al.*, eds (1978) *African Perspectives on South Africa: A Collection of Speeches, Articles and Documents*, Stanford, CA: Hoover Institution Press, pp. 101–5.

DAN MONTSISI TESTIFIES AS TO THE ORIGINS OF THE SOWETO **Document 7**
UPRISING, 1976

In 1976 Dan Montsisi was a high school student and one of the organisers of the protests that began on 16 June in Soweto. With the fall of apartheid, he became an ANC member of parliament and continues to represent his constituents in Soweto.

When we organised the demonstration [16 June 1976] for instance a number of meetings started quite earlier because as members then of the then existing student organisations we were aware of problems which were taking place . . . obviously Afrikaans was something quite difficult and we couldn't conceive of Afrikaans being taught as a medium of instruction in the township of Soweto, because most publications and magazines are English and most people around, I mean we were more acquainted with English rather than Afrikaans. We do speak Afrikaans and we do Afrikaans as a language, but now for maths for instance to be taught in the medium of Afrikaans, Science and Economics and all those subjects to be taught in the medium of Afrikaans that was highly unthinkable.

So we met with, firstly it was in May 1976. . . . One of the issues came up about what we are going to do on the issue of Afrikaans as a medium of instruction. Sometime in April, May 1976 the students . . . voiced out their concerns. Now the announcement was actually made sometime in 1975 in December by the then existing Minister of Education. Now the spiral went on of this concern within the school community and also within the teachers because some of them were quite aware of the fact that they were not competent enough to teach in the medium of instruction which they actually designed to do.

A number of meetings were held . . . the . . . school board in Meadowlands [to which Sophiatown residents had been removed in 1954–55] refused to acknowledge and accept that their own schools and the teachers should actually teach in Afrikaans. They tried to talk to the Department and even explained to the district officials of education that there is no way in which you can introduce Afrikaans as a medium. The Department refused to listen. The circuit inspector refused to listen.

Now there was no way in which the parents and the teachers could have been able to do anything because the powers that be (the inspector) had actually refused, in a period of about five months, to negotiate and actually resolve the issue of Afrikaans as a medium of instruction. Treurnicht later said that where the government actually funds, the government will decide the policy regarding education.

Now in a way it was a challenge to the young people of Soweto, and the young people of South Africa because he (Treurnicht) was saying you are going to take Afrikaans whether you like it or not and you are going to do it. . . .

When we met finally on the 15th of June in order to inform the students about the day there was a lot of enthusiasm and excitement among students because the government was reluctant to actually withdraw Afrikaans as a medium and the students were prepared that they are not going to let Afrikaans ruin their future, because already the type of education system that we were receiving left quite a lot to be desired. So on the placards, as we reported to them, firstly they had to condemn Afrikaans as a medium and secondly while they had a lot to say about the Nationalist Party leadership, Verwoerd for instance and Vorster, B.J. Vorster. And then the student leadership at the same time made known their displeasure about apartheid government in general so that the placards that came on June 16 were a reflection of what the students were up against in addition to Afrikaans as a medium of instruction. The major issue as it is was Afrikaans as a medium of instruction.

Now on the 16th we met in my school immediately after the assembly. The teachers were not informed. Only a few teachers knew about this and immediately after the assembly the official prayer meeting in the morning, we took up the rostrum. So I had, together with my colleagues explained the route that we were going to take . . . obviously when we marched we were not aware that this was a chapter actually in the history of South Africa. We had not gone out to really bring about the transformation and change that took place. We only went out into the demonstration hoping that tomorrow we will come back to our classes, sit down and begin with our lessons. That is what we thought. So we moved out of our school.

All along when we began to march, I mean the contingent was gaining its momentum and it was becoming stronger. So already while we were heading towards Morris Isaacson there was something like four to six thousand students and people in general who were on the march, because those parents were not at work, you know the unemployed and the young people who were out there in the township, actually joined the march, but nevertheless the march was peaceful. No single stone was thrown up to that moment [then the police began shooting and teargassing the protesting students]. . . .

Now if one has to comment about the condition in which those students [who had been shot] were, you had girls for instance who were clad in gym dress but now those gyms were actually cut into two by the fence and they were just exposed, and some of them were actually bleeding. There is one particular girl whom I saw who had a gash on the head and all the time they had been trying to stop the blood that was flowing profusely and a number of them did not even have their shoes on. It was terrible. It was almost as if these people had come from a battlefield, not a demonstration.

Now on our way to Morris Isaacson we met a van, it was a green bakkie [pick-up truck], one of these Municipality vans, it was driven by a White man. That is when violence started with our group. Mostly the girls were in the forefront. I have never seen so many stones in my life raining on a car or on a target. I don't know where most of the stones came from. In no time the bakkie had no windows. And the student girls themselves actually struggled and fought among each other to get hold of the White man who was inside the car. They dragged him out. They pelted him with stones, with bottles, with their shoes as they were screaming. There was a young boy who was also looking for a way through to the White man. Finally when they made space for him he produced a knife and he stabbed a number of times in the chest of the White man.

Source: Personal testimony, available at: http://www.doj.gov.za/trc/hrvtrans/ Soweto/montsisi.htm.

Document 8   DAN MONTSISI IS TORTURED BY THE POLICE, 1977

Dan Montsisi was detained by the police in Johannesburg on 10 June 1977, and interrogated and tortured by them on several occasions before being incarcerated on Robben Island. Here he describes, in testimony given to the Truth and Reconciliation Commission in 1996, how agents of the apartheid state treated those they viewed as enemies.

[The police] fetched me from John Vorster Square [the main police station in Johannesburg] and we drove down to Protea Police Station, and they used the rubber truncheon to beat you all over the head and it was quite difficult because I was blindfolded and I couldn't see the direction from which the truncheon was coming from, so it was quite easy for them. It went on for quite some time. And then you could also be kicked and beaten with fists, stomach and so on. And there was also one other method they used, the rifle. They used the rifle to stamp on your toes. So every time you talk what they do not agree with they use the rifle on your toes. And one method they referred to as an airplane, I didn't know what they were talking about, but I was grabbed and they swung me and they threw me right into the air but when you land, fortunately it was a wooden floor so they did that several times. All along I mean they were like laughing and so on and so on, ridicule you and so on. And they were pulling the muscles on the back to put a strain on you so they come from behind and they pull the muscles with their own hands. And so they also forced me to squat. That time I was quite weak and I didn't have much power left in me. I could have collapsed any time but they still continued, so I had to squat against the wall and a brick was placed on my hands as I squatted against the wall. I don't know what happened because I think the brick fell and it hit me on the head and when I regained consciousness they had poured water all over me. So the first person I saw looking down at me was Visser, Captain Visser from Protea Police Station. So all I said to him when I saw him was that 'Baas they are killing me', that is what I said to him. And I never thought I would say 'baas' but I did. So they explained to him that – they used very strong language, 'hardegat', so they were going to continue. That time they had removed the blindfold and he left the room, and then as soon as he left I could see the people who were instrumental in the torture. Although there were something like eight policemen inside there were two others Trollip and Van Rooyen, those were the ones who were the leaders and the senior was this Lieutenant Van Rooyen. So they blindfolded me again and this time they took off my pants and my underpants and they used what we referred to later as we were talking about it as a USO, an unidentified squeezing object, but probably it was a plier, to actually press my testes. They did that twice or thrice and when they do that it becomes very difficult for you to scream because you like choke. When they leave you then you are able to scream. So they did that twice, thrice. I don't know what happened and again they poured water all over me. And I was taken to John Vorster and ja [yes] I was dumped there. Later I saw a doctor, a district surgeon Williamson, so he was able to treat me. He wasn't supposed to see me, it was just a mistake on the part of the police, because in the cells in John Vorster Square when they were opening the cells they opened my own cell by mistake. Those who were tortured must not be seen by the doctor because they will be . . . (indistinct), so this policeman opened my door unaware and then I couldn't go on my own so I used the wall to walk towards the part of the cells was a surgery where the doctor saw us, so I crawled and so on and so on. When the security police saw me they wanted to take me back to the cells so I screamed, so fortunately the doctor came out and he saw me, then he said I want to see that man. . . . My whole body was swollen, there were stripes all over the body and so on. So the doctor was able to see me and he made a profile of a human being to indicate all areas of injury. My medical record was subsequently submitted in court so it's properly recorded. When I recovered this was sometime in September they took me again. This time it was on the 10th Floor of John Vorster Square and there it was De Meyer, Sergeant de Meyer, Captain . . . they didn't touch the face and Stroewig was just concentrating on the head. He didn't hit anything except the head. So he just focused on the head and so on and so forth. For the whole day he did not hit anything except the head and I think I collapsed and again I was taken to hospital. So this time they took me to the Florence Nightingale Clinic in Hillbrow. It was a White hospital so no Africans can see one of the student activist casualties, unlike if you had to take him to an African clinic, quite a number of people could have seen him. So I was smuggled into an exclusive White clinic. There they did brain scanning and well they checked me and they wanted to do a lumbar puncture. At that time I didn't understand what a lumbar puncture was so they explained that they are going to stick a needle in my spine and extract the liquid. I refused because I wasn't quite sure whether I could trust them to do that to me. I knew the spine to be quite sensitive so I refused. So the security cops came again to try and talk to me to do the lumbar puncture, I refused. They promised that they would take me back to prison and beat me up and bring me . . . (indistinct) and so on and so on, but once I was with the doctor I was able to tell the doctor that he shouldn't, so fortunately the doctor did not do it. I recovered after some time. I was taken back to the cells. Later well we were tried I was sentenced to Robben Island and Mandela wanted a report about June 16 including Mr. Sisulu there and Govan Mbeki. So together . . . we had . . . to write a comprehensive report about the events.

Source: Personal testimony, available at: http://www.doj.gov.za/trc/hrvtrans/Soweto/montsisi.htm.

Document 9   AN ORDINARY POLICEMAN EXPLAINS HIS INVOLVEMENT IN THE KILLING OF STEPHEN BIKO, 1977

Daniel Petrus Siebert, a member of the team of policemen who interrogated and tortured Stephen Biko to death, and who subsequently was promoted to head of the detective branch in the Eastern Transvaal and retired with the rank of police brigadier in 1995, submitted his personal overview statement to the Truth and Reconciliation commissioners as part of his application for amnesty.

Mr. Siebert   [I was born] on the 20th of September 1945 in Bloemfontein. I am the youngest of four children. I grew up in a conservative and Christian home. I am a member of the Dutch Reformed Church and have been actively involved in the Dutch Reformed Church since my childhood and have, for the past 26 years, served on the local Church Council. I grew up, during my formative years, in the apartheid era. The apartheid policy would, as a consequence, have been acceptable and justifiable to me since I was of the opinion, at that time, that this policy was necessary for the continued survival of the White and South African at the southern end of Africa. This point of view, in subsequent years, was additionally influenced and strengthened by the policy expressions or statements of political leaders as well as cultural and church leaders.

As a result of these statements and rhetoric, I was convinced that the White Afrikaans-speaking person would have to fight

	for the right of survival and for the right to continue to live as our ancestors did, with particular reference to our heritage, background, culture and political way of life. . . .
Question	And I want to ask you not to give us or repeat to us any political speeches, but in a nutshell, what did Mr. Vorster [whom Siebert knew personally] communicate to you with regard to his beliefs regarding the security situation and so forth?
Mr. Siebert	That the security situation was becoming far more intense and that serious attention would have to be paid to it to control it and, perhaps, entirely to eliminate it, since this damaged the image of the Republic, particularly with the view to sanctions, which was operative at that time, with regard to development and foreign investment. . . .
Question	[in response to Siebert's denial that Biko was assaulted by the police but that what took place was more akin to a wrestling match]: However, we do know that this [assault on Biko] did occur. What would your impression have been with regard to your direct Commanding Officer and so forth? Was such assault condoned or was there objection against it when it did occur?
Mr. Siebert	I would admit that such events did occur and the statement would then have been, if this was not damaging or to the disadvantage of the State and the Security Branch, then this would not be acted against. . . .
Question	[regarding the transportation of Biko, after his interrogation in Port Elizabeth, by bakkie to Pretoria where he died within 24 hours]: . . . was Mr. Biko dressed in the back of the Land Rover?
Mr. Siebert	Your Honour, he was wearing only a pair of underpants. I asked the members who accompanied me, those members whom I had asked to prepare the vehicle and obtain the vehicle had also received instructions from me to process Mr. Biko at the police station and to collect him. I joined them at a later stage since I had some other arrangements, personal arrangements to make. I had to collect clothes for myself, I had to purchase food for the road and just outside Blouwater Baai, outside Port Elizabeth we stopped to eat. When I got out of the car and looked back in the vehicle to see whether the deceased had any interest in food I noticed his right leg, I noticed that it was open and naked. I then determined that he was only wearing underpants. I asked the members why this was the case, why he was not fully dressed and they informed me that it was very difficult to dress him since he was clumsy and stiff. I then realised that it would be even more difficult to dress him in the back of the Land

Rover. I accept that I made no effort to dress him. I also accept that this was inhumane. However, I do want to mention at the same time, that there were a number of cell mats on which he was lying as well as a number of blankets and a pillow, that he was fully covered. It was not as if he was publicly naked or anything like that.

[Biko received medical assistance only a day after his 1,100 kilometre trip from Port Elizabeth to Pretoria, and then only while standing handcuffed to a security gate. He died within a few hours of brain injuries inflicted during his interrogation.]

Source: Personal testimony, available at: http://www.justice.gov.za/trc/amntrans/pe/siebert.htm.

Document 10   F.W. DE KLERK ANNOUNCES THE UNBANNING OF THE ANC AND THE FREEING OF MANDELA, 1990

Speaking at the first session of parliament on 2 February 1990, de Klerk made the announcement that his government would release Mandela and other political prisoners, grant legal recognition to the ANC, the PAC, the SACP and other banned organisations, and enter a process of negotiation to recognise and incorporate all Africans as citizens of South Africa, a stunning and unexpected change from previous NP policy.

The general election on 6 September 1989 placed our country irrevocably on the road of drastic change. Underlying this is the growing realisation by an increasing number of South Africans that only a negotiated understanding among the representative leaders of the entire population is able to ensure lasting peace.

The alternative is growing violence, tension and conflict. That is unacceptable and in nobody's interest. The well-being of all in this country is linked inextricably to the ability of the leaders to come to terms with one another on a new dispensation. No one can escape this simple truth.

On its part, the Government will accord the process of negotiation the highest priority. The aim is a totally new and just constitutional dispensation in which every inhabitant will enjoy equal rights, treatment and opportunity in every sphere of endeavour – constitutional, social, and economic. . . .

The Government accepts the principle of the recognition and protection of the fundamental individual rights which form the constitutional basis of most Western democracies. We acknowledge, too, that the most practical way of protecting those rights is vested in a declaration of rights justifiable by an independent judiciary.

However, it is clear that a system for the protection of the rights of individuals, minorities and national entities has to form a well-rounded and balanced whole. South Africa has its own national composition, and our constitutional dispensation has to take this into account. The formal recognition of individual rights does not mean that the problems of a heterogeneous population will simply disappear. Any new constitution which disregards this reality will be inappropriate or even harmful.

Naturally, the protection of collective, minority and national rights may not bring about an imbalance in respect of individual rights. It is neither the Government's policy nor its intention that any group – in whichever way it may be defined – shall be favoured over or in relation to any of the others. . . .

Practically every leader agrees that negotiation is the key to reconciliation, peace, and a new and just dispensation. However, numerous excuses for refusing to take part are advanced. Some of the reasons being advanced are valid. Others are merely part of a political chess game. . . .

Against this background I committed the Government during my inauguration to giving active attention to the most important obstacles in the way of negotiation. Today I am able to announce far-reaching decisions in this connection.

I believe that these decisions will shape a new phase in which there will be a movement away from measures which have been seized upon as a justification for confrontation and violence. The emphasis has to move, and will move now, to a debate and discussion of political and economic points of view as part of the process of negotiation. . . .

The steps that have been decided on are the following:

- The prohibition of the African National Congress, the Pan Africanist Congress, the South African Communist Party and a number of subsidiary organisations is being rescinded.
- People serving prison sentences merely because they were members of one of these organisations or because they committed some other offence which was merely an offence because a prohibition on one of the organisations was in force, will be identified and released. Prisoners who have been sentenced for other offences such as murder, terrorism or arson are not affected by this.
- The media emergency regulations as well as the education emergency regulations are being abolished in their entirety. . . .
- The period of detention in terms of the security emergency regulations will be limited henceforth to six months. Detainees also acquire the right to legal representation and a medical practitioner of their own choosing. . . .

I wish to put it plainly that the Government has taken a firm decision to release Mr. Mandela unconditionally. I am serious about bringing the matter to finality without delay. . . .

Today's announcements in particular go to the heart of what Black leaders – also Mr. Mandela – have been advancing over the years as their reason for having resorted to violence. The allegation has been that the Government has not wished to talk to them and that they have been deprived of their right to normal political activity by the prohibition of their organisations.

Without conceding that violence has ever been justified, I wish to say today to those who have argued in this manner:

- The Government wishes to talk to all leaders who seek peace.
- The unconditional lifting of the prohibition on the said organisations places everybody in a position to pursue politics freely.
- The justification for violence which has always been advanced therefore no longer exists.

Source: Hansard (1990) South African Parliament, *Debates of Parliament*, cols 1, 2, 6, 12, 13 and 16, Cape Town: Hansard.

Document 11   EUGENE DE KOCK TALKS ABOUT KILLING PEOPLE, 1990

Barely two months after de Klerk made his speech calling for negotiations and the end of violence, Eugene de Kock, though officially suspended from duty and his covert organisation, like others operated by the state, supposedly under investigation (by an official commission that concluded that there was no proof that the government had ever engaged in a dirty tricks campaign), got orders from his military superiors to kill again.

In April 1990, when the Harms Commission was in full swing and I had been suspended, Brigadier [later General] Nick Van Rensburg summoned me to his office. Brigadier [later General] Krappies Engelbrecht [head of counter-intelligence for the South African police] was also there. Van Rensburg asked me to carry out an attack on a house in Botswana that belonged to a family called Chand. . . .

Van Rensburg mentioned that the Chands had helped a large group of PAC terrorists to infiltrate South Africa. I knew that the Chands worked as double agents for the . . . South African Defence Force. . . .

During this meeting with Van Rensburg, he also told me to make a 'plan' about Brian Ngqulunga. Van Rensburg said Ngqulunga had become unstable after giving testimony at the Harms Commission. He had seriously injured his pregnant wife when he shot her one evening. . . .

The only information available about the Chands was that they were a man and a woman who lived alone near a border post. I can't remember the name of the border post. We were told that there were no guards and everybody else on the property could be regarded as a PAC member.

I put Lieutenant Martiens Ras in charge of the operation as I was busy training him to take over operations from me. I took part in the operation as an attack group member and as overall commander and adviser. Van Rensburg said the attack should have the trademarks of a PAC operation and ordered us to use Scorpion machine guns. I also ordered that all members carry AK-47 assault rifles in case we landed up in a full-scale firefight; Scorpion machine pistols have very little stopping power. The Scorpions were fitted with silencers. We also took 30 kg to 40 kg of explosives to destroy the house.

When we approached the house, we bumped into a night watchman, which was very unexpected. The other men hesitated so I walked up from behind and shot the man three or four times in the head. The guard began screaming and someone jumped over the fence and shot him dead with a Makarov pistol.

While I was firing, I had fallen into a hole and injured my knee badly, so I ordered the rest of the group to launch the attack on the house. According to reports, everyone in the house was shot dead. I later learnt that two of those killed in the house were Sam and Hajira Chand's two deaf sons, Redwan and Ameen.

No one had known that the boys would be in the house. Our instructions had been clear: all the occupants had to be eliminated. If I had known that we were going to have to shoot those innocent boys, I would not have been prepared to go ahead with the operation.

Or, if it was vital that the operation be carried out, I would have seen to it that they were not killed.

We killed the four Chand family members, the watchman and the family dog. We planted our explosives in the main bedroom and they exploded about 40 minutes later.

The attack group went on to Empangeni and spent two days there to provide an alibi. . . . The details of the operation were related to Van Rensburg. He took full note of them. . . .

Ngqulunga, a member of C1 and former ANC member had been called as a witness by Judge Louis Harms. Ngqulunga had also been stationed at Vlakplaas at one time. . . .

Engelbrecht said clearly during the [original] meeting that Ngqulunga should be silenced ('*Hy moet stilgemaak word*'). I did not have any doubt that Ngqulunga had to be killed. I also clearly understood that Van Rensburg and Engelbrecht had taken the decision to kill. But I decided to ignore the order to kill Ngqulunga and give my full attention to planning the Botswana operation against the Chand house.

Then, about a month and a half later, I spoke to Van Rensburg again and he asked me to give urgent attention to the 'elimination' of Ngqulunga. The reason for the urgency lay in the fact that Ngqulunga had already put out feelers to the ANC, saying that he wanted to reveal the truth about the murder of Griffiths Mxenge.

After my discussion with Van Rensburg, I discussed the killing of Ngqulunga with Major David Baker, who was connected to our unit. We decided that he should be killed in Bophuthatswana. . . .

The task was carried out on Friday, 20 July 1990. I was told that Ngqulunga was abducted in a Kombi, dragged out and shot dead.

Baker and I went back to Van Rensburg's office to report back. I asked if the Pretoria murder and robbery squad would lend assistance in the investigation of the murder so that the police could monitor and control the investigation properly. I learnt later that this had not been done.

Source: Eugene de Kock (1998) *A Long Night's Damage: Working for the Apartheid State*, Saxonwold, South Africa: Contra Press, pp. 191–5.

Document 12   NELSON MANDELA CAUTIONS THAT THE STRUGGLE FOR FREEDOM REMAINS TO BE WON, 1990

Nelson Mandela walked out of prison on 11 February 1990 and immediately travelled to the main public square in Cape Town to speak to the thousands of people who had gathered to hear the first legal speech in over 30 years by the leader of the ANC.

Friends, comrades and fellow South Africans.

I greet you all in the name of peace, democracy and freedom for all.

I stand here before you not as a prophet but as a humble servant of you, the people. Your tireless and heroic sacrifices have made it possible for me to be here today. I therefore place the remaining years of my life in your hands.

On this day of my release, I extend my sincere and warmest gratitude to the millions of my compatriots and those in every corner of the globe who have campaigned tirelessly for my release. . . .

The large-scale mass mobilisation of the past few years is one of the key factors which led to the opening of the final chapter of our struggle.

I extend my greetings to the working class of our country. Your organised strength is the pride of our movement. You remain the most dependable force in the struggle to end exploitation and oppression.

I pay tribute to the many religious communities who carried the campaign for justice forward when the organisations for our people were silenced.

I greet the traditional leaders of our country – many of you continue to walk in the footsteps of great heroes like Hintsa and Sekhukune.

I pay tribute to the endless heroism of youth, you, the young lions. You, the young lions, have energised our entire struggle.

I pay tribute to the mothers and wives and sisters of our nation. You are the rock-hard foundation of our struggle. Apartheid has inflicted more pain on you than on anyone else. . . .

Today the majority of South Africans, black and white, recognise that apartheid has no future. It has to be ended by our own decisive mass action in order to build peace and security. The mass campaign of defiance and other actions of our organisation and people can only culminate in the establishment of democracy. The destruction caused by apartheid on our subcontinent is incalculable. The fabric of family life of millions of my people has been shattered. Millions are homeless and unemployed. Our economy lies in ruins and our people are embroiled in political strife. Our resort to the armed struggle in 1960 with the formation of the military wing of the ANC, Umkhonto we Sizwe, was a purely defensive action against the violence of apartheid. The factors which necessitated the armed struggle still exist today. We have no option but to continue. We express the hope that a climate conducive to a negotiated settlement will be created soon so that there may no longer be the need for the armed struggle. . . .

Mr. De Klerk has gone further than any other Nationalist president in taking real steps to normalise the situation. However, there are further steps . . . that have to be met before negotiations on the basic demands of our people can begin. I reiterate our call for, *inter alia*, the immediate ending of the State of Emergency and the freeing of all, and not only some, political prisoners. Only such a normalised situation, which allows for free political activity, can allow us to consult our people in order to obtain a mandate.

The people need to be consulted on who will negotiate and on the content of such negotiations. Negotiations cannot take place above the heads or behind the backs of our people. It is our belief that the future of our country can only be determined by a body which is democratically elected on a non-racial basis. Negotiations on the dismantling of apartheid will have to address the overwhelming demand of our people for a democratic, non-racial and unitary South Africa. There must be an end to white monopoly on political power and a fundamental restructuring of our political and economic systems to ensure that the inequalities of apartheid are addressed and our society thoroughly democratised.

It must be added that Mr. De Klerk himself is a man of integrity who is acutely aware of the dangers of a public figure not honouring his undertakings. But as an organisation we base our policy and strategy on the harsh reality we are faced with. And this reality is that we are still suffering under the policy of the Nationalist government.

Our struggle has reached a decisive moment. We call on our people to seize this moment so that the process towards democracy is rapid and uninterrupted. We have waited too long for our freedom. We can no longer wait. Now is the time to intensify the struggle on all fronts. To relax our efforts now would be a mistake which generations to come will not be able to forgive. The sight of freedom looming on the horizon should encourage us to redouble our efforts.

It is only through disciplined mass action that our victory can be assured. We call on our white compatriots to join us in the shaping of a new South Africa. The freedom movement is a political home for you too. We call on the international community to continue the campaign to isolate the apartheid regime. To lift sanctions now would be to run the risk of aborting the process towards the complete eradication of apartheid.

Our march to freedom is irreversible. We must not allow fear to stand in our way. Universal suffrage on a common voters' role in a united democratic and non-racial South Africa is the only way to peace and racial harmony.

In conclusion I wish to quote my own words during my trial in 1964. They are true today as they were then:

'I have fought against white domination and I have fought against black domination. I have cherished the ideal of a democratic and free society in which all persons live together in harmony and with equal opportunities. It is an ideal which I hope to live for and to achieve. But if needs be, it is an ideal for which I am prepared to die.'

Source: http://www.anc.org.za/ancdocs/history/mandela/1990/release.html.

Document 13   MANDELA SPEAKS OF FREEDOM ATTAINED, AT HIS INAUGURATION AS PRESIDENT OF SOUTH AFRICA, 1994

Standing on 10 May 1994 on the steps of the Union Buildings in Pretoria, where every segregationist and apartheid white politician had had his office since the turn of the century, Nelson Rolihlahla Mandela spoke to the gathered dignitaries and supporters as the first leader of South Africa elected by a majority of the country's inhabitants.

Your Majesties, Your Highnesses, Distinguished Guests, Comrades and Friends.

Today, all of us do, by our presence here, and by our celebrations in other parts of our country and the world, confer glory and hope to newborn liberty. Out of the experience of an extraordinary human disaster that lasted too long, must be born a society of which all humanity will be proud. Our daily deeds as ordinary South Africans must produce an actual South African reality that will reinforce humanity's belief in justice, strengthen its confidence in the nobility of the human soul and sustain all our hopes for a glorious life for all. All this we owe both to ourselves and to the peoples of the world who are so well represented here today. To my compatriots, I have no hesitation in saying that each one of us is as intimately attached to the soil of this beautiful country as are the famous jacaranda trees of Pretoria and the mimosa trees of the bushveld. Each time one of us touches the soil of this land, we feel a sense of personal renewal. The national mood changes as the seasons change. We are moved by a sense of joy and exhilaration when the grass turns green and the flowers bloom. That spiritual and physical oneness we all share with this common homeland explains the depth of the pain we all carried in our hearts as we saw our country tear itself apart in a terrible conflict, and as we saw it spurned, outlawed and isolated by the peoples of the world, precisely because it has become the universal base of the perni- cious ideology and practice of racism and racial oppression. We, the people of South Africa, feel fulfilled that humanity has taken us back into its bosom, that we, who were outlaws not so long ago, have today been given the rare privilege to be host to the nations of the world on our own soil. We thank all our distinguished international guests for having come to take possession with the people of our country of what is, after all, a common victory for justice, for peace, for human dignity. We trust that you will continue to stand by us as we tackle the challenges of building peace, prosperity, non-sexism, non-racialism and democracy. We deeply appreciate the role that the masses of our people and their political mass democratic, religious, women, youth, business, traditional and other leaders have played to bring about this conclusion. Not least among them is my Second Deputy President, the Honourable F.W. de Klerk. We would also like to pay tribute to our security forces, in all their ranks, for the distinguished role they have played in secur- ing our first democratic elections and the transition to democracy, from blood-thirsty forces which still refuse to see the light. The time for the healing of the wounds has come. The moment to bridge the chasms that divide us has come. The time to build is upon us. We have, at last, achieved our political emancipation. We pledge ourselves to liberate all our people from the continuing bondage of poverty, deprivation, suffering, gender and other discrimination. We succeeded to take our last steps to freedom in conditions of relative peace. We commit ourselves to the construction of a complete, just and lasting peace. We have triumphed in the effort to implant hope in the breasts of the millions of our people. We enter into a covenant that we shall build the society in which all South Africans, both black and white, will be able to walk tall, without any fear in their hearts, assured of their inalienable right to human dignity – a rainbow nation at peace with itself and the world. As a token of its commitment to the renewal of our country, the new Interim Government of National Unity will, as a matter of urgency, address the issue of amnesty for various categories of our people who are currently serving terms of imprisonment. We dedicate this day to all the heroes and heroines in this country and the rest of the world who sacrificed in many ways and surrendered their lives so that we could be free. Their dreams have become reality. Freedom is their reward. We are both humbled and elevated by the honour and privilege that you, the people of South Africa, have bestowed on us, as the first President of a united, demo-cratic, non-racial and non-sexist government. We understand still that there is no easy road to freedom. We know it well that none of us acting alone can achieve success. We must therefore act together as a united people, for national reconciliation, for nation building, for the birth of a new world. Let there be justice for all. Let there be peace for all. Let there be work, bread, water and salt for all. Let each know that for each the body, the mind and the soul have been freed to fulfil themselves. Never, never and never again shall it be that this beautiful land will again experience the oppression of one by another and suffer the indignity of being the skunk of the world. Let freedom reign. The sun shall never set on so glorious a human achievement! God bless Africa! Thank you.

Source: http://www.anc.org.za/ancdocs/history/mandela/1994/inaugpta.html.

Guide to further reading

Since the end of the apartheid era in South Africa, an increasing amount of information has gradually come to light concerning the activities of the government as well as of individuals. The most revealing documentary evidence is available through the records of the Truth and Reconciliation Commission. The full text of the testimonies of the more than 29,000 witnesses who appeared before the TRC is available online (http://www.justice.gov.za/trc/amntrans/index.htm). The website also includes formal submissions to the TRC made by political parties (including the ANC and the NP) and other organisations such as the South African military. The TRC has evaluated and summarised this evidence in a seven-volume report, available in CD and printed format, *Report* (Cape Town: The Truth and Reconciliation Commission, 1998), and on the web (http://www.justice.gov.za/trc/report/index.htm). The ANC's website contains a large number of full-text historical documents detailing its struggle against apartheid (http://www.anc.org.za/show.php?doc=ancdocs/history/index.html&title=Historical+Documents). Two other expanding online resources provide access to fully digitised books, magazines, and journals that illuminate the anti-apartheid struggle in South Africa, Digital Innovation South Africa (DISA), http://www.disa.ukzn.ac.za/, and in southern Africa, ALUKA (from a Zulu word meaning 'to weave'), http://www.aluka.org/action/doBrowse?sa=3&sa_sel=. There is a useful index of all South African government websites (often containing full text reports reaching back into the 1990s) at http://www.gksoft.com/govt/en/za.html. For insight into the thinking of white supremacists, past and present, visit the website of the late Eugene Terre'Blanche's AWB, http://www.awb.co.za/english.htm.

Key collections of printed documents include D.W. Krüger, ed., *South African Parties and Policies, 1910–1960: A Select Source Book* (Cape Town: Human & Rousseau, 1960), A.N. Pelzer, ed., *Verwoerd Speaks: Speeches 1948–1966* (Johannesburg: APB Publishers, 1966), Edgar Brookes, *Apartheid: A Documentary Study of Modern South Africa* (London, Routledge & Kegan Paul,

1968), and the publications edited by Muriel Horrell of the South African Institute of Race Relations, especially *Laws Affecting Race Relations in South Africa (to the end of 1976)* (Johannesburg: South African Institute of Race Relations, 1978).

The best collections of documents detailing the actions of people opposing segregation and apartheid are Gwendolen Carter and Thomas Karis, eds, *From Protest to Challenge: A Documentary History of African Politics in South Africa, 1882–1964* (Stanford, CA: Hoover Institution Press [1972]–97), 5 vols, and Sheridan Johns and R. Hunt Davis, eds, *Mandela, Tambo, and the African National Congress: The Struggle Against Apartheid* (Oxford: Oxford University Press, 1991). *The United Nations and Apartheid, 1948–1994* (New York: Department of Public Information, United Nations, 1994) documents part of the international dimension of the anti-apartheid struggle, while Hassen Ebrahim, *The Soul of a Nation: Constitution-making in South Africa* (Cape Town: Oxford University Press, 1998) examines the process of negotiations for a new South Africa that took place between 1985 and 1996.

Most academic writing about South Africa reflects the historic divisions within the country, focusing on particular racial, ethnic or economic groups, and few synthetic studies of apartheid South Africa have been produced. Researchers had difficulty spanning these divisions during the apartheid era, when the complete separation of racial groups extended even into the archives where records pertaining to each group were housed separately. Some of the best works giving both a full background on pre-1900 developments and covering the broad trend of events in the twentieth century have been general histories written for students. Nigel Worden, *The Making of Modern South Africa: Conquest, Segregation, and Apartheid* (4th edition, Oxford: Blackwell, 2007) provides a concise overview of the history of South Africa, and is particularly useful because of its historiographical references. Leonard Thompson, *A History of South Africa* (3rd edition, New Haven, CT: Yale University Press, 2001) is more detailed, especially on the development of African societies. Other relevant books by Thompson, the pre-eminent historian of South Africa, include, *The Political Mythology of Apartheid* (New Haven, CT: Yale University Press, 1985), which dissects the historical accuracy of Nationalist Party justifications and, edited with Monica Wilson, *The Oxford History of South Africa* (New York: Oxford University Press, 1969–71), volume 2, which includes useful chapters on the implementation of urban and rural apartheid policies.

Among the extensive specialist literature on apartheid, the following are especially important. Philip Bonner, Peter Delius and Deborah Posel, eds, *Apartheid's Genesis, 1935–1962* (Braamfontein, South Africa: Ravan Press, 1993) contains chapters covering all aspects of apartheid policies, including education, influx control, labour strikes, etc. Deborah Posel has also written

The Making of Apartheid 1948–1961: Conflict and Compromise (Oxford: Clarendon Press, 1991), in which she explains the incremental construction of apartheid legislation and ideology as Nationalist Party politicians balanced ideological and economic considerations. Ivan Evans has provided a detailed examination of the laws and policies applied to Africans in his *Bureaucracy and Race: Native Administration in South Africa* (Berkeley, CA: University of California Press, 1997). Dan O'Meara, *Volkskapitalisme: Class, Capital and Ideology in the Development of Afrikaner Nationalism, 1934–1948* (Cambridge: Cambridge University Press, 1983) focuses on the class origins of Afrikaner nationalism and apartheid. O'Meara has also produced a comprehensive study of Nationalist Party politics, *Forty Lost Years: The Apartheid State and the Politics of the National Party, 1948–1994* (Randburg, South Africa: Ravan Press, 1996). On the religious element in Afrikaner nationalism, see Dunbar Moodie, *The Rise of Afrikanerdom: Power, Apartheid, and the Afrikaner Civil Religion* (Berkeley, CA: University of California Press, 1975). Three fascinating works on the connections between Afrikaner nationalism, white supremacy and apartheid are Brian Bunting's polemical *The Rise of the South African Reich* (Harmondsworth: Penguin, 1969), J.H.P. Serfontein's exposé, *Brotherhood of Power: An Exposé of the Secret Afrikaner Broederbond* (Bloomington, IN: Indiana University Press, 1978), and Vincent Crapanzano's fieldwork-based *Waiting: The Whites of South Africa* (New York: Random House, 1985). The fullest and most recent account of the development of Afrikaner politics is Hermann Giliomee, *Afrikaners: Biography of a People* (Charlottesville, VA: University of Virginia Press, 2003); that on apartheid is David Welsh, *The Rise and Fall of Apartheid* (Charlottesville, VA: University of Virginia Press, 2010). Both reflect the Cape 'liberal' tradition of historiography in South Africa (see ch. 1), and tend to be relentlessly political in their focus, with little or no mention of blacks.

There is a solid body of literature on the long history of resistance to apartheid and earlier segregation. The classic work is Peter Walshe, *The Rise of African Nationalism in South Africa: The African National Congress, 1912–1952* (Berkeley, CA: University of California Press, 1971), and this has been augmented for an earlier period by Andre Odendaal, *Vukani Bantu!: The Beginnings of Black Protest Politics in South Africa to 1912* (Cape Town: David Philip, 1984). Picking up chronologically from where Walshe leaves off is Tom Lodge, *Black Politics in South Africa since 1945* (London: Longman, 1983). Gail Gerhart, *Black Power in South Africa: The Evolution of an Ideology* (Berkeley, CA: University of California Press, 1978) examines the subsequent emergence of Black Consciousness, especially after the banning of the ANC in the 1960s. The outbreak of African protest in Soweto in 1976 is discussed in Baruch Hirson, *Year of Fire, Year of Ash: The Soweto Revolt, Roots of a Revolution?* (London: Zed Press, 1979). The subsequent brutal and often covert crackdown on African opposition is detailed in Stephen Davis, *Apartheid's Rebels: Inside South Africa's Hidden War* (New Haven, CT: Yale University Press, 1987). On the growth of the African trade union movement, see Denis MacShane, Martin Plaut and David Ward, *Power!: Black Workers, Their Unions and the Struggle for Freedom in South Africa* (Nottingham: Spokesman, 1984). On the grassroots struggles of the 1980s, see Anthony Marx, *Lessons of Struggle: South African Internal Opposition, 1960–1990* (New York: Oxford University Press, 1992), Ineke van Kessel, *Beyond Our Wildest Dreams: The United Democratic Front and the Transformation of South Africa* (Charlottesville, VA: University of Virginia Press, 2000), Jeremy Seekings, *The UDF: A History of the United Democratic Front in South Africa, 1983–1991* (Cape Town: David Philip, 2000), and Belinda Bozzoli, *Theatres of Struggle and the End of Apartheid* (Athens, OH: Ohio University Press, 2004).

Some of the most insightful works on South Africa during the apartheid era are biographical and autobiographical. Among many books by and about Nelson Mandela three stand out: an early collection of Mandela's writings, *No Easy Walk to Freedom* (London: Heinemann, 1973), his magisterial autobiography, *Long Walk to Freedom: The Autobiography of Nelson Mandela* (Boston: Little, Brown and Co., 1994), and Tom Lodge, *Mandela: A Critical Life* (Oxford: Oxford University Press, 2007). Two forerunners of Black Consciousness are the subjects of Robert Edgar and Luyandaka Msumza, eds, *Freedom in Our Lifetime: The Collected Writings of Anton Muziwakhe Lembede* (Athens, OH: Ohio University Press, 1996), and Benjamin Pogrund, *How Can Man Die Better: Sobukwe and Apartheid* (London: P. Halban, 1990). While most opposition in South Africa was silenced by bannings and censorship laws after the 1960s, Govan Mbeki, *Learning from Robben Island: The Prison Writings of Govan Mbeki* (London: J. Currey, 1991) reveals the rich development of anti-apartheid ideology, even in prison. Other notable accounts include Albert Luthuli, *Let My People Go: An Autobiography* (London: Collins, 1962), Oliver Tambo, *Preparing for Power: Oliver Tambo Speaks* (New York: G. Braziller, 1987), Ellen Kuzwayo, *Call Me Woman* (London: Women's Press, 1985), Emma Mashinini, *Strikes Have Followed Me All My Life: A South African Autobiography* (New York: Routledge, 1991), Frank Chikane, *No Life of My Own: An Autobiography* (London: Catholic Institute for International Relations, 1988), Mamphela Ramphele, *Across Boundaries: The Journey of a South African Woman Leader* (New York: Feminist Press at the City University of New York, 1997), and Gatsha Buthelezi, *South Africa: My Vision of the Future* (London: Weidenfeld & Nicolson, 1990).

The lives of white supporters and opponents of apartheid are also the subject of many studies. Marq De Villiers, *White Tribe Dreaming: Apartheid's Bitter Roots as Witnessed by Eight Generations of an Afrikaner Family* (New York: Penguin, 1987) provides a semi-fictionalised account of his own family.

Alexander Hepple, *Verwoerd* (Harmondsworth: Penguin, 1967), and Henry Kenney, *Architect of Apartheid: H.F. Verwoerd, an Appraisal* (Johannesburg: J. Ball, 1980) are the best studies of the man popularly regarded as the main architect of apartheid. F.W. de Klerk, *The Last Trek – A New Beginning: The Autobiography* (London: Macmillan, 1998) provides the views of a supporter of apartheid who now finds it necessary to justify a policy seen by all as morally bankrupt. The lives of some of apartheid's white opponents are most eloquently recounted in Helen Joseph, *Side by Side: The Autobiography of Helen Joseph* (London: Zed Books, 1986), Helen Suzman, *In No Uncertain Terms: A South African Memoir* (New York: Knopf, 1993), and Frederik van zyl Slabbert, *The Last White Parliament: The Struggle for South Africa by the Leader of the White Opposition* (New York: St Martin's Press, 1987).

There is a growing literature on the transition from apartheid. Robert Price, *The Apartheid State in Crisis: Political Transformation in South Africa 1975–1990* (New York: Oxford University Press, 1991) presents a political analysis of some of the factors that weakened the apartheid state from within. Lindsay Eades, *The End of Apartheid in South Africa* (Westport, CT: Greenwood Press, 1999) chronicles the chain of events in the late 1980s and early 1990s, as does Patti Waldmeir, *Anatomy of a Miracle: The End of Apartheid and the Birth of the New South Africa* (New York: W.W. Norton, 1997). Eugene de Kock, *A Long Night's Damage: Working for the Apartheid State* (Saxonwold, South Africa: Contra Press, 1998), and Richard Goldstone, *For Humanity: Reflections of a War Crimes Investigator* (New Haven, CT: Yale University Press, 2000) document the violent nature of the last few years of apartheid. Important works on the problems of transition from apartheid to black majority rule, in which the Truth and Reconciliation Commission is the key institution around which debate revolves, are Martin Meredith, *Coming to Terms: South Africa's Search for Truth* (New York: Public Affairs, 1999), Antjie Krog, *Country of My Skull: Guilt, Sorrow and the Limits of Forgiveness in the New South Africa* (New York: Crown Publishing Group, 1999), Alex Boraine, *A Country Unmasked* (Cape Town and New York: Oxford University Press, 2000), and Deborah Posel and Graeme Simpson, eds, *Commissioning the Past: Understanding South Africa's Truth and Reconciliation Commission* (Johannesburg: Witwatersrand University Press, 2003).

The difficult legacy of apartheid in post-1994 South Africa has been discussed in a multitude of studies, among the most illuminating of which are Tom Lodge, *Politics in South Africa: From Mandela to Mbeki* (Cape Town: David Philip, 2003), Jeremy Seekings and Nicoli Nattrass, *Class, Race, and Inequality in South Africa* (New Haven, CT: Yale University Press, 2005), Gillian Hart, *Disabling Globalization: Places of Power in Post-Apartheid South Africa* (Berkeley, CA: University of California Press, 2002), Didier Fassin, *When Bodies Remember: Experiences and Politics of AIDS in South Africa* (Berkeley, CA:

University of California Press, 2007), and Cherryl Walker, *Landmarked: Land Claims and Land Restitution in South Africa* (Athens, OH: Ohio University Press, 2008).

Finally, an intellectually stimulating and empirically rich group of studies have examined South Africa in comparative perspective. The best of these include Stanley B. Greenburg, *Race and State in Capitalist Development: Studies on South Africa, Alabama, Northern Ireland, and Israel* (New Haven, CT: Yale University Press, 1980), John W. Cell, *The Highest Stage of White Supremacy: The Origins of Segregation in South Africa and the American South* (Cambridge: Cambridge University Press, 1982), George M. Fredrickson, *White Supremacy: A Comparative Study of American and South African History* (Oxford: Oxford University Press, 1982) and his *Black Liberation: A Comparative History of Black Ideologies in the United States and South Africa* (Oxford: Oxford University Press, 1996), Gay W. Seidman, *Manufacturing Militance: Workers' Movements in Brazil and South Africa 1970–1985* (Berkeley, CA: University of California Press, 1994), Anthony W. Marx, *Making Race and Nation: A Comparative Study of the United States, South Africa, and Brazil* (Cambridge: Cambridge University Press, 1998), and Ivan Evans, *Cultures of Violence: Lynching and Racial Killing in South Africa and the American South* (Manchester: Manchester University Press, 2010).

References

Biko, Stephen (1986) *I Write What I Like: Steve Biko – A Selection of His Writings*, edited with a personal memoir and a new preface by Aelred Stubbs. San Francisco: Harper & Row.

Boraine, Alex (2000) *A Country Unmasked*. Cape Town and New York: Oxford University Press.

Bunche, Ralph (1992) *An African American in South Africa: The Travel Notes of Ralph J. Bunche, 28 September 1937–1 January 1938*, edited by Robert R. Edgar. Athens, OH: Ohio University Press; Johannesburg, South Africa: Witwatersrand University Press.

Bundy, Colin (1979) *The Rise and Fall of the South African Peasantry*. Berkeley, CA: University of California Press.

Carter, Gwendolen (1958) *The Politics of Inequality: South Africa since 1948*. New York: F.A. Praeger.

De Klerk, F.W. (1999) *The Last Trek – A New Beginning: The Autobiography*. New York: St Martin's Press.

De Kock, Eugene (1998) *A Long Night's Damage: Working for the Apartheid State*. Saxonwold, South Africa: Contra Press.

Economist Intelligence Unit (2002) *Economist Intelligence Unit*. London: The Unit.

Eiselen, W.M. (1948) 'The meaning of Apartheid', *Race Relations*, 15/3.

Eybers, G.W., ed. (1969) *Select Constitutional Documents Illustrating South African History, 1795–1910*. New York: Negro Universities Press, reprint of the 1918 edition, New York.

The Freedom Charter. Available at: http://www.anc.org.za/ancdocs/history/charter.html.

Gann, L.H. and Duignan, Peter (1991) *Hope for South Africa?* Stanford, CA: Hoover Institution Press/Stanford University Press.

Giliomee, Hermann (2003) *Afrikaners: Biography of a People*. Charlottesville, VA: University of Virginia Press.

Hansard (1956, 1984, 1988, 1990) South African Parliament, *Debates of Parliament*. Cape Town: Hansard.

Horrell, Muriel, compiler (1978) *Laws Affecting Race Relations in South Africa (to the end of 1976)*. Johannesburg: South African Institute of Race Relations.

Huddleston, Trevor (1956) *Naught for Your Comfort*. London: Collins.

Kessel, Ineke van (2000) *Beyond Our Wildest Dreams: The United Democratic Front and the Transformation of South Africa*. Charlottesville, VA: University of Virginia Press.

Krüger, D.W., ed. (1960) *South African Parties and Policies, 1910–1960: A Select Source Book*. Cape Town: Human & Rousseau.

Lelyveld, Joseph (1985) *Move Your Shadow: South Africa Black and White*. New York: Penguin.

MacShane, Denis, Plaut, Martin and Ward, David (1984) *Power!: Black Workers, Their Unions and the Struggle for Freedom in South Africa*. Nottingham: Spokesman.

Mandela, Nelson (1953) 'No Easy Walk to Freedom', Presidential address to the ANC (Transvaal Branch), 21 September. Available at: http://www.anc.org.za/ancdocs/history/mandela/1950s/sp530921.html.

Mandela, Nelson (1994) *Long Walk to Freedom: The Autobiography of Nelson Mandela*. Boston, MA: Little, Brown.

Marks, Shula and Trapido, Stanley (1979) 'Lord Milner and the South African State', *History Workshop*, 8: 50–80.

Matshoba, Mtutuzeli (1979) *Call Me Not a Man*. Johannesburg: Ravan Press.

Meredith, Martin (1999) *Coming to Terms: South Africa's Search for Truth*. New York: Public Affairs.

Merwe, Hendrik van der *et al.*, eds (1978) *African Perspectives on South Africa: A Collection of Speeches, Articles and Documents*. Stanford, CA: Hoover Institution Press.

Modisane, Bloke (1963) *Blame Me on History*. New York, NY: Dutton.

Mokgatle, Naboth (1971) *The Autobiography of an Unknown South African*. Berkeley, CA: University of California Press.

Moodie, T. Dunbar (1975) *The Rise of Afrikanerdom: Power, Apartheid, and the Afrikaner Civil Religion*. Berkeley, CA: University of California Press.

Mphahlele, Ezekiel (1959) *Down Second Avenue*. London: Faber & Faber.

Newton, P. and Benians, E.A. with Walker, Eric A. (1936) *The Cambridge History of the British Empire*. Vol. 8: *South Africa, Rhodesia and the Protectorates* (8 vols). Cambridge: Cambridge University Press.

Nkosi, Lewis (1965) *Home and Exile*. London: Longmans.

Nzula, A.T., Potekhin, I.I. and Zusmanovich, A.Z. (1979) *Forced Labour in Colonial Africa*, edited and introduced by Robin Cohen, translated (from the Russian) by Hugh Jenkins. London: Zed Books.

Odendaal, Andre (1984) *Vukani Bantu!: The Beginnings of Black Protest Politics in South Africa to 1912*. Cape Town: David Philip, in association with the Centre for African Studies at the University of Cape Town.

Pelzer, A.N., ed. (1966) *Verwoerd Speaks: Speeches 1948–1966*. Johannesburg: APB Publishers.

Plaatje, Solomon Tshekisho (1987) *Native Life in South Africa*, edited and introduced by Brian Willan. Harlow, UK: Longman; first published, 1916, London.

Platzky, Laurine and Walker, Cherryl (1985) *The Surplus People: Forced Removals in South Africa*. Johannesburg: Ravan Press.

Posel, Deborah (1991) *The Making of Apartheid, 1948–1961: Conflict and Compromise*. Oxford and New York: Clarendon Press.

Price, Robert M. (1991) *The Apartheid State in Crisis: Political Transformation in South Africa, 1975–1990*. New York: Oxford University Press.

Saunders, Christopher (1988) *The Making of the South African Past: Major Historians on Race and Class*. Totowa, NJ: Barnes & Noble.

Simons, H.J. and Simons, R.E. (1969) *Class and Colour in South Africa, 1850–1950*. Harmondsworth, Penguin.

Smith, Ken (1988) *The Changing Past: Trends in South African Historical Writing*. Johannesburg: Southern Book Publishers.

South African Native Affairs Commission (SANAC) (1904–05) *Report*. Cape Town: Cape Times.

Themba, Can (1985) *The World of Can Themba*. Braamfontein, South Africa: Ravan Press.

Truth and Reconciliation Commission of South Africa (1998, 2003) *Report* (vols 1–7). Cape Town: The Truth and Reconciliation Commission.

United Nations (1994) *The United Nations and Apartheid, 1948–1994*. New York: Department of Public Information, United Nations.

Verwoerd, H.F. (1954) *Bantu Education: Policy for the Immediate Future – statement by the Hon. Dr H.F. Verwoerd, Minister of Native Affairs, in the Senate of the Parliament of the Union of South Africa, 7th June 1954*. Pretoria: Information Service of the Department of Native Affairs.

Verwoerd, H.F. (1958) *Separate Development: The Positive Side*. Pretoria: Information Service of the Department of Native Affairs.

Walker, Cherryl (2008) *Landmarked: Land Claims and Land Restitution in South Africa*. Athens, OH: Ohio University Press.

Welsh, David (2010) *The Rise and Fall of Apartheid*. Charlottesville, VA: University of Virginia Press.

Worger, William H. (1999) 'Southern and Central Africa', in Robin W. Winks, ed., *The Oxford History of the British Empire*. Vol. 5: *Historiography*. Oxford: Oxford University Press.

Yudelman, David (1983) *The Emergence of Modern South Africa: State, Capital, and the Incorporation of Organized Labor on the South African Gold Fields, 1902–1939*. Westport, CT: Greenwood Press.

Index

The Index includes Chapters One to Six, the Documents, the Glossary, and Who's Who, but not the Chronology, Guide to Further Reading or References. Locators in **bold** indicate definitions or explanations. The abbreviation *illus.* after a locator denotes a plan or chart.